D0732767

# GROUP PRO

## SOCIOLOGICAL ANALYSES

### Date Due

FEB 1 4 1998

**The Nelson-Hall Series in Sociology**
Consulting Editor: Jonathan H. Turner
*University of California, Riverside*

# GROUP PROCESSES

## SOCIOLOGICAL ANALYSES

**Edited by**
Martha Foschi
University of British Columbia

Edward J. Lawler
Cornell University

NELSON–HALL PUBLISHERS    CHICAGO

Project Editor: Rachel Schick
Cover Painting: *Crossroad* by Kae Guhl Campbell

**Library of Congress Cataloging-in-Publication Data**

Group processes : sociological analyses / edited by Martha Foschi,
    Edward J. Lawler.
       p.    cm.
    Includes bibliographical references and index.
    ISBN 0-8304-1232-8
    1. Intergroup relations.  2. Social groups.  3. Social
interaction.  I. Foschi, Martha, 1937-    .  II. Lawler, Edward J.
HM131.G7185   1994
302.3—dc20                                      93-40581
                                              CIP

Manufactured in the United States of America

10  9  8  7  6  5  4  3  2  1

TM The paper used in this book meets the
minimum requirements of American
National Standard for Information
Sciences—Permanence of Paper for
Printed Library Materials, ANSI
Z39.48-1984.

# CONTENTS

# PREFACE

The study of how people behave in groups has always received special attention in the social sciences. The reason for this extends beyond intellectual curiosity. Since we all spend a substantial part of our lives in group settings, it is of practical utility as well as academic value to know how groups function. When do status differences emerge in informal groups? How is group leadership gained and kept? How is power used to achieve influence? Why are some task groups more efficient than others? What rules are group members more likely to follow in allocating rewards to each other? These are a few examples of the questions often posed in this field.

A large interdisciplinary literature has now accumulated in the study of groups, encompassing a variety of theoretical approaches and research orientations, and focusing on a range of substantive topics. It is not our intention to cover this literature in its entirety. Rather, we focus on a specific segment of the work.

Within sociology, an important tradition has developed in the way questions such as those posed above are approached. Often referred to as the "group processes tradition," it is rooted in the writings of Lewin and Mead. Other, more recent precursors are Heider, Schachter, Festinger, Bales, Thibaut, Kelley, Homans, and Emerson. The combination of three features characterizes this approach. First, it has an analytical, theory-driven orientation. Thus, the work involves an emphasis on formulating knowledge claims as precisely as possible, stating them in abstract rather than concrete terms, and formally deriving hypotheses from more general propositions. The explicit inclusion of scope limitations is central to this tradition's theoretical strategy, as are a strong commitment to cumulative knowledge and a conviction that successful practical application is not possible without a good theory. The theoretical emphasis is further reflected by an interest in conceptualizing the processes that underlie group behavior, rather than accumulating empirical observations of it. Secondly, the tradition is closely associated with the notion that theories should be put to empirical test, and that the more rigorous the test, the better. In the study of groups, this often translates into a preference for experimental designs. A third characteristic relates to the choice of unit of analysis. Although the work carried out within this approach has a distinct methodological affinity with experimental social psychology, the link is with its sociological rather than its psychological variety. Thus, the tradition is characterized by an emphasis on social structures, how they emerge and change, and how they affect and are affected by individuals. In other words, the social context (or network, or system of relations) in which an individual finds him or herself, rather than the characteristics of this person, are most central to the explanation of group phenomena, and the unit of analysis is the person-in-a-context.

Since 1988, members of this tradition have organized annual conferences on theory and research on group processes. The conferences, held in connection with the meetings of the American Sociological Association, received assistance from Emory University (1988), Stanford University (1989), the University of Maryland (1990), the University of Cincinnati (1991), the University of Pittsburgh (1992), and the University of South Carolina (1993). In the course of discussions at these conferences it became apparent that, in addition to holding such specialized meetings, there was a need for a book that would introduce the tradition to a student audience.

We have organized the presentation of the material around two main objectives. The first is to familiarize students with the key assumptions of the approach; the second is to illustrate these assumptions by reviewing and assessing the major contributions to the study of group processes. Thus, the first three chapters provide theoretical and methodological background, while the remaining seven examine basic group processes. All the chapters are original pieces, written expressly for this volume by specialists on each of the topics.

Barry Markovsky begins Chapter 1 with a discussion on how scientific knowledge differs from common knowledge, and then proceeds to identify and examine the components of a theory. David G. Wagner's Chapter 2 deals first with criteria, both formal and empirical, for evaluating theoretical assertions, followed by a review of the various ways in which such assertions may be improved. Chapter 3, by Murray Webster, Jr., focuses on experiments—the tool most widely used in this field for the evaluation of theoretical claims. After a discussion of research designs and their most common sources of confounding factors, several central issues in the conduct of experiments, namely artificiality, generalizability, and ethics, are examined.

Chapters 4 through 10 look at basic group processes. Their selection was guided both by their centrality to group interaction, and our judgment as to whether or not there had been sufficient work carried out within this tradition to merit a separate chapter. It should be noted, however, that this work has taken different forms for the various processes represented here: in some cases a single, well-established theory dominates the area (e.g., performance evaluation, status), whereas in others the theoretical linkages are both more diverse and less developed (e.g., person perception, affect).

We asked each of these seven authors to identify classical and contemporary studies in his or her topic, and to show the theoretical linkages among them. Thus analysis, rather than thorough coverage of the findings, is emphasized. The common thread throughout these chapters is provided by this focus and by the authors' shared assumptions and goals for research in the field, as outlined earlier. Efforts have also been made to avoid unnecessary differences in terminology across all chapters, although we did not attempt to superimpose a common presentation format or writing style. In some instances an interesting dimension is added to the discussions by the fact that two or more authors look at the same material from different perspectives. These cases are noted by cross-references.

Chapter 4, by Barry Markovsky, reviews issues in social perception, concentrating on the common forms of perceptual bias (e.g., the use of preconceived notions and the reliance on anecdotes). Two features of special interest in this chapter are that Markovsky then proceeds to show how these biases operate in each of the six processes discussed in the other chapters, and that this analysis is extended from the group level to larger-scale phenomena.

Barbara Foley Meeker's Chapter 5 examines how patterns of inequality develop in task groups whose team-oriented members initially perceive each other as equal in status (e.g., sex, social class, competence at the task at hand). Basing her discussion on expectation states theory, Meeker describes how those patterns are the result of a "fundamental sequence of interaction" involving expectations, action opportunities, performance evaluations, and influence. In Chapter 6, James W. Balkwell also examines team-oriented task groups, but focuses on those exhibiting differences in initial status. The chapter presents a series of analyses based on predictions from status characteristic theory (a major branch of the expectation states program), which show that experimental results provide strong support for the theory.

Chapter 7, by John F. Stolte, analyzes the role of power differences in social relations. He overviews several approaches to power and influence and then devotes special attention to power-dependence theory, including a discussion of two types of exchange (productive versus distributive). The chapter also examines how actors' strategies can foster power balance, and how these strategies are stimulated by and also affect the larger social network.

Chapter 8 on justice, written by Karen A. Hegtvedt, assesses the impact of differences in outcomes or benefits on social relations. She examines how shared definitions or conceptions of justice come about in group contexts, how self-interest affects choices among competing justice principles, and how social comparisons shape justice judgments. Actors' responses to perceptions of injustice, and the effects of procedural rules on justice principles, are also discussed.

In Chapter 9, Cecilia L. Ridgeway considers the role that emotions and sentiments play in group interaction, and in particular, how they result in the creation of an "affective structure" of relations. This structure is not very different from the status order of a group and, moreover, the two hierarchies are interdependent: while status position is a factor in what emotions and sentiments are experienced, these affective reactions, in turn, modify the status order.

In Chapter 10, Rebecca Ford integrates selected theory and research on bargaining and negotiation. The chapter analyzes the nature and sources of conflict in social relations, contrasts tacit versus explicit bargaining, and shows how hostile and conciliatory tactics affect the prospects for conflict resolution. The chapter uses studies on the prisoner's dilemma to point to the difficulties of conflict resolution, and studies on threats and coercion to suggest that such tactics are often counterproductive. Finally, research on power is used to illustrate how bilateral deterrence processes can forestall hostile action.

The book is designed primarily for the upper-level undergraduate in sociology but it should also be useful to students at a similar level in related disciplines, such as psychology, organizational behavior, political science, and education. We also believe it will be helpful to the beginning graduate student in those fields, as well as to any intellectually curious reader seeking an overview of theoretical, methodological, and substantive issues in this tradition. Accordingly, the book could be used either as a primary text or as supplementary/reference reading material. The chapters are organized so that theoretical and methodological background is presented before the analyses of group processes, and the processes themselves appear in a sequence whereby they build upon each other. While we suggest reading the chapters in the order in which they are presented, the chapters remain individual contributions and may be read independently of each other. For example, the reader who is already well versed in issues of theory and experimentation may want to concentrate on the basic processes chapters.

This book was truly a group effort. We thank the authors for their enthusiastic response to the project and for their readiness to make revisions for the sake of greater consistency across chapters. Marie Lembesis and Kirsten Sigerson contributed many perceptive comments on earlier versions of the manuscript. At Nelson-Hall, we thank Rachel Schick for first-rate copyediting, and Stephen A. Ferrara and Richard Meade for facilitating this endeavor in many ways and providing sound professional advice.

Martha Foschi and Edward J. Lawler

# THE EDITORS

*Martha Foschi* is Professor of Sociology at the University of British Columbia. She received her Ph.D. in Sociology from Stanford University in 1970. Her areas of specialization are theory construction, social psychology (particularly the effects of gender and ethnicity in group interaction), and experimental research. Her work has appeared in *Acta Sociologica, Advances in Group Processes,* the *Canadian Journal of Sociology,* the *Canadian Journal of Behavioural Science,* the *Canadian Review of Sociology and Anthropology,* the *Journal of Mathematical Sociology,* and *Social Psychology Quarterly,* as well as several edited books. She is also co-editor (with Murray Webster, Jr.) of *Status Generalization: New Theory and Research* (Stanford University Press, 1988). Her research interests lie in the social psychology of ability evaluation, and her current project is a series of experiments on the use of gender-based double standards in the assessment of competence.

*Edward J. Lawler* was the Duane C. Spriestersbach Professor of Liberal Arts at the University of Iowa during the preparation of this volume. He received his Ph.D. in Sociology from the University of Wisconsin in 1972. In 1994 he moved to the Department of Organizational Behavior, New York State School of Industrial and Labor Relations, Cornell University. He has done research on power, bargaining tactics, conflict resolution, and revolutionary coalitions. His interests span social psychology and organizations. His work has appeared in the *American Sociological Review,* the *Industrial and Labor Relations Review,* the *Journal of Personality and Social Psychology, Social Forces,* and *Social Psychology Quarterly.* He is co-author (with Samuel B. Bacharach) of *Power and Politics in Organizations* (Jossey-Bass, 1980) and *Bargaining: Power, Tactics, and Outcomes* (Jossey-Bass, 1981). He is series editor of the annual, *Advances in Group Processes,* and became the editor of *Social Psychology Quarterly* in 1993. His current research deals with commitment formation and conflict resolution in bargaining and negotiation.

# THE AUTHORS

*James W. Balkwell* is Associate Professor of Sociology at the University of Georgia. He received his Ph.D. in Sociology from Michigan State 'University. His areas of specialization are small groups, criminal violence, and quantitative methods. His publications include articles in *Advances in Group Processes,* the *American Sociological Review,* and *Social Forces.* Current research projects investigate the development of performance expectations in task groups, and ethnic inequality and homicide rates.

*Rebecca Ford* is currently Assistant Professor of Sociology at the University of Florida. She received her Ph.D. in Sociology in 1988 from the University of Iowa, and specializes in power relations in bargaining and in status-organizing processes. Ongoing projects involve an experimental investigation of unilateral initiatives and punitive tactics in bargaining (with Edward J. Lawler), and a study of the impact of framing on the use of such tactics. She has published in the *American Sociological Review* and *Social Psychology Quarterly.*

*Karen A. Hegtvedt* is Associate Professor of Sociology at Emory University. She received her Ph.D. in Sociology in 1984 from the University of Washington. Her areas of expertise are social psychology, group processes, and emotions (with particular emphasis on issues of justice, power, and social perception). Her work appears in such publications as the *Journal of Social Issues, Social Forces,* and *Social Psychology Quarterly,* as well as several edited volumes. At present she is researching the effects of social identity factors, wage-setting beliefs, and gender role attitudes on the perceived fairness of income inequalities based on sex and education. In addition, she is working on a series of experiments on the negotiated resolution of conflict between individuals promoting different conceptions of justice.

*Barry Markovsky* is currently Associate Professor at the University of Iowa. He received his Ph.D. in Sociology in 1983 from Stanford University. Areas of research include distributive justice, status, power, social networks, judgments and decision making, computer simulations, and socio-physiology. His work has appeared in *Advances in Group Processes,* the *American Sociological Review,* the *Journal of Political and Military Sociology, Personality and Social Psychology Bulletin, Social Forces, Social Justice Research, Social Networks, Social Psychology Quarterly,* and *Sociological Theory,* as well as in a number of edited works. Present research addresses the emergence of power in social exchange networks, and the formation and maintenance of individual and collective beliefs in paranormal claims.

*Barbara Foley Meeker* has a Ph.D. in Sociology from Stanford University (1966) and is currently Professor of Sociology at the University of Maryland, College Park. Prior to this, she taught at the University of Washington. Her areas of specialization are social psychology, theory, and mathematical sociology. She has co-authored *Mathematical Sociology* with Robert K. Leik (Prentice-Hall, 1975) and *Social Causality* (Unwin Hyman, 1988) with Jerald Hage. Her articles have appeared in the *American Sociological Review, Human Relations,* the *Journal of Personality and Social Psychology,* the *Journal of Political and Military Sociology, Sex Roles,* and *Social Psychology Quarterly.*

*Cecilia L. Ridgeway* is Professor of Sociology at Stanford University. She received her Ph.D. from Cornell University in 1972, and has taught at the University of Wisconsin (Milwaukee) and the University of Iowa. Her specializations are social psychology and gender relations, with a particular focus on group processes. She is the editor of *Gender, Interaction, and Inequality* (Springer-Verlag, 1992) and the author of *The Dynamics of Small Groups* (St. Martin's Press, 1983). She has written numerous articles as well, published in the *American Journal of Sociology,* the *American Sociological Review, Social Forces,* and other journals. Her current work deals with the role of groups in the social construction of status dimensions, and with the role of affect in mediating the relationship between power and status.

*John F. Stolte* completed his Ph.D. in 1972 at the University of Washington and is currently Professor of Sociology and Director of the Gerontology Program at Northern Illinois University. His areas of specialization include group processes, socialization, social stratification, experimental research methods, and aging. His research has been published in *Advances in Group Processes,* the *American Sociological Review,* the *Journal of Social Psychology,* and *Social Psychology Quarterly.*

*David G. Wagner* is Associate Professor of Sociology at the State University of New York at Albany. He received his Ph.D. in 1978 from Stanford University. He has previously taught at the University of Toronto and the University of Iowa. His primary research interests are issues of cumulative knowledge growth in sociology, reward expectations and distributive justice, and the social control of status deviance. His journal publications include articles in the *American Journal of Sociology* the *American Sociological Review,* and *Social Forces.* In addition, he has published two books, *The Growth of Sociological Theory* (Sage, 1984) and *Postmodernism and Social Theory* (co-edited with Steven Seidman; Basil Blackwell, 1992). He is currently working on *Strategies, Theories, and Pro-*

*grams,* a book concerned with questions of theory generation, analysis, and growth.

*Murray Webster, Jr.,* received his Ph.D. in Sociology from Stanford University in 1968. His publications include *Sources of Self-Evaluation* (with Barbara Sobieszek; Wiley-Interscience, 1974), *Actions and Actors: Principles of Social Psychology* (Winthrop, 1975), *Status Generalization: New Theory and Research* (co-edited with Martha Foschi; Stanford University Press, 1988), and chapters in several edited collections. His research and theoretical work has appeared in the *American Journal of Sociology,* the *American Sociological Review,* the *Canadian Review of Sociology and Anthropology, Social Forces, Social Psychology Quarterly, Sociology of Education,* and other journals. He has taught at Johns Hopkins University, the University of South Carolina, San Jose State University, and Stanford University. From 1989 through 1991 he was Director of the Sociology Program at the National Science Foundation. He is now Professor of Sociology at the University of North Carolina, Charlotte. His current areas of interest are status processes, legitimation, and effective team decision making.

# PART I

# Theory and Methods

# ONE

# The Structure of Theories[1]

BARRY MARKOVSKY

## WHAT ARE SCIENTIFIC THEORIES?

In science, theories are accorded a very special status: they become focal points of controversy and debate, egos and enmity, conjectures and inquiries. Some take on lives of their own, some have offspring, some are sterile, others never reach maturity. Most are stillborn and never see daylight. This organic analogy runs deeper still: theories contain differentiated substructures, they grow and change, and they interact with other theories—sometimes harmoniously and sometimes in battles to the death.

Common sense has it that theories can be one of two things: guesses about something that is not fully understood, or prescriptions for doing something correctly. In the first case, we may hear the word used by a detective who has a theory linking a particular suspect to a crime; or by a friend who has a theory about why she smokes too much. In the second common use of the term, chronic gamblers frequently develop elaborate (and usually baseless) theories for "beating the odds" in various games of chance; or an author may attempt to add a tone of

1. Many social scientists have suggested methods for constructing theories. Most appear to assume that their field's subject matter is so unique that it requires an approach different from that already employed in the natural sciences, and that knowledge accumulated during more than a century of debate and refinement in the philosophy of science is not particularly relevant. The result is nearly always an idiosyncratic blend of method and substance, quite inconsistent with the goal of providing a general, content-free theoretical method. An important exception to this is Bernard P. Cohen's *Developing Sociological Knowledge*. With a clarity that is easy to take for granted, and without detracting at all from sociology's uniqueness, Cohen provides a theoretical method fully distinguishable from sociological metatheorizing—a method that transcends sociology and is consistent with methods employed by other sciences. This note acknowledges Cohen's strong influence on this chapter. Many other teachers and colleagues will find bits of their lectures, conversations, and wisdom embedded in these pages and I thank them, too, for their various contributions.

scientific legitimacy to an otherwise adequate book title—*The Theory of Achieving Financial Success.*

This chapter does not use the word "theory" in these ways. Rather than argue that such uses are improper, however, this chapter concentrates on defining and illustrating the nature and workings of *scientific* theories. Their purposes, components, relationship to reality, and the potential benefits they can bring to the social sciences are examined.

A suitable working definition for "scientific theory" ("theory" for short) is the following: *a set of explicit, abstract, rigorous and logically related statements that explains or predicts a general class of phenomena.* Before discussing the several parts of this definition, let us consider some of the differences between theories and alternative approaches best classified as "common sense."

## THEORY VERSUS COMMON SENSE

In addition to the above working definition, it is useful to characterize scientific theory by considering what it is not. Theory is not common sense. "Common sense" or "common knowledge" is a storehouse of beliefs, expectations, and inferential techniques dealing with everyday objects, events, and relationships. Individuals and their cultures fill this storehouse over time, and they draw upon its contents on a regular basis. One writer (Hofstadter 1985, p. 640) characterized it this way:

> Common sense is . . . a general—that is, domain-independent—capacity that has to do with fluidity in representation of concepts, an ability to sift what is important from what is not, an ability to find unanticipated analogical similarities between totally different concepts.

Hofstadter, along with some influential philosophers of science (e.g., Popper 1979, Chapter 1), believes it is possible or even advisable to begin the theory-building process from common sense foundations, for science may be thought of as a process of elaborating and refining common sense. This does not imply that common sense and theories are synonymous, however, and Popper explicitly warns that we must be critical of all that is claimed true in the name of common sense. Two reasonable questions, therefore, are "What are the differences between theory and common sense?" and "How can theory improve upon common sense?"

These questions are especially relevant for social scientists whose research findings are often accused of being obvious, that is, readily predictable using only common sense. Is common sense really this powerful? Research clearly indicates that it is not. Investigations of the "hindsight bias" show that *once people know a particular research finding,* they often presume that it was highly likely and knowable in advance. In fact, when it comes to actually predicting the outcomes of experiments before their results are known, observers' powers of common sense turn out to be not much better than blind guessing (Slovic and Fischoff 1977).

Common sense is often equated with "that which virtually everyone believes to be true." As pointed out by Quine and Ullian (1978), however, such "strength in numbers" assertions do not generally provide solid grounding for arguments. Throughout history, popular beliefs have frequently proven unverifiable or false despite the firmest and most widespread of convictions. Quine and Ullian suggest that "what backing suffices depends on what it is to suffice for." When seeking acceptance by a group, it may be sufficient to grasp its members' shared beliefs. When seeking objective knowledge, it is better to evaluate the evidence for and against a claim rather than popular belief about it.

Philosopher Ernest Nagel (1979) found no strict dividing line between science and common sense, but pinpointed several differences. Often, for example, common sense is accurate but the reasons for its accuracy are false or unknown. For instance, members of some group may know that the sun will rise at 6:00 A.M. tomorrow morning, but firmly believe that sunrise occurs at the same time everywhere on a flat and stationary earth. In this way, common sense is often practical but not explanatory. It does not include rigorously tested general propositions from which accurate, specific predictions may be derived. Scientific theories, in Nagel's words, seek the "organization and classification of knowledge on the basis of explanatory principles" (1979, p. 4). In contrast, common sense is unaware of the limits of its validity and applicability. It functions best when prevailing conditions are constant because it does not incorporate those conditions in its descriptions and prescriptions. Scientific theories seek to understand the underlying mechanisms of phenomena and how they are affected by prevailing conditions.

It is undeniable that without common sense, the world would seem incoherent and unpredictable. We literally could not survive without extraordinary aid from others (who do have common sense). Even so, there are many aspects of reality with which common sense is never called upon to deal, many questions that it is never asked, and many answers that are simply accepted without critical examination. For these and other reasons discussed below, a common sense approach to acquiring knowledge about the social world is inadequate for our purposes. Scientific theories overcome these limitations. Obviously, if theories were no better than common sense at explaining and predicting phenomena, they would have no special value to us. Moreover, to the degree that research is not theoretically-driven, there is some validity to the criticism that research findings tend to simply confirm what we already know or could have intuited through common sense. This chapter takes the position that theories can and do fare better than common sense in explaining social phenomena. They do so by avoiding the problems endemic to common sense.

## Common Sense Explanations Can Be Circular

In a circular explanation, that which is to be explained appears as part of the explanation, often in a disguised form. A simple example appears in the following exchange:

*Person A:* "Do you believe in God?"
*Person B:* "Yes."
*Person A:* "Why do you believe this?"
*Person B:* "Because the Bible says He exists."
*Person A:* "Why do you believe what the Bible says?"
*Person B:* "Because it's the word of God, of course!"

Saying that the Bible is the word of God already presumes a belief in God's existence, and it is that belief that was supposed to have been justified. Usually, circular explanations are much more difficult to identify. They may be hidden within layers of text, spread across lengthy discourse, or obscured by changes in terms. Importantly, however, the conclusion of a circular argument is not automatically wrong. For instance, circularity in the above argument obviously does not preclude the existence of God. In general, circular arguments are merely irrelevant to the issues for which explanations are being sought.

Scientific theories employ several methods to help guard against circularities. These include (1) the adoption of a formal syntax (e.g., a set of logical or mathematical rules) for organizing a theory's statements, (2) an effort to make the terms of the theory as few in number and as clear in meaning as possible, and (3) the critical evaluation of theories by peer reviewers and/or others with the knowledge to do so. A formal syntax guards against circularities by making them immediately evident and defining them as problematic. Minimizing the number of terms used to express a theory simplifies its analysis and, again, helps to make circular statements more evident. Having the theory critically evaluated by others is a powerful method for locating problem areas and often leads to suggestions for remedies.

---

## Common Sense Explanations Can Be Ad Hoc

An *ad hoc* explanation is one that is formulated for a specific observation. As such, it will tend to ignore more general factors which may be relevant to that observation. For example, a sexual assault may be "explained" by blaming the victim: "She was attacked because she was dressed so provocatively that night." This *ad hoc* reasoning ignores many possible factors that may not be apparent to the casual observer: the location of the assault is a frequent site of similar violent crimes; the attacker had been stalking the victim for days; the victim was beaten and robbed; the attacker has a history of such crimes. The *ad hoc* explanation ignores larger patterns of which the particular incident is but a part. Social, geographical, and economic factors may combine to make certain areas dangerous. The attacker's history may show that his victims fit a general physical profile, making style of dress irrelevant. There may have been numerous others who dressed similarly and were nearby, but who were not attacked that night. *Ad hoc* explanations are attractive as tools of common sense because they give us a feeling of security and control—that we understand life's complexities and thus may by our own volition seek pleasant outcomes and avoid the harmful ones. Common sense says that by dressing conservatively one may avoid sexual assault. It is not that simple.

In science, *ad hoc* explanations are frequently offered in a provisional way to account for anomalous findings. They are also regarded as virtually useless for the growth of theoretical knowledge because, as Popper noted (1979, p. 16), they "are not independently testable" and "can be had for the asking." Such explanations may prove fruitful by motivating the development of alternative theories and new directions for research. By themselves, however, *ad hoc* explanations take us no further than the observation for which they were concocted.

## Common Sense Explanations Can Be Particularistic

The scope of common sense is frequently limited to particular times, places, and things. This is not usually a problem. It is useful to be able to anticipate a friend's responses to your words and actions, or to know how your car behaves on wet roads. Most of us are also interested in certain worldly events and we turn to journalists who, as part of their job, gather information on them. Such a "particularistic" approach is self-defeating, however, when the goal is to acquire knowledge that can be generalized to other times, places, and things. No amount of detailed information about the workings of the board of directors of General Motors will by itself increase our theoretical knowledge about group processes.

Berger, Zelditch, and Anderson (1972), Cohen (1989), and Popper (1961) have all expressed quite similar views on the distinction between historical (or particularizing) and generalizing strategies. If we accept the construction of *general* theories as a goal of science, then particularizing approaches do not provide much benefit. As Berger et al. (1972, p. xii) note:

> That [general scientific] laws are not of any intrinsic interest in a purely historical investigation makes it possible for the investigation to be content with a relatively unsystematic collection of relatively unformulated, relatively concrete, and relatively common sense propositions about social behavior. . . . The difficulty is that it is an effect, not a law or set of laws, that is of central concern.

To summarize: the greater the depth of knowledge acquired with regard to any particular phenomenon or entity, the less the degree to which that knowledge will apply to anything else. This runs counter to the goal of theoretical generality.

In contrast to a particularistic focus, theories are designed to be generalizable by virtue of their abstractness. In some quarters, abstractness is considered a bad quality because it implies detachment from reality. Of course, a theory with no connection to reality is not going to be of any use in explaining real events.

However, total concreteness would prevent any generalization beyond the case at hand. Imagine what the field of physics would be like if different theories were required to explain every distinct physical event.

## Common Sense Explanations Can Be Post Hoc

This may be the most serious problem with common sense explanations, and one of the easiest to overcome using standard scientific procedures. The *post hoc* fallacy is the claim that event a caused event b because b followed a. Humans learn by recognizing "temporal contiguities"—events that follow one another relatively closely in time—and inferring from such observations that the earlier event caused the later one. Undeniably, the inference of causality is oftentimes quite valid: lightning does cause thunder, and a wound causes pain. Sometimes, however, this logic backfires and false inferences are made. For example, millions of people believe that all sorts of phenomena, from crime waves to hospital emergency ward admissions to losing car keys, are caused by full moons. Study after study finds no such effect, but it still seems very real to those who believe in it.

The logic of scientific theorizing and testing is actually incapable of proving that a causal relation exists between events a and b. However, theories can generate testable hypotheses for empirical relationships that should hold for causally related phenomena. Data analytic techniques may then be applied to determine whether those observed relationships are unlikely to have been due to chance alone. To use the example just mentioned, many people believe that increases in crimes, natural disasters, and other phenomena are caused by the full moon (Lieber 1978). To support this claim, believers ignore the lack of a theoretical basis for such relationships, and instead recall specific events that occurred around the time of a full moon, or others' claims about such events.

Can temporally contiguous events, such as an apparent rise in emergency room admissions during a full moon, be taken as causally related? The answer is no, not without more information. The following categories define the cells of Table 1.1, which displays the results of a hypothetical two-year experiment. In addition to knowing the number of times that (1) such admissions were abnormally high during the full moon (see cell A), you would also need to know how often (2) comparable increases occurred during other lunar phases (see cell B), (3) no increases occurred during full moons (see cell C), and (4) no increases occurred during other phases (see cell D).

For emergency room workers reflecting on events of the last two years, cells B, C, and D would require recalling "non-events," i.e., non-full moons and/or non-rises in admission. Perhaps because cell A is the only one in which both of the rarer events occur, the five times that admissions were above normal during full moons may be very memorable to emergency room workers—sufficiently so

**Table 1.1 Moon Effects on Number of Days with Above Normal Versus Normal Emergency Room Admissions**

|  |  | Moon Phase | | Total |
|---|---|---|---|---|
|  |  | Full | Other |  |
| Emergency Room Admissions | Above Normal | A 5 | B 15 | 20 |
|  | Normal | C 20 | D 60 | 80 |
|  | Total | 25 | 75 | 100 |

to lead them to conclude that full moons caused the rises. An analysis of the information in the table leads to a very different conclusion, however. Multiplying the totals for the row and column of a given cell (e.g., 25 × 80 for cell c) and dividing by the grand total (100) yields the cell values that would be expected to be found when there is no association at all between moon phase and emergency room admissions. The values appearing in the four cells represent just such a case. Common sense tends to ignore cells B, C, and D, all of which are required to transcend the *post hoc* bias and determine whether there really is a statistical relationship.

## Common Sense Often Deals with Surface Features

A good example of this practice is the formation of first impressions. We all quite readily formulate hunches about the deeper aspects of acquaintances' personalities, often based on very limited information. Even though we may feel confident about such impressions, they often turn out to be ill-informed and they are seldom checked for accuracy.

Another example is the tendency, given some set of unexplained events, to readily accept explanations that violate thousands of years of accumulated knowledge. Thus we often view as credible any scenario that appears to account for the surface features of a complex phenomenon. Sometimes, in fact, the *lack* of a thorough, conventional explanation is claimed to be *supportive* of an unorthodox explanation. For example, a newspaper in upstate New York reported that citizens and scientists alike were at a loss to explain colored lights in the evening sky over a certain small city. Members of a state UFO-enthusiast network, when questioned by the press, announced that this inability to identify the lights provided further evidence that the earth is under surveillance by alien life forms. The failure to account for the unidentified objects, however, does not increase the likelihood that they are the spacecraft of alien visitors. "Unidentified" means *unidentified.* In general, there is no scientific shame in having insufficient data to draw conclusions. The only shame is promoting speculations whose only merit is an ability to weave surface features of phenomena into a whimsical fabric.

## Common Sense Allows Contradictions

A contradiction amounts to saying that something is both true and untrue. When friends are separated, we may wish to predict whether their relationship will strengthen or weaken. Two famous maxims generate contradictory predictions: "Absence makes the heart grow fonder," and "Out of sight, out of mind." Each statement contains a measure of common sense, but both cannot be true for the same pair of friends at the same point in time without some type of reinterpretation. And yet both bits of folk wisdom remain in our storehouse of common sense, telling us in essence that separated friends will either forget about each other or grow closer. In science, if we wish to know whether or not event x will occur, it is altogether unsatisfying to be told that "either x will happen, or else x will not happen."

It is worth noting that if we allow a contradiction in our explanation, then any false statement that you can imagine may be logically derived and proven true. Take the contradiction (1) "The sky is blue and the sky is not blue." Now take the false statement (2) "Humans have no heads." At this point we may derive from (1) and (2) the following valid conclusion: (3) "Either the sky is blue, or humans have no heads." Now from statement (1) we may also obtain (4) "The sky is not blue." But if (3) *"Either* the sky is blue, *or* humans have no heads," and (4) "The sky *is not* blue," then it must be true that *humans have no heads!* Contradictions lead to absurdities. That is why we should take great pains to exclude them from our theories. This chapter later shows that adopting an explicit logical framework helps to eliminate contradictions.

## Common Sense Is Unconditionalized

A condition is a statement that places limitations on another statement. For example, "grass is green" is an unconstrained, unconditional statement to which "in the spring" may be added as a limiting condition. For those times when common sense does reach beyond particulars in search of generality, it is too often unconditionalized. That is, the conditions under which claims of knowledge apply are either not considered or left unstated. Before my first science class I learned that water freezes at 32 degrees—an unconditional statement. What a rude complication it was for me to learn that standing water in the pond near my childhood home froze before moving water in the river that fed it, and that ocean water 25 miles away could be much colder than "freezing" without freezing! The actual freezing point is conditional on such factors as the purity of the water, its rate of flow, and the barometric pressure. Notice that just because the statement is conditional does not prevent it from being general. The statement applies any time, any place, to any vessel of water, if the appropriate conditions are satisfied. That amounts to a potentially infinite number of times and places.

Conditionalization adds precision to theoretical claims and prevents their application to phenomena outside of the intended purview of the theory. Another benefit of conditionalization is its capacity to resolve apparent contradictions. In reference to (and rephrasing) the contradiction cited earlier, it may be reasonable to assert that for two people who have regular face-to-face contact and positive evaluations of one another, physical separation increases emotional attachment *under the condition* that the relationship has progressed beyond the level of an acquaintanceship by the time the separation takes place. The effect of separation may be asserted to be the opposite under the condition that the relationship has not progressed beyond this critical stage.

## Common Sense is Not Systematically Tested

It is far easier and more psychologically satisfying to simply believe that we are correct about something than it is to carefully test our beliefs and risk being wrong. This is not to say that we must all endeavor to test every opinion we hold, observation we make, or statement we utter. Much of what we believe, observe and say is based on time-tested practical knowledge, and little would be gained— and much time and energy lost—by subjecting this knowledge to systematic examination. It does suggest, however, that we should not be surprised to find that common sense errs from time to time. If we are concerned with the truthfulness of particular explanations and beliefs, and also with the possible consequences of acting on their behalf, then testing is the best way we know of verifying those beliefs, eliminating false alternative explanations, and resolving differences of opinions.

Systematic testing, as described in Chapter 3, is part of a method for improving upon untested common sense. This is because we may legitimately attach more confidence to claims or beliefs that have survived pointed attempts at disconfirmation than those that have not been so tested. This is doubly important in view of the issue raised in the next section.

## Common Sense Allows Subjective Validation

Subjective validation is a method that we all employ to verify our beliefs. It is a form of nonsystematic testing which involves attending to evidence that supports a belief, and discounting or ignoring neutral or unfavorable evidence. Whereas *post hoc* inferences and other common sense methods may plant the seed of a belief, subjective validation permits it to flourish indefinitely.

In the example of belief in the "lunar effect" on human affairs, once the possibility is allowed that moon phases affect people, attention is drawn to those events that can be interpreted as supporting the belief. Quite often this involves granting a good deal of latitude in those interpretations. A rise in emergency room admissions a few days either prior or subsequent to the full moon may suggest an effect—as might reading about a moderate earthquake in Europe, a hefty drop in the Dow Jones Industrial Average, or a riot involving ardent fans at a London soccer match. During other lunar phases, the believer simply fails to note the frequency at which such events occur. During or close to the full moon, virtually any unusual event may be interpreted as caused by the moon. Overlooked is the fact that such events actually occur very frequently and during all lunar phases.

Many people can recount a time when they saw something in a dream that later came true, and so believe that dreams are capable of foretelling the future. For example, some have reported prescient dreams in which a certain loved one dies, followed soon thereafter by his or her actual death. In fact, such dreams turn out to be fairly common—especially when the loved one is elderly or ailing. We also tend to forget that the contents of the vast majority of our dreams are not played out in reality, and that we are prone to fill in many of a dream's details long after awakening. Still, the coincidence of dream and reality can produce such an emotional impact that subjective validation of dreams' abilities to foretell the future almost inevitably follows. In this example, the belief is quite harmless. Unfortunately, however, subjective validation is also at the root of many harmful beliefs and perceptions. The same mechanism that allows us to validate unfounded beliefs about dreams or moon phases also permits us to hold onto harmful and false stereotypes, and to misplace faith in our abilities to make accurate judgments under complex or ambiguous circumstances.

Scientists are humans too, and they often engage in a process of subjectively validating their theories. This alone, however, is not (and should not be) sufficient to convince others of the truthfulness of a theory's claims. To be generally accepted in a field, a theory's tests must survive the collective scrutiny of skeptics. These skeptics are bound and determined to point out when a test is too weak to rule out alternative explanations. Subjective evaluation fails as a theory-testing method precisely because it systematically ignores information (e.g., cells B, C and D in Table 1.1) that would suggest alternative explanations for observed phenomena.

## *Common Sense Is Unorganized and Vague*

Common sense is unorganized because it lacks a system for keeping track of what is known already, the amount of evidence backing that knowledge, and how existing information can be used to garner further knowledge. The difference between the ways that common sense and theory are organized is something like the difference between a long list of independent sentences and a book with sentences organized into paragraphs, sections, and chapters. Long, unstructured lists are extremely inefficient storehouses for knowledge. In constructing new theories, a great deal of attention is paid to what theories already exist, the kinds of evidence offered for them, and how they can be improved upon by making them simpler, more compact, and still as accurate and comprehensive as possible.

Common sense is vague in that its terms lack unambiguous definition. What do we really mean when we say that someone has a good personality? A strong will? A mean streak? What are we actually talking about when using the ideas of "power," "status," "love," or "justice" in everyday discourse? If you and nine of your friends wrote down definitions for each of these words, the chances are good that you would wind up with ten different definitions for each. This is a problem because any explanations involving "power," "love," etc., could only be of use if we first agree on meanings for such terms.

In the construction of a scientific theory, it is perfectly reasonable to assume that there are no absolute, "true" definitions for the terms it contains. Instead, the theorist will try to guarantee accurate communication by stating the exact meanings that he or she intends to communicate. This is done using various types of explicit definitions, as discussed below. For example, it is reasonable to have "injustice" defined in one theory as "the violation of objective allocation standards," but in another theory as "the emotional response to the violation of objective allocation standards," without implying that at least one of the definitions must somehow be wrong.

To summarize, common sense methods of acquiring knowledge have a variety of limitations that can lead to faulty explanations. Despite their necessity and utility for a wide range of everyday purposes, these methods are generally inadequate to address most of the problems of long-standing interest in the social sciences. On the other hand, the methods of science do not provide a universal panacea for all of the inadequacies of common sense. Therefore, it is worthwhile to next consider the proper role of scientific theorizing in terms of its requirements and benefits.

## THE ROLE OF SCIENTIFIC THEORIZING

Although theories provide a method for improving upon common sense, it is important to realize that not all phenomena addressed by common sense are potential targets for scientific theories. Two criteria distinguish phenomena that are candidates for theoretical analysis from those which are not: repeatability and testability.

## Repeatability

Is the phenomenon of interest—or important properties of the phenomenon—reproducible or naturally recurrent? Laboratories in different sciences serve the purpose of reproducing phenomena of interest while controlling and manipulating surrounding conditions. Not all properties of any natural phenomenon can be reproduced in a laboratory, of course. It is not feasible to create civil wars or cultural revolutions in a laboratory at will. Nevertheless, certain properties of revolutions and wars may be abstracted and studied in laboratories, e.g., conflicts of interest, knowledge about opponents, relative levels of resources, capacities to benefit or harm the other, access to strategic information, etc.

Alternatively, there may have been a large enough number of naturally occurring revolutions that historical records provide all the information necessary to test a particular explanation. Thus, some phenomena recur in nature with sufficient frequency that their determinants and consequences may be studied without the need for experimental control. An astronomer cannot manipulate the cosmos, but she or he can (1) make repeated observations using instruments sensitive to different properties of the objects of interest, such as radiation emanating from a star in both the visible and infrared ranges of the radiation spectrum; (2) observe different phenomena that are within the same abstract class, such as different binary star systems; or (3) investigate naturally occurring periodic events such as planetary orbits, eclipses, visits by comets, and so on.

More and more, it seems, we are bombarded with advertisements for books and television programs about "strange phenomena that baffle scientists." One television commercial for a series of books on the supernatural tells of a mother who felt a sharp pain in her hand at the very instant that her daughter, one thousand miles away, scalded her hand with some hot water. The implication is that this must be more than mere coincidence. It is not so much that this type of event leaves scientists baffled, but rather that they simply tend not to be very interested. This is because such events are relatively unique, there is usually no way to verify the claims, and we do not know how often the events occur naturally. Does the daughter scald herself on a regular basis? Does the mother have arthritis? All that we may conclude from such a claim (or from a collection of one hundred such claims) is that it would be foolhardy to conclude anything.

## Testability

The second criterion for determining whether a phenomenon is amenable to scientific theorizing is whether statements about the phenomenon are testable. In other words, such statements must be falsifiable. As indicated earlier in this chapter, it is possible to make statements in such an ambiguous way that they cannot be disproved. Take, for example, "Small groups may have role structures." This statement is unfalsifiable: it is supported by the observation of a small group with a role structure, but it is not refuted by the observation of a small group without one. Such statements have absolutely no predictive power.

Falsifiability and predictive power actually go hand in hand. Think of falsifiability not as the likelihood that a statement is false, but rather as the vulnerability of a statement to being disproved. For instance, "Water boils when it gets hot enough" is both testable and falsifiable, but it is not nearly as vulnerable to falsification as the statement "Water boils at 100 degrees centigrade at sea level." The latter has a much narrower range of acceptance than the former, which means it has many more ways to be wrong. It is a more precise statement and has greater predictive power. It is *riskier.*

For excellent examples of statements that are usually either impossible to falsify or that simply go untested, examine the predictions given by psychics and astrologers in supermarket tabloids. Most are virtually invulnerable to falsification ("Elvis' Ghost Will Occupy a Des Moines Family's Microwave") or could have been predicted by anyone ("There Will Be Tension in Some Part of the Middle East"). Predictions that are both falsifiable and risky are rare in these publications, and when made are usually not borne out. To see this, save a publication containing "Psychic Predictions for the Coming Year." After a year passes, check to see how many of the predictions that were both risky and falsifiable came to pass. Also check to see how many major world events occurred that were not predicted by any of the psychics. It is extremely unlikely that you will find evidence of extraordinary psychic powers.

## The Benefits of Scientific Theorizing

To summarize thus far, scientific theories provide a means of improving upon common sense. In fact, they open new worlds of knowledge where common sense rarely ventures. They are able to do this by employing methods designed to eliminate circularities and contradictions; by striving toward abstraction, generality, and conditionalization without sacrificing applicability; by probing below the surface characteristics of phenomena; by organizing and structuring knowledge in a way that promotes testability, depth, and explanatory power; and by using clearly defined terms whose meanings may be communicated accurately, facilitating the ongoing refinement and expansion of the theory containing those terms.

All this may seem a tall order for a device so ephemeral as a theory, especially for those attempting to address human social behavior. In fact, a theory can do all this and more, but there is a price: great care is required to assemble all of its parts into a coherent and parsimonious whole. The goal in the following section is to describe the parts of a theory and how they fit together.

## ELEMENTS OF THEORIES

First, it is necessary to distinguish theories from related entities known variously as "metatheories," "paradigms," "orientations," "perspectives," "frameworks," etc. A theory makes rigorous, explicit, abstract, general, and testable statements. In contrast, metatheories (and the like) are usually loosely organized and often implicit sets of ideas and value statements that identify important problems, appropriate modes of theoretical discourse, broad assumptions about human nature, philosophical positions, and so on. They also may consist of discussions about a theory's components or its relationships to other theories. Metatheories are not directly testable, and ambiguities in their language almost always inhibit comparisons that are mutually satisfying to adherents of different metatheories. The theory–metatheory distinction is crucial, though, because theories always contain testable provisional knowledge claims, but metatheories need not do so.

### *Concepts*

Ordinary language is usually inadequate for expressing the non-intuitive ideas in which theories often deal. The elements of common languages relate to the world of everyday objects. They tend to be evocative but imprecise. This does not present a problem for most purposes. Words uttered by one person to another generally evoke the intended meanings and responses from others. On the other hand, because theories are used to develop and communicate *new* knowledge, meanings for their specialized terms are generally not widely shared. This is the case whenever the theory uses ideas that are not from the realm of common sense experience: quarks, role structures, and black holes are examples. Although such terms are generally understood in a vague way, they also have explicit, highly specialized meanings in the context of particular theories. For example, the definition of "role" in a theory of group structure should determine what properties an object must possess in order to be classified as either a role or not a role (Freese and Sell 1980). In this way, anyone using the theory can employ the definition to determine, for any object in the universe, whether or not it is an instance of a role. To the extent that this ideal can be achieved, the theorist can be assured that others are comprehending the theory exactly as he or she intended it to be understood.

In the context of theories, expressions like "role" and "black hole" serve as labels for "concepts." Concepts are specialized, well-defined ideas that are brought together and communicated by theories. Although we frequently encounter arguments about the true meaning or "essence" of a variety of concepts, here we assume that theorists provide their meanings as part of the theory-building process. This means that concepts cannot be proven true or false. Instead, they are evaluated according to the precision of the ideas they communicate, by their utility in explanations of phenomena, and by the extent to which they are useful in a large number and broad range of theoretical statements.

To construct meanings or definitions for concepts requires the use of expressions which, in turn, are labels for other concepts. Thus, a theory actually employs a conceptual system in which more complex concepts are built from simpler ones. To prevent an infinite regress, the very simplest are assumed to be widely understood and are left undefined in the theory. These are called the theory's "primitive concepts." In contrast, "defined concepts" use expressions for primitive and/or previously defined concepts to establish their meanings through definitions. Conceptual systems may range from relatively "flat" and simple to extremely "deep" and complex, depending upon the needs and purposes of the theory. Concepts and their definitions are always provisional and subject to refinement and revision as theoretical needs dictate.

Cohen (1989) distinguished between three types of definitions: "denotative," "connotative," and "nominal." A denotative definition provides meaning for a concept by indicating examples. Gift-giving, household economics, or national trade deficits may be used in a denotative definition of the concept of "social exchange system." This type of definition may be very useful and is often the best we can hope for until we are willing or able to assign more abstract and general properties to a concept, as discussed next.

Connotative definitions specify the properties of the concept being defined in abstract and general terms, not via examples. We may say, for example, that x is a social exchange system if and only if x consists of two or more actors among which are distributed two or more objects that are valued by and traded among those actors. Connotative definitions are the most rigorous and demanding of the three types, and therefore can be very difficult to devise. At the same time, the process of developing a connotative definition or a system of connotatively defined concepts for a theory can be very informative and rewarding. For example, even a little attention to the definitions of concepts can have great payoffs in terms of the theory's precision and communicability. When examining a given piece of scholarly work, we often find that what appeared to be a straightforward, intuitively appealing theory actually contains much ambiguity and redundancy. In general, failing to adequately define concepts may confer a false sense of precision and, even worse, indicate a form of intellectual dishonesty. Thus, one should always be very skeptical of theories with poorly defined or undefined concepts.

A nominal definition is simply the substitution of a new label for an existing concept's label. For example, a theorist may wish to substitute the term "s" for every appearance of "exchange system" in his or her theory, where "exchange system" is already connotatively defined. Stating a nominal definition does not add meaning to the term being defined. However, it does facilitate communication by contributing to a well-defined lexicon whose meanings are shared across members of some relevant audience. For this reason, and contrary to popular misconceptions, some "jargon" is essential in scientific theories; only ill-defined jargon is objectionable.

## Statements

The terms used to express a theory's concepts are combined to form "statements." The most explicit methods for accomplishing this employ one of a variety of "logical calculi." These are sets of logical or mathematical procedures that provide (1) methods for combining theoretical terms into statements, and (2) a set of rules for deriving new statements.

Sentential logic, for example, provides rules for truth-preserving manipulations of statements, regardless of their content. Take a statement such as "If a social group has a sanctioning system, then the sanctioning system serves the interests of higher status members." This can be shown to have the simple logical form "If x then y," or "x implies y," or "x → y." The x statement is "A social group has a sanctioning system" and y is "The sanctioning system serves the interests of higher status members." Other basic forms include "not x," "x and y," "x or y (but not both)," "x and/or y," and "x if and only if y."

Now let "z" stand for the statement "The lower class revolts," and form the statement "If y then z." This simple theory now contains two basic statements: "x → y" and "y → z." Call these statements "assumptions" because we will accept them as true. (We could also call them "axioms," "postulates," or "propositions.") Sentential logic contains a law or transformation rule that, when applied to these two true statements, forces a new statement that must also be true: "x → z." Such statements are usually called "derivations" or "theorems." In general, the transformation rules of a logical calculus allow us to obtain new knowledge from prior statements that are assumed to be true. Sometimes the statements comprising this new knowledge are obvious, as in the above example. For more complex systems of statements, or with richer logical calculi (e.g., higher level mathematics), derived statements may be unanticipated or even counterintuitive—but still true given the truth of the assumptions.

There are benefits to the use of logical calculi that build upon and go beyond their organizational and transformational services. When properly constructed and distinguished from definitions of concepts, logically related theoretical statements avoid the circularities, contradictions, and vagaries to which less rigorous approaches are vulnerable. The "tautology" is one example of an invalid form of theoretical argument. A tautology exists when "If x then y" is asserted as an assumption and, additionally, y is defined partly or wholly in terms of x. For example, consider a theory that contains the assumption "In groups, reward systems lead to solidarity." Elsewhere the theorist defines solidarity as "a group condition characterized by the existence of a reward system." The first statement assumes that the reward system *determines* solidarity. According to the second statement, solidarity can exist *only* if there is a reward system; the correspondence of solidarity with reward systems is declared to be true by definition. This makes the assumption unfalsifiable. We can never have both the absence of a reward system and solidarity, because the absence of the reward system means, by definition, that solidarity is not present. This problem has not prevented a good many theorists from declaring their assumptions to be verified, however.

Employing an explicit logical calculus also helps to focus attention on the concepts, assumptions, and derivations of a theory rather than on who wrote the theory, what perspective the theory embodies (e.g., neofunctionalist, Marxist, interactionist, rationalist), the intellectual evolution of the theory, etc. All of these issues can be interesting in their own right, but none has any reliable bearing on the truth or falsity of the theory. In particular, the so-called "argument from authority" is very pervasive in speculative social scientific theorizing. In piecing together their own theories, many writers believe that it is sufficient to note that a given assertion is corroborated by a famous scholar, without concern for whether or not the assertion has been borne out through empirical test.

## Scope

The scope of a theory is the domain of phenomena to which it applies, and "scope conditions" are provisional statements which delineate that domain. For example, a theorist may wish to apply a theory of justice only in social exchange situations, a theory of status only in collective task situations, or a theory of power only when there are negotiations occurring. In each case, scope conditions would express, in abstract theoretical terms, exactly the properties that must or must not be present in a situation before the theory is deemed applicable.

Like assumptions, scope conditions are not bound to any particular time or place, so theories remain general, i.e., applicable in a potentially infinite number of instances. Moreover, scope conditions are not evaluated in the same way as assumptions. When they are not satisfied by a given set of empirical circumstances, this simply indicates that the theory is not relevant in those circumstances. So if a theory of power has a scope condition saying that the theory is applicable "when every actor prefers to receive higher rewards than other actors," and if a group is identified in which all members look out for everyone else's welfare before their own, then whether or not the theory's predictions turn out to be true for that group is irrelevant for purposes of evaluating the theory. The falsification of predictions would not weaken the theory. When scope conditions are satisfied *and* theoretical assumptions are falsified, however, then we must return to the proverbial drawing board and carefully reconsider one or more aspects of the theory or the methods by which it was tested.

Regretfully, few social scientific theories come with explicit scope conditions and there are no widely shared norms or conventions requiring their use. It also turns out to be quite challenging to devise even provisional scope conditions. We naturally tend to more readily conceive of possible applications of our theories than we do of non-applications. Perhaps for these reasons, many of our theories are written in a way that conveys a false image of universality even though, when pressed, virtually every theorist will admit that there are limitations to the domain of his or her theory's applicability.

Darker motives may also inhibit the use of scope conditions. Those whose theories appear deep, broad and consistent with many empirical observations receive professional accolades. Why should a theorist tarnish this success by pointing out scope *limitations*? Is this not an admission of weakness? Perhaps, but in the long run, if theoretical advancement is valued over theorists' self-promotion, then it behooves theorists to assert explicit scope conditions. Otherwise, negative instances are too easily declared irrelevant ("My theory was obviously never intended to explain *everything!*") and the theory fails to benefit from its mistakes. Like the organisms alluded to at the beginning of this chapter, in order to become stronger, theories must evolve within a challenging environment.

## The Link to Reality

Although scope conditions provide abstract guidelines for the application and testing of theories, they provide only limited help in deciding what specific phenomena a theory may actually predict and explain. How do we make this crucial link from theory to reality? More specifically, how do we connect a general and abstract theoretical derivation like "If x, then z" to something that we can actually observe?

Many scientists like to think of a theory as an idealized model of processes and events occurring in an imaginary universe. At the same time, the "unreal" theory can be extraordinarily useful for understanding real processes and events *if* we are able to build bridges from its concepts to observable phenomena. It is the concept definitions, described in preceding pages, that serve as the blueprints for such bridge-building. In short, a concrete (or "real") object or event that satisfies the abstract (or "idealized") conditions set forth in a definition is employed to "instantiate" or "operationalize" that concept, i.e., to serve as an observable manifestation of the idealized concept. When all of the concepts represented in a theoretical statement are instantiated, the result is a new kind of statement—one that makes a prediction about relationships between real objects and/or events. This "observation statement" is most commonly known as a "hypothesis."

As an example, Theorem 1 in a theory of power in social exchange networks (Markovsky, Willer, and Patton 1988) stated: "If i has no alternative relations, then i seeks exchange with j." Obviously, this is a highly abstract statement. Earlier in the article in which it appeared, however, its terms were defined with sufficient clarity so that a laboratory test that satisfied the theory's scope conditions could be constructed. Actors i and j were assumed to be decision-making individuals or groups that could negotiate and exchange goods with each other to obtain profit. In the experimental test, (1) human subjects with mutual visual contact served as instances of i and j in an exchange relationship; (2) one of the subjects, i, had a single potential exchange partner, j; (3) i perceived that j may have had other potential exchange partners; and (4) the predicted behavior "i seeks exchange with j" was operationalized as i making negotiation offers to j that were competitive with others that j may have been receiving. Linking the earlier abstract statement with instantiations of its theoretical concepts, we can derive a hypothesis:

> In an experiment conducted at the University of Kansas on February 17, 1986 at 2:00 P.M., if subject i (who has subject j as a potential exchange partner) does not have visual contact with any subjects other than j, then i will make negotiation offers to j that are competitive with other offers that j may receive.

Quite often researchers blur the distinction between theoretical statements and hypotheses, thereby committing a type of "reification error." That is, they forget that theories do not speak directly to real objects and events, but that they must first be translated, concept by concept, term by term, into statements about observable phenomena. (See also Chapter 3 on this point.) Willer and Webster (1970) addressed a related issue: the focus on "empirical explanations" of relationships among observables; that is, mistaking summaries of statistical relationships among measured variables for theories. The authors recognized several benefits associated with empirical explanations. For instance, they tend to account for a larger number of the specific details of the situation in which observations were made, and they are more readily linked to observables and so are easier to test than theories. The sacrifice that is suffered for these advantages, however, is generality. An empirical explanation may be said to "generalize" to situations that are highly similar to that in which the explanation is developed. In contrast, a theory generalizes to situations that satisfy its scope conditions. For example, the theory of power in social exchange networks generalizes not only to similar laboratory settings, but also to such diverse contexts as dating networks, economic markets, auctions, and inter-organizational relations that are subsumed within the theory's scope. Willer and Webster argued that too much attention to relations among empirical indicators hinders the development of cumulative theories in sociology.

Just as empirical observation without theory retards the development of general knowledge, theory-building without recourse to stringent empirical testing is at least as inefficient a route to knowledge. The former leads to rich but non-generalizable descriptions; the latter to "castles in the air." A balance must be struck between our interest in phenomena and our interest in general knowledge. These interests cannot be satisfied simultaneously. A particularly useful metaphor that brings the two together likens theories to abstract, psychological lenses. Through the lenses of theory we can obtain accurate but limited images of a broad range of specific phenomena. Much is filtered out, but this is the cost we willingly bear in order that other phenomena may be brought into clearer view.

## SUMMARY

Before discussing the structure of theories, this chapter examined some of the pitfalls that theories are designed to avoid. Common sense reasoning is indispensable, but it proves to be limited as an alternative to theory-building. Due to their lack of built-in safeguards, arguments made on the basis of common sense may be circular, *ad hoc, post hoc,* unconditionalized, unorganized, vague, particularistic, superficial, untested, subjectively validated, and self-contradictory. When phenomena of interest are repeatable or recurrent, and if the statements made in their regard are testable, then the theoretical and empirical methods of science may be applied toward improving our understanding of those phenomena.

In addition to being testable, the statements of well-formed theories are rigorous, explicit, abstract, and general. Toward these ends, efforts are made to provide explicit definitions for the ideas or concepts in theories. To the degree that a statement "x" contains concepts whose meanings are not accurately communicated to others wishing to test the theory, this ambiguity is transmitted from x into any derived statements that depend upon x. Furthermore, ambiguity will also infect the hypotheses to be tested and thus create a situation in which observers may disagree in their interpretations of the observations upon which the hypotheses are presumed to bear.

A theorist can employ one of a variety of logical calculi to help safeguard against internal contradictions and invalid derivations from his or her theory, and to promote its efficient communication and testing. Such procedures also allow one to explore logical consequences of a theory—consequences that may not be readily apparent without the use of a systematic method for generating derivations. When a researcher is interested in testing one or more of a theory's consequences, he or she does so by identifying observable instances of theoretical terms and generating testable hypotheses. If hypothesis testing is to have any impact on the theory, however, the researcher must also locate or create a research setting that satisfies its scope conditions. If the theory survives attempts to falsify it, we may feel more confident in its truthfulness and go about extending and/or refining it. If the theory fails its test, then one or more aspects of the theory must be re-examined, including testing procedures, instantiations, concept definitions, logical integrity, or even its basic assumptions if problems cannot be found elsewhere. Importantly, the weakness is unlikely to be identified without further research.

Only a very small proportion of social scientific theories ever achieve these ideals. An examination of our journals finds some theories stated with explicit assumptions but no definitions for concepts, and others with key concepts defined but no explicit assumptions. Rarely are scope conditions asserted or theoretical derivations explored. Even rarer are well-developed theory programs—sets of multiple, interrelated theories—a topic discussed in the next chapter. This is due in part to the relative youthfulness of social research, but also to the fact that social scientists generally lack training in, or concern with, theory construction. The ideals of clarity, precision, rigor, falsifiability, etc., are not yet institutionalized.

This is not to imply that our theoretical landscapes are barren. There are growing numbers of highly rigorous and creative theories being constructed, tested, and extended, and countless theory-fragments (often confusingly referred to as "theories") awaiting assemblage by clever and insightful theorists. The area of sociology concerned with group processes is especially vibrant and particularly theory-oriented, while still containing a variety of perspectives and plenty of room to grow. This volume exemplifies the level of theoretical development in the group processes area, displaying a broad spectrum of interesting topics and degrees of theoretical development. Some of the ideas are highly developed, some are best thought of as theories-in-waiting.

Readers who take to heart this chapter's prescriptions will undoubtedly discover for themselves many ways to integrate, clarify, and extend the theoretical ideas in the chapters of Part II. One advantage of learning about research and theory in a "younger" science is that, relative to more highly evolved disciplines, students are more likely to discover areas where work needs to be done, and to offer viable solutions to important intellectual questions. Discovering these answers is not only of great value; it is also great fun. Theories are the playgrounds where most of the fun takes place.

## SUGGESTED READINGS

Alcock, James E. 1981. *Parapsychology: Science or Magic?* Oxford, England: Pergamon.
   Through his careful, in-depth analysis of the field of parapsychology, Alcock sheds light on elements that distinguish between science and non-science. His reviews of the human judgment literature on perceptual limitations, and the parapsychological literature itself, are enlightening. At the heart of the classification of parapsychology as a pseudo-science is its lack of explicit theorizing.

Cohen, Bernard P. 1989. *Developing Sociological Knowledge: Theory and Method,* 2nd ed. Chicago: Nelson-Hall. Chapter 7.
   This chapter discusses the need for specialized, explicitly defined concepts in scientific theories. It also provides a thorough treatment of the different types of definitions and the objectives that each satisfies or fails to satisfy.

Flew, Antony. 1977. *Thinking Straight.* Buffalo, NY: Prometheus.
   This concise work provides an entertaining compendium of common methods for logical argumentation, and for recognizing invalid argument forms.

Freese, Lee and Jane Sell. 1980. "Constructing Axiomatic Theories in Sociology," Part 1 and Part 2. Pp. 263–368 in *Theoretical Methods in Sociology,* edited by L. Freese. Pittsburgh, PA: University of Pittsburgh Press.

In the first of these two related chapters, the authors justify the need for formal languages and logical calculi in sociological theorizing. The second chapter emphasizes criteria for the development of cumulative theories, demonstrating the services that axiomatic theoretical methods provide through the analyses of actual theories. Together, these chapters provide a strong case for raising the level of theoretical rigor in the social sciences.

## REFERENCES

Berger, Joseph, Morris Zelditch, Jr., and Bo Anderson. 1972. "Introduction." Pp. ix-xxii in *Sociological Theories in Progress,* vol. 2, edited by J. Berger, M. Zelditch, Jr., and B. Anderson. Boston: Houghton Mifflin.

Cohen, Bernard P. 1989. *Developing Sociological Knowledge: Theory and Method,* 2nd ed. Chicago: Nelson-Hall.

Freese, Lee and Jane Sell. 1980. "Constructing Axiomatic Theories in Sociology," Part 1. Pp. 263–309 in *Theoretical Methods in Sociology,* edited by L. Freese. Pittsburgh, PA: University of Pittsburgh Press.

Hofstadter, Douglas R. 1985. *Metamagical Themas: Questing for the Essence of Mind and Pattern.* New York: Basic Books.

Lieber, Arnold L. 1978. *The Lunar Effect.* Garden City, NJ: Anchor Press.

Markovsky, Barry, David Willer, and Travis Patton. 1988. "Power Relations in Exchange Networks." *American Sociological Review* 53:220–36.

Nagel, Ernest. 1979. *The Structure of Science: Problems in the Logic of Scientific Explanation.* Indianapolis: Hackett.

Popper, Karl R. 1961. *The Poverty of Historicism.* New York: Harper and Row.

———. 1979. *Objective Knowledge,* revised ed. Oxford, England: Oxford University Press.

Quine, W.V. and J.S. Ullian. 1978. *The Web of Belief,* 2nd ed. New York: Random House.

Slovic, Paul and Baruch Fischoff. 1977. "On the Psychology of Experimental Surprises." *Journal of Experimental Psychology: Human Perception and Performance* 3:544–51.

Willer, David and Murray Webster, Jr. 1970. "Theoretical Concepts and Observables." *American Sociological Review* 35:748–57.

# TWO

# The Growth of Theories

## DAVID G. WAGNER

We confront claims to theoretical knowledge about social processes almost every day of our lives. We read about such claims in the newspapers, see and hear experts express their opinions about them on radio and television, and debate them ourselves with family, friends, or coworkers. One person claims that blacks and whites have different learning styles, and that therefore different pedagogical techniques are required for each to learn effectively. Another argues that women who have recently had abortions experience increased stress as a result. And others debate (or at least worry about) the consequences of either negotiating or engaging in armed conflict with dictators.

What are we to make of such claims? Some choose simply to ignore them as "only one person's opinion." Others attribute ideological bias to those making the claims. If a claim can be traced to "fuzzy-thinking liberals at the University" or "reactionary conservatives on the school board," then it must be inherently wrong. Still others throw up their hands in despair at ever knowing which claims to believe.

At the other extreme, some people treat claims of theoretical knowledge as holy writ. If a person with the right credentials has made the claim, it must be inherently right. Similarly, if the claim is consistent with a social policy one supports, the worth of the claim may be unquestioned. Even the most skeptical social scientists often assume that once a claim has been supported by empirical observations, it must be true (and, of course, that once it has been refuted by data, it must be false).

None of these responses is appropriate. First, all claims to theoretical knowledge must be evaluated, both logically and empirically. Their worth must be determined on the basis of grounds other than one's own personal beliefs or policy preferences. Second, no matter what their established worth, claims to theoretical knowledge are always subject to improvement. Good ideas can be made better; bad ones can be revised to make them good.

## EVALUATING THEORETICAL CLAIMS

We begin by evaluating our claims to theoretical knowledge. Do the ideas make sense? Unfortunately, answering such a question is not a simple task. "Making sense" involves a large number of distinct issues, from the breadth of a claim's scope of application to the reproducibility of the empirical observations that support it. Furthermore, the success of a claim with respect to one of these criteria is largely independent of its success with respect to other criteria. One theoretical argument may apply to an especially broad range of social situations, but make only vague claims about how people are likely to act in those situations. Another argument may apply only to a limited range of situations, but make very specific claims about how people will behave. A simple "yes" or "no" answer to questions of the worth of theoretical claims is seldom possible.

It is perhaps more distressing that social scientists and philosophers cannot reach consensus about the meaning of some of the criteria to be used in evaluating theoretical claims. Even such apparently straightforward criteria as "simplicity" are notoriously difficult to articulate and apply. As a result, we often cannot readily determine whether one claim fares better than another with respect to such criteria.

Nevertheless, we can identify some of the most basic criteria for evaluating theoretical claims, ones about which there is a fairly high degree of consensus and which do not require special technical knowledge to apply. There are two primary types of criteria to consider: structural and empirical.

### Structural Criteria

Consider the claim that blacks and whites have different learning styles. How can we go about evaluating this statement? We do *not* begin by reviewing the relevant empirical evidence. There are in fact several questions about the nature of the theoretical argument being made that must be answered before we can even consider empirical evidence. These questions pertain to the structure, logic, and meaning of the argument. Unless we understand clearly what is being claimed, it is nearly impossible to evaluate whether empirical observations support a theoretical argument. So we begin with structural criteria for evaluating theoretical claims.

*Clarity.* Perhaps the single most important criterion in evaluating the structure of theoretical arguments is clarity. Explicitness in the expression of our claims to knowledge is a prerequisite for evaluating any other aspect of these claims. Otherwise, we have no way of knowing what to evaluate.

Unfortunately, social scientists are often notoriously vague in stating their claims. The claim about learning styles is a good example. What, for example, is meant by the phrase "learning styles"? Does it refer to the manner in which individuals absorb information? Does it instead refer to the cognitive content of the information being learned? Might it involve some combination of both ideas? Might it involve something else entirely? The way the argument is generally stated (and even the way much of the research literature on the topic is framed) fails to answer these questions. Consequently, the claim is not sufficiently explicit to permit clear, unambiguous empirical evaluation.

Similar questions of clarity arise in other parts of our sample claim, too. The terms "black" and "white" seem quite unambiguous. In fact, they are not. What kind of learning style should we expect from someone who has one black parent and one white parent, or grandparents with, for example, German, Italian, Japanese, and Native American backgrounds? Would each small difference in ancestral history generate a different learning style? If not, where do we draw the boundary lines? The terms can actually obscure the meaning of the claim put forward.[1]

As stated, our sample claim seems to suggest to many people some sort of biological or genetic reason for the difference. However, as we attempt to clarify the idea we soon discover the difficulty in classifying people in terms of their genetic racial composition. This may suggest that what the person making the claim about learning styles "really" means has more to do with the way people are treated on the basis of perceived skin color than with their genetic history. But this is a far different claim from what most people assume when it is initially presented.

*Generality.* It is also important to evaluate how broadly applicable our claims are. An argument is certainly more valuable if it pertains to a broad range of people or social situations than if it deals only with a very limited set. We are able to say more about the social world with a more general theory. Further, an argument is more valuable if it uses only a limited set of theoretical principles in making those claims. Our understanding of the social world is more compact. If we are fortunate, more general arguments may permit us to understand features of the social world more completely *and* more compactly at the same time; fewer theoretical principles can be used to say more.

As Markovsky notes in Chapter 1, stating an argument more generally usually involves expressing its terms more abstractly. For example, we might consider the application of the claim about learning styles to differences between men and women, not just to differences between blacks and whites. At first glance, this may seem a rather far reach. What do race and ethnicity have to do with sex and

---

1. The problem has nothing to do with the term itself, but with the meaning we intend to communicate when we use the term. This is made most evident by the fact that the problem is made neither simpler nor more difficult by substituting the earlier term "Negro" or the more recent term "African American" for "black" in the sample claim.

gender? However, as we have seen in trying to clarify the meaning of our sample claim, the argument may have more to do with perceptions of easily visible differences than with actual biological make-up. In this respect, sex may be just like race. It too involves an often easily visible difference that may affect how people are treated. We might be wise to state the argument even more abstractly to focus on individuals who have social advantages or disadvantages that are tied to easily visible differences in their appearance, rather than on either race or sex.

Of course, stating an argument more generally or abstractly does not solve all our problems. However, it does allow us to bring to bear information that otherwise might be ignored. Perhaps we could draw on our knowledge of attractiveness or of physical handicaps in our evaluation of claims about differences in learning style, since these too are easily visible differences that often affect the way people are treated.

*Precision.* It is important also to attempt to state our theoretical claims as precisely as possible. Hypothesizing that a relationship between two social phenomena exists is only a first step. Several other steps are possible. We can specify the *causal order* of a relation (which phenomenon is responsible for changes in the other phenomenon?), the *direction* of a relation (does a change in one phenomenon lead to an increase or decrease in the frequency of the other?), its *directness* (is the relation mediated by another phenomenon?), its *strength* (how consistently does the relation hold?), its *form* (how rapidly do changes in one phenomenon create changes in the other? does the direction of this change ever differ?), and even its *limits* (is there some threshold above or below which the relation no longer holds?).

The more of this information we can provide, the more precise is our understanding of the claim we are making and the easier it becomes to generate empirical observations that test it. Our sample claim states that easily visible differences are related to learning styles. It also seems to involve (at least implicitly) the notion that these differences are the cause of differences in learning style, not the other way around. However, nothing is either said or implied about the directness of the relation. How, specifically, do visible differences come to affect learning styles? Is the effect mediated by family socialization practices? Peer pressure? The availability of models of one or another learning style? Further details regarding the directness of the relation (and, of course, the remaining issues) would enhance our claim considerably.

As claims come to be stated with increasing precision they often are formulated using an abstract calculus like symbolic logic, set theory, or any of a variety of forms of mathematics. Logic and mathematics encourage us to describe our claims in terms of a common set of basic abstract properties (such as "similarity" or "transitivity"). These properties are all well-defined and applicable to a very broad range of phenomena. Thus, formalization with an abstract calculus helps enhance the clarity and generality of our claims as well, not just their precision.

*Completeness.* A theoretical argument may be clearly stated, abstract and precise, yet still not be complete. For most social phenomena, at least three basic kinds of processes are involved. *Emergence* concerns the processes by which the phenomenon arises in the first place. *Maintenance* focuses on the processes by which the phenomenon comes to be established as a stable part of the social world. *Change* deals with the processes by which the phenomenon may come to be transformed or extinguished by the world in which it exists. All three are necessary for a complete explanation.

Our sample argument is far from complete. As we saw in discussing precision, that argument claims only the fact of a relation and never directly considers the processes that ought to govern the emergence, maintenance, or change of that relation. We have little or no information about what circumstances are likely to generate a link between visible differences and learning styles in the first place, about how the link is maintained once it is generated, or about how and under what circumstances the link may cease to exist. The sample argument would become much more useful if it more directly attempted to deal with at least one of these issues.

## Errors and Confusion

As long as we allow our ideas to remain implicit, concrete, vague and incomplete, they will yield little but confusion. Who now can truly say what we should expect to be the relation between race and learning styles?

But are we not likely to make mistakes if we demand that our theoretical claims be clear, general, specific, and complete? Yes! And that is exactly the point of theorizing in the first place. Once we begin to state our claims more explicitly, more abstractly, more precisely or more completely, our understanding begins to improve. We learn more through error than we do through confusion; even wrong answers teach us something about the social process we are studying.

Thus, if we never go beyond the simple claim that race is related to learning styles, we never come to understand when, how, or why this relation might occur, let alone test the relation empirically. When we do attempt to develop this understanding we often make mistakes. Perhaps we may suggest that peer pressure is most directly responsible for learning style. Empirical observations may or may not bear this out. If they do, we have learned something quite valuable about how the relation works. Even if they do not, we have learned something. We have learned that we must look for some other process (e.g., modelling others' behavior) to understand the relation.

## Empirical Criteria

Thus far we have considered only structural criteria in evaluating claims to theoretical knowledge. The four mentioned certainly do not exhaust the list of such criteria. However, they do represent a set of issues that must be considered before one even begins to explore the empirical evaluation of theoretical claims. As we have noted, one cannot adequately test an argument that is only implicitly stated or too concretely stated to allow for application beyond the original conjecture.

Suppose now that a claim has satisfied these structural concerns sufficiently. How then does one test and evaluate theoretical claims empirically? The answer to this question is considered much more directly and completely by Webster in Chapter 3. A few comments are necessary here to deal with aspects of the ways in which empirical evidence bears on theoretical claims.

*Relevance.* Before one can evaluate any empirical observations, one must determine that they are indeed relevant to the claims being made. This is primarily an issue of ascertaining whether the research situation fits the scope of the theory. It may also involve considering whether the people whose behavior is observed in fact represent examples of the people to whom the theory applies.

In the United States it is common to mistake particularly dark-skinned Hispanic or Mediterranean peoples for blacks or African Americans. Suppose that an investigator gathers evidence about the relative learning styles of a group of these people and a group of white-skinned Caucasians. None of the evidence the investigator has gathered is at all relevant to evaluating the claim that blacks and whites have different learning styles. It does not matter at all what results the investigator obtains; the data are meaningless in evaluating this theoretical claim.

Interestingly, if we state the claim more abstractly as before (i.e., as concerned with easily visible differences in appearance), then the evaluation of the relevance of the observations made is likely to be quite different. It is the dark skin that is more important in the more abstract formulation, not the genetic background. Hence, the data should be quite relevant; the investigator's results will be important in evaluating the theory.

Stressing the importance of relevance may seem obvious. It is surprising how often this problem appears, however. Perhaps it occurs so often because even professional social scientists rarely state the scope of application of their theoretical claims explicitly (as Markovsky indicates in Chapter 1).

*Reproducibility.* It is also important that the evidence an investigator gathers be reliably observable. If the results cannot be repeated under the same observational conditions, then they are not likely to be very useful because the phenomenon may not be a recurrent one.

Many social scientists treat this issue in a very concrete manner. They assume that the observations to be compared must be made under the same *empirical* conditions (or at least under conditions as empirically similar to the original ones as possible). Thus, if the first study was performed at the State University of New York at Albany in October of 1990, then any study that attempts to replicate its findings should be conducted in as similar a setting as possible. Unfortunately, this becomes increasingly difficult as we state more explicitly what those empirical conditions are. Suppose we specify that the study was done by Professor Wagner in his Social Psychology class in October 1990, a class composed of twenty-seven whites and four blacks, nineteen females and twelve males. . . . Where does one stop? How do we determine what empirical conditions are actually relevant to observing the phenomenon?

In fact, the conditions it is important to reproduce in a replication study are the *theoretical* ones. If our theoretical argument proposes that the phenomenon is to be observed in formal learning settings in which actors are aware of differences in physical appearance (such as skin color), then any setting in which those features appear may yield observations relevant to evaluating the theoretical claims. A kindergarten classroom in France in 1960 might present relevant evidence, as might a carpentry shop in Mexico in 1860. And, perhaps surprisingly, observations from a second class covering the same subject matter, taught by the same instructor in the same semester at the same institution, with the same class composition may be entirely irrelevant if the African American students are sufficiently light-skinned (or the Caucasian students are sufficiently dark-skinned) that no member of the class is aware of a visible difference in skin color. Again, evaluating our theoretical claims empirically depends on a clear statement of those claims structurally.

*Consistency.* At last, we turn to the criterion most obviously related to the worth of empirical evidence in evaluating a theoretical argument. We expect the results of our observations to be consistent with each other and with the claims of the theories they test. If observations are consistent with the theory, it is regarded as "true"; if observations are inconsistent with the theory, it is considered "false."

Unfortunately, the scientific world is seldom this simple. Empirical investigations hardly ever test all of a theoretical argument. They also often provide evidence of phenomena that goes well beyond what the theory specifies. Moreover, research seldom unambiguously supports or challenges all the theoretical claims made. It is much more common for observations to support some theoretical claims, not support others, and be unable to resolve at all still others. Under these circumstances, it is very difficult to tell whether a theory is "true" or "false."

Even more important, whether a theory is regarded as "true" or "false" also depends on what other theories are available for comparison. Science is replete with theories their creators know to be wrong in at least some respects, but which continue to be used because they are better (more "true"?) than any available alternatives. Even the most advanced physical theories (such as Einstein's theory of relativity) are known to be inadequate in some respects, yet they continue to guide our understanding of the physical world, because no alternative theory is as adequate as they are.[2] Thus, even if our sample argument about visible physical differences and learning styles were consistently supported by observation (which is clearly not the case), there may still remain valid alternative arguments.

## The Comparative Value of Theoretical Claims

What we have just applied to the consistency of observations with theoretical claims applies equally as well to *all* of the criteria we may use to evaluate theoretical claims. No theory ever fully satisfies all the criteria we might consider. Most theories fare well by some criteria and worse by others. The features of one theoretical argument are seldom consistently better than those of all other arguments.

As a result, it is often difficult to state unequivocally whether our theories are true or false. The assessments we make depend on which criteria we choose to apply. In fact, we may have several theories about similar processes that are sufficiently successful for us to regard them all as true. We may have no theories about a process that are regarded as true, but these theories may still be used appropriately because they are better than any alternatives. In short, *ultimate "truth" has very little to do with the worth of our theoretical claims*. Instead, it is the comparative value of our ideas with which we should be concerned. The best theories are the ones that are clearer, more general, more precise, or more complete, and have more relevant, more reproducible, or more consistent observations supporting them than their alternatives. If a theory fares well by several of these criteria, so much the better, although we seldom reach the point of endorsing a single theory without qualification.

## IMPROVING THEORETICAL CLAIMS

Suppose a researcher has just finished testing a theoretical argument empirically. What should the investigator do now? It seems rather obvious that the next step depends on the outcome of the empirical test.

### Failure to Support Theoretical Claims

Consider first the consequence of a failure to support the theoretical argument. Some would suggest that the failed theory ought to be immediately rejected as false. However, our discussion of the evaluation of theoretical claims does not so easily yield such a strong negative result. First, there may be methodological

---

2. This argument applies even to Newtonian mechanics, which has been superseded by relativity theory as the basis of our understanding of the physical world, yet continues to be used regularly and successfully by scientists and engineers because it is simpler to use for physical problems that do not involve the speed of light.

flaws in the tests we make; our inference of failure may be in error. But even if the tests are not flawed and the theory is understood to be false, it may be better than any alternative and therefore a poor candidate for outright rejection.

Instead, the investigator might be wiser to revise the theoretical argument in some way (perhaps modifying its clarity, generality, precision, or completeness) and to test it again. But now suppose the new test again fails to support the theoretical claims. Should the investigator reject the theory? Perhaps surprisingly, the same advice holds as before. Rather than scuttle the theory, the investigator might be better off revising the argument once more and testing still further. In fact, there is rarely a point at which the investigator must unquestionably interpret a failure to support the theory as a requirement that the theory be rejected. Theoretical arguments may be modified indefinitely.

An admittedly imperfect analogy may help to explain why this is so. Imagine the explanatory domain of social science as a jigsaw puzzle and the theories we propose as puzzle pieces. We use those pieces to reveal a picture of the social world. Now suppose that one of the pieces fails to "fit" where we first try to insert it in the puzzle. Would we be wise to set aside that piece immediately or even to throw it out as useless in solving the puzzle? Obviously not. Few puzzles would ever get completed if we had to put them together perfectly the first time. Instead, what we are likely to do is to rotate the piece or try it in several different locations before we even temporarily set it aside to consider other pieces. Furthermore, there is no specific step at which it becomes more rational to move on to the next piece than to continue to search for the appropriate placement of the piece we have. Some people's successful puzzle-solving strategies depend almost entirely on determining the location of each specific piece before moving on to the next one. The process is slow but ultimately effective.

Further, suppose a piece does not fit our theoretical puzzle, no matter how hard we try. We may then reject the piece as not part of the puzzle we are trying to solve. But that does not necessarily mean the piece is worthless. It may simply belong to a different puzzle—that is, it still may be useful in helping us to solve different theoretical problems.

Why should we not give theoretical arguments at least as much chance to demonstrate their worth as we give jigsaw puzzle pieces? It makes sense to "rotate" (modify) the theory a few times or to "try it in new locations" (apply it to other situations) before we consider moving on to another argument. Thus, the most likely outcome of a failure to support the theoretical argument is not rejection but revision of the theory.

---

## Success in Supporting Theoretical Claims

Suppose the investigator's observations did support the theory. Now what should the investigator do? Some social scientists would say at this point: "Do nothing!

Your work is finished." For these people, the statement of a successful theoretical argument is the endpoint of the investigative process.

However, this strategy has some problems. First, recall that theoretical arguments are seldom unequivocally supported by the data that test them. Even if such claims were thoroughly consistent with the data, they remain limited in their scope of application; hence, theories are always subject to improvement. And what does our lazy investigator do when someone else appears with a more successful theory? Now he or she must attempt to revise the theory in such a way that it outshines its new competitor, *even though the observations are just as consistent with the original theory as they always were*. In other words, even though observations supported the theory, it is still useful to attempt to improve it through modification.

In fact, this is what social scientists sometimes do (and need to do more often). Once a theoretical argument has shown its mettle initially, investigators begin to challenge it with ever more sophisticated problems to solve. Each challenge it overcomes improves the theory.

There are at least five types of challenges with which a theory may be presented.

*Elaboration.* One of the most common kinds of challenges an investigator takes on is to make the theory's account of a particular social process clearer, more precise, more general, or more complete. The goal is for the theory to make additional or better predictions about the domain to which it applies.

For example, in 1946 Fritz Heider proposed a simple theory suggesting that actors organize their cognitions in a consistent manner. Among other things, we tend to like those we see as similar to us and to dislike those we see as different. Further, our friends' friends tend to become our own friends as well. Perhaps a little more surprisingly, our enemies' enemies also tend to become our friends. Actor p may dislike actor o and perceive that o dislikes actor q. P's cognitions will be most consistent if p likes q; the enemies of p's enemies are likely to be p's friends.

Heider's claims dealt with a maximum of three relations among three cognitive entities at any one time. If we ask about the implications of adding a fourth actor r, or a fourth relation (e.g., that p also sees himself as similar to o), the theory could not give us an answer. However, in 1956 Cartwright and Harary *elaborated* Heider's claims using graph theory. The consequence was an argument that could accommodate any number of relations among any number of cognitive entities. The theory made more and better predictions about the consistency of actors' cognitions.

*Proliferation.* Somewhat less frequently, investigators attempt to apply their arguments to new problems or new explanatory domains. In this case the goal is to say something about a new or different issue, not to enlarge or improve the theory's account of an existing one. Proliferation is more a challenge to discover new explanatory domains than it is a challenge to explore already charted ones.

In 1966 Berger, Cohen, and Zelditch presented a theory that explained how status differences in task groups come to affect the character of a group's interaction. In particular, they were interested in who influences whom when group decisions are made. They theorized that status differences generate expectations for task performance, which in turn govern the manner in which actors distribute chances to contribute to the group's task, evaluations of those contributions, and deference to others' evaluations. Six years later the same investigators, along with Anderson, used many of the same ideas to explain how actors come to see their reward allocations in task groups as just or unjust (Berger et al. 1972). They argued that status differences also sometimes generate expectations for reward allocation, which in turn govern the manner in which actors allocate group rewards and assess the justice of allocations made by others. The latter argument (about reward expectations) was a *proliferant* of the earlier one (about task expectations) because it was designed to make claims about a new domain—justice and injustice—that was not part of the domain of the original theory—power and prestige behavior.

*Competition.* Another task investigators seem to enjoy tackling with their theories is to challenge another theory's account of an explanatory domain the two theories share. Competing theories tend to have little in common but the social phenomena or processes they try to explain. As a consequence, it is often quite difficult to determine which theory presents a more satisfactory account of the issue. Proponents of competing theories will seldom even agree on what observations should be considered relevant in evaluating the theories.

In 1966 Thomas Scheff published a "labelling" theory of mental illness. He explained the deviant patterns of behavior exhibited by those classed as mentally ill as a result of the attachment by others of the label "mentally ill" to what would ordinarily be random and transitory behavior. Those who are so labelled are then rewarded for behaviors that are consistent with the label and punished for behaviors that are inconsistent with it. Then in 1970 Walter Gove began developing a *competing* theory to challenge Scheff's labelling theory. Gove's argument is that the deviant behavior of the mentally ill results more from psychophysiological conditions of the mentally ill themselves than from outside societal forces; deviance is patterned and persistent because the internal conditions remain, not because others reward the deviant behavior.

Scheff and Gove and their respective supporters have been raising challenges to each other's claims ever since. For example, they have debated whether those with social advantages (e.g., the rich, powerful, or well-educated) are more likely or less likely to be treated for mental illness than those with social disadvantages (e.g., the poor, powerless, or uneducated). The labelling argument suggests the latter should be the case; the psychophysiological argument suggests the former. It has taken many years for researchers on mental illness to discover that both predictions may be true—under different conditions. Those who are socially advantaged are in fact more likely to seek out treatment for mental problems; however, those who are socially disadvantaged are much more likely to be involuntarily committed for treatment. The extensive conflicts over even basic principles between the competing theories have obscured the resolution of some of their discrepancies in predictions.

*Variation.* A much less visible, but still important, task an investigator may pursue is to build alternative versions of the same theory in order to make evaluations of the theory more discriminating. Usually such theories differ only with respect to the specific mechanism they propose to account for behavior within their common explanatory domain.

For example, in 1960 Deutsch and Krauss presented a theory of bargaining behavior suggesting that threats by one party to the bargaining generally lead to counterthreats by the other party, ultimately creating a spiral of conflict between the parties. Almost a decade later Horai and Tedeschi (1969) developed a *variant* argument suggesting that threats by one party tend, under some circumstances, to deter the other party from engaging in punitive action, and therefore to reduce the level of conflict. Others (notably Bacharach and Lawler 1981; Lawler 1986) have since shown how similar these variant theories are, despite their apparently conflicting claims about the consequences of threat behavior in bargaining. Both theories assume that bargaining relationships involve punitive capabilities, threats, and punitive tactics. Both assume that actors attempt to alter each other's outcomes in a manner that improves their own outcomes. However, the two arguments differ with respect to the cognitive mechanisms they suggest motivate bargaining behavior. The earlier "conflict spiral" argument focuses on the actor's temptation to use punitive capabilities, while the later "deterrence" argument emphasizes the actor's fear of retaliation for such use. (See also Chapter 10 regarding these theories.)

*Integration.* By far the most honored form of challenge an investigator may seek to meet is to integrate previously distinct theoretical arguments into a single theory. In effect, the goal is to make two (or more) different explanatory domains one. This may be accomplished in any of several ways. It may be as limited as specifying different conditions under which each of two previously separate (usually variant) theories apply. It may be as complex as inventing an entirely new theoretical language and structure to incorporate ideas from each earlier argument.

This last is what Guillermina Jasso has attempted in her 1978 theory of distributive justice. She proposed a "justice evaluation function" that incorporates elements of both the theory of Berger and his associates (1972) discussed above and a competing theory developed by Homans (1961) and Adams (1965). As Jasso points out, Berger and his colleagues' theory proposes that evaluations of the justice or injustice of a reward distribution are based on a comparison of actual with just (i.e., expected) rewards, as follows:

**justice evaluation = actual reward − just reward**  (1)

In contrast, the Homans and Adams theories assume that justice evaluations are based on a comparison of actual rewards with actual investments, as follows:

**justice evaluation = (a's rewards/a's investments) −**
**(b's rewards/b's investments)**  (2)

Jasso proposes a "generalized justice evaluation function" that incorporates elements of both earlier equations. Specifically, she suggests that:

**justice evaluation = ln (actual amount of good/just amount of good)**  (3)

That is, an evaluation of the justice of a reward distribution is a function of the natural logarithm of the ratio of an actor's actual rewards to the rewards he or she assesses as just. Note that the evaluation may also be described as the difference between the logarithms of the actual amount and the just amount, a difference that is mathematically equivalent to the logarithm of the ratio. Status-value theorists like Berger and his associates would probably prefer the former reading, whereas equity theorists like Adams and Homans would probably prefer the latter. However, since the forms are mathematically equivalent, Jasso's justice evaluation function satisfactorily integrates features of both theories.

While Jasso's argument is quite sophisticated, general, and well-developed mathematically, it does not attempt to capture all the ideas represented in the two earlier sets of theories. Performing such a task would be herculean and probably not worth the effort.

## The Tentativeness of All Theoretical Claims

Thus, whenever observations support a theory, the wisest next step is to modify the theory in an attempt to improve it. This may be accomplished in any one of the five ways outlined above (and probably many more). Because it is always possible to improve a theory, modifying the theoretical argument is always available as the next step.

Ironically, this is exactly the action suggested for circumstances when observations *fail* to support a theory as well. Intuition would seem to suggest that "successful" theories (i.e., ones that are well supported by observations) ought simply to be accepted as true and that "unsuccessful" ones (i.e., those generally inconsistent with observations) ought to be rejected unequivocally as false. In fact, both situations should generally involve the same response: modification of the theory. Of course, the specific actions taken are likely to be quite different; failure focuses attention on what can be done to resolve the inconsistency, while success focuses attention on what new ideas can be developed and tested. Nevertheless, the impetus is always to modify the theory.

Perhaps the most important reason this action is appropriate is that theoretical arguments are always tentative. We do not have, and cannot ever have, an entirely finished theory. Our claims are always subject to revision and improvement, regardless of their current status.

In this sense social science (as with any science) is basically a playful activity. We ask "What if?" and then send our theories out to see what happens. Sometimes they come back with a tag that says "This didn't work," so we tinker with our ideas a little and send them out once again asking "What if?" Sometimes our theories come back with a tag that says "Aha! This worked." Once again, we tinker with our ideas a little and send them back out once more asking "Well! That's nice. What if this *and* this too?" And the process never ends.

## What Theoretical Knowledge Can and Cannot Provide

Social scientific theorizing is certainly an enjoyable and creative activity that can accomplish many things. We hope our enthusiasm and optimism about that activity comes through to you as you read about the group processes we consider here. However, there are several kinds of things that social science theorizing—about group processes or about any other processes—cannot accomplish. These limitations of theoretical work apply regardless of the level of interest, enthusiasm, or optimism that is brought to the work.

First, no amount of theory improvement will ever allow us to answer the ultimate questions of human existence. For example, our theories cannot determine whether human beings are inherently good or evil. The question is simply beyond any possible scope of application of scientific theorizing. Such basic philosophical questions deal with what is essential and universal about the species. Social scientific inquiry deals only with conditional claims about human behavior—*if* certain social conditions arise, *then* certain behaviors result. Our theories do not address issues of what must always occur or what must be universally characteristic of the species.

Similarly, our theories cannot answer moral questions. For example, they cannot tell us whether we should support or oppose the death penalty. Nor can our theories by themselves solve social problems. They cannot, for example, show us how to reduce crime on city streets. Finally, our theories do not allow us to predict the future. We cannot specify who will win the next presidential election.

These constraints on the use of our knowledge seem quite limiting. After all, issues of human existence and morality, of the resolution of social problems, and of predicting the future are questions most of us wish to have answered. But these qualifications are not nearly as limiting as they first appear; our theorizing can say some things that are relevant to these important questions, even if it cannot answer them for us.

Theorizing can help to reveal some of the most basic characteristics of human life. This is largely because theorizing forces us to focus on those features of human behavior that appear to be most recurrent. While such a focus does not tell us the meaning of life, it does enable us to understand in what aspects of our lives we generally search for meaning and how we come to attach importance to those meanings.

Theorizing also provides insights into some of the reasons we behave the way we do. We focus on those features that relate us to other people: power, sentiment, status, authority, kinship, and a hundred others. This emphasis does not tell us who we are, but it does enable us to understand what we share with other people.

Finally, theorizing enables us to make conditional predictions regarding our social behavior. We consider the implications our social situations have for the ways in which we interact with each other. Thus, although we cannot make categorical prophecies about the future, we can predict the consequences that are likely to follow from particular social policies or circumstances: *If* a specific social situation is created, *then* certain social attitudes and behaviors are likely to result.

In the long run, then, social science theorizing does help us *think* about ultimate questions, consider moral questions, solve social problems, and plan for the future more responsibly. And we get to be creative as a bonus.

## SUMMARY

Improving our theoretical knowledge depends first on our ability to evaluate theoretical claims. Personal beliefs and policy preferences are *not* satisfactory grounds upon which to base these evaluations. Further, empirical observations provide a necessary standard of judgment, but they are not sufficient to determine the worth of our ideas.

There are, in fact, many criteria for evaluating our claims to knowledge. Structural criteria include *clarity, generality, precision*, and *completeness*. Clarity concerns the explicitness with which we state our claims. Generality deals with the breadth of application our arguments have. Precision focuses on the specificity of the predictions our theories permit us to make. Completeness refers to the number of different kinds of social processes we include in our accounts of social phenomena.

Other criteria are empirical. We must be concerned with the *relevance* and *repro-ducibility* of our observations, not just with the *consistency* of those observations with our theoretical claims. Relevance involves determining whether the conditions under which our observations are made reflect the abstract conditions to which the theory applies. Reproducibility requires that we be able to make the same observations under similar theoretical conditions. Finally, consistency entails a judgment of the similarity of our observations with theoretical predictions.

Evaluating a theory is a complex process, involving the application of all these criteria (and more). Theories are seldom evaluated as unequivocally "true" or "false." Instead, they are evaluated comparatively; one theory may be regarded provisionally as better than another because it is successful with respect to one (or several) of the criteria we have discussed. If different criteria are considered, another theory may be preferred.

In any case all these judgements are temporary, since theories can always be improved. Certainly, when observations fail to support our arguments, we are wise to spend at least some time modifying our claims to determine whether we can overcome the inconsistency. Even when observations support our arguments, we are still wise to invest effort in revising our theories to present them more challenges. We may choose to *elaborate* our argument by attempting to make it clearer, more general, more precise, or more complete. We may *proliferate* our theory to apply it to a new sociological problem. We may reconstruct it to *compete* with another theory's account of a social process. Alternative theories may be formulated that *vary* from the original only in limited ways and which permit a more refined test of how things really work. More comprehensive theories may be built that *integrate* the ideas from two (or more) different explanatory domains.

Whatever theoretical steps are taken, there are always more than can be pursued. Our analysis of social processes is tentative, forever subject to revision and improvement.

## SUGGESTED READINGS

Berger, Joseph, Morris Zelditch, Jr., and Bo Anderson, eds. 1966. *Sociological Theories in Progress*, vol. 1. Boston: Houghton Mifflin; Berger, Joseph, Morris Zelditch, Jr., and Bo Anderson, eds. 1972. *Sociological Theories in Progress*, vol. 2. Boston: Houghton Mifflin; Berger, Joseph, Morris Zelditch, Jr., and Bo Anderson, eds. 1989. *Sociological Theories in Progress: New Formulations*. Newbury Park, CA: Sage.

These three books constitute the most concentrated compilation available of theories undergoing regular modification and improvement. Many, though not all, of the theories considered are directly concerned with the group processes discussed in this volume. A few are quite technical—generally, the ones that have undergone the most development—but most are understandable to the intelligent lay reader.

Cohen, Bernard P. 1989. *Developing Sociological Knowledge: Theory and Method*. 2nd ed. Chicago: Nelson-Hall. Chapters 1–4, 15, and 16 especially.

Although Cohen presents a somewhat different view of the growth of theories through "cumulative research programs," his analysis of what social scientific theorizing can and cannot accomplish is consistent with the perspective presented here. The first four chapters of his book provide a detailed examination of the advantages and limitations we face scientifically; the last two chapters discuss Cohen's ideas about theory growth most directly.

Lakatos, Imre. 1968. "Criticism and the Methodology of Scientific Research Programmes." *Proceedings of the Aristotelian Society* 69:149–86.

Much of the foundation for the ideas about theory growth expressed in this chapter was laid by Imre Lakatos. This article presents his ideas primarily as they apply to the physical sciences, but the principles remain the same when applied to the social sciences.

Lawler, Edward J., ed. 1984–present (additional editors since 1987). *Advances in Group Processes: A Research Annual*, vols. 1–present. Greenwich, CT: JAI Press.

The articles written for these volumes generally also represent contributions to developing programs of theory and research on group processes. In most cases, the material presented here is somewhat more accessible than in the volumes by Berger and his associates.

Wagner, David G. 1984. *The Growth of Sociological Theories*. Beverly Hills, CA: Sage; Wagner, David G. and Joseph Berger. 1985. "Do Sociological Theories Grow?" *American Journal of Sociology* 90:697–728.

These two publications spell out in much greater detail the discussion of ways to improve successful theoretical arguments. The book is, of course, much longer and provides a more complete presentation of examples. In the article, the discussions of examples are considerably abbreviated.

## REFERENCES

Adams, J. Stacy. 1965. "Inequity in Social Exchange." Pp. 267–99 in *Advances in Experimental Social Psychology*, vol. 2, edited by L. Berkowitz. New York: Academic Press.

Bacharach, Samuel B. and Edward J. Lawler. 1981. *Bargaining: Power, Tactics and Outcomes*. San Francisco: Jossey-Bass.

Berger, Joseph, Bernard P. Cohen, and Morris Zelditch, Jr. 1966. "Status Characteristics and Expectation States." Pp. 29–46 in *Sociological Theories in Progress*, vol. 1, edited by J. Berger, M. Zelditch, Jr., and B. Anderson. Boston: Houghton Mifflin.

Berger, Joseph, Morris Zelditch, Jr., Bo Anderson, and Bernard P. Cohen. 1972. "Structural Aspects of Distributive Justice: A Status Value Formulation." Pp. 119–46 in *Sociological Theories in Progress*, vol. 2, edited by J. Berger, M. Zelditch, Jr., and B. Anderson. Boston: Houghton Mifflin.

Cartwright, Dorwin P. and Frank Harary. 1956. "Structural Balance: A Generalization of Heider's Theory." *Psychological Review* 63:277–93.

Deutsch, Morton and Robert M. Krauss. 1960. "The Effect of Threat on Interpersonal Bargaining." *Journal of Abnormal and Social Psychology* 61:181–89.

Gove, Walter R. 1970. "Societal Reaction as an Explanation of Mental Illness: An Evaluation." *American Sociological Review* 35:873–84.

Heider, Fritz. 1946. "Attitudes and Cognitive Organization." *Journal of Psychology* 21:107–12.

Homans, George C. 1961. *Social Behavior: Its Elementary Forms*. New York: Harcourt, Brace and World.

Horai, Joann and James T. Tedeschi. 1969. "Effects of Credibility and Magnitude of Punishment on Compliance to Threats." *Journal of Personality and Social Psychology* 12:164–69.

Jasso, Guillermina. 1978. "On the Justice of Earnings: A New Specification of the Justice Evaluation Function." *American Journal of Sociology* 83:1398–419.

Lawler, Edward J. 1986. "Bilateral Deterrence and Conflict Spiral: A Theoretical Analysis." Pp. 107–30 in *Advances in Group Processes: A Research Annual*, vol. 3, edited by E. J. Lawler. Greenwich, CT: JAI Press.

Scheff, Thomas J. 1966. *Being Mentally Ill*. Chicago: Aldine.

# THREE

# Experimental Methods[1]

## MURRAY WEBSTER, JR.

## SOCIAL SCIENTIFIC KNOWLEDGE

A central purpose of social science is to develop cumulative, verified knowledge of social structures and processes. In this volume, Chapters 4 through 10 describe research showing progress towards achieving this goal. Recent work builds on previous work and extends it.

Developing cumulative knowledge is promoted by understanding the steps involved. How do social scientists come to know more? Briefly, the answer is that they formulate theories of social structures and processes, assess and modify the theories using evidence, and then extend them further. Here I elaborate this view of social science knowledge and describe the central place of experimental research methods in the enterprise of developing this knowledge. I also consider principles of experimental design, potential problems and ways to deal with them, and particular ethical problems of experimenting on humans.

When someone wants others to believe something, or faces challenges from the question "How do you know?" he or she could, in principle, choose any of three different bases discussed below to support an argument. All three bases have uses. However, only the third one is valid in social science. To understand why, it is helpful to distinguish "knowledge" from "knowledge claims." Knowledge is what people believe, claims are what someone asks others to believe. Extending knowledge thus involves persuading others to accept knowledge claims. What bases are available to support such claims?

1. Knowledge based upon authority. This type assumes that certain people have specific qualifications for understanding, so that others can trust their claims. People rely on critics to tell whether a painting, a book, or a movie is good.

---

1. Brian T. Marti read a draft of this chapter and kindly advised on style and phrasing.

Some believe in the authority of mystics and psychics. Many trust priests, doctors, and judges.

However, appeals to authority do not persuade others in social science, nor in any other scientific discipline. Only a naive person believes something just because a famous man or woman says it is true. Foolish pronouncements by self-proclaimed experts are too common for an intelligent scientist to accept unsupported claims.

2. Internal verification. The basis here is, "I know this is true because something inside me says so." For example, people cite internal verification under different names—higher order morality or natural law—on moral issues such as the ethics of a war, or terminating a pregnancy. Everyone may reach his or her judgment, and any opinion formed by careful introspection is correct. The type of music two individuals enjoy may differ, but each is, in this way of thinking, "right."

What makes internal verification unsatisfactory for science is that it provides no way to resolve disputes. Science requires clear, intersubjective verification. Otherwise, a discipline degenerates into competing opinions, with no way to choose among them.

3. External verification. In science, knowledge claims are tested using standards of external verification. This method assumes that any (normally competent) person can assess an idea, given evidence. Evidence decides, not authority or an internal sense of what is right.

The first and most important feature of scientific knowledge is that its claims stand or fall on evidence. That is why research and data are so important in any scientific study of group interaction. A second result of basing knowledge on external verification is that science is self-correcting. Most times, error correction results when investigators try to replicate previous findings. External verification provides a structure of norms legitimating and encouraging open sharing of research methods, results, and evidential bases for conclusions. The other two knowledge bases do not provide for error correction. Third, externally verified knowledge is public. Science has no secrets, either of knowledge or supporting evidence, since other scientists always can test and verify knowledge claims. This property, incidentally, is the primary distinction between science and mysticism.

This chapter begins by addressing some common fallacies, or impediments to developing scientific knowledge, which sometimes appear in the social sciences. Then we see how research, ideally, can change the knowledge base. Next we examine the primary methodological challenges in research design, and see how experimental designs deal with those challenges. The points are illustrated by tracing development of one standardized experimental design. I offer a view of the most common concern voiced over experimental studies of social behavior, that they are artificial. The chapter closes with an examination of ethical concerns in human research, and contemporary professional guidelines for protection of participants in the studies.

## EVIDENCE AND FALLACIES

In conducting research, an investigator formulates a hypothesis, usually by derivation from a more general theory, and gathers evidence by collecting data. (Chapter 1 provides more detail on the logical form and structure of hypotheses.) A hypothesis is a knowledge claim in sentence form. With acceptable evidence, it becomes part of knowledge, and bears on theoretical ideas from which the hypothesis was derived. Research has as its purpose collecting evidence for deciding whether to accept hypotheses, using the method of external verification.

Certain implications follow from the above, revealing some common fallacies, or misuses of evidence. First, we legitimately reject a claim if the evidence supporting it is weak or disconfirming. However, we may not cavalierly reject it in the face of good supporting evidence. That is the "Wishing can make it so" fallacy. Second, when we have considerable evidence, most of it supporting a claim, we require more than one piece of counter evidence before rejecting the idea. If fifteen studies including millions of people show that smoking cigarettes increases the risk of cancer, we do not reject that link because we find someone who smoked for fifty years and never developed cancer. That is the "I know a person who" fallacy. Third, whether or not we like something is irrelevant to whether it is true. Considerable evidence shows that men enjoy many interaction advantages over women in the United States (and in most other societies). If a person did not believe that because it is unfair, he or she would be using internal verification. That produces the "Why can't I be God?" fallacy. Fourth, evidence cannot be perfect. It might be tempting to say that we will not believe anything until the evidence is overwhelming, but if we did, we would have very little knowledge. That would be the "sophomoric sophistication" fallacy. The world is always more complicated than our understanding of it, and at any given time, some evidence will be either incomplete or difficult to interpret. The appropriate goal is to judge wisely how confident to be about the truth of knowledge claims given the available evidence.

The above fallacies obviously work against the accumulation of scientific knowledge. What may not be so apparent is that fallacies also work against *using* knowledge for desirable ends. To change things, it is first necessary to understand how things are now, and the theoretical reasons why. If part of the social world is upsetting—and many aspects of it are upsetting—indignation by itself does not change that fact. Instead, a social engineer must know how things are, and what theoretical processes are producing the results. Then theoretical understanding may be used to intervene effectively.

## HOW RESEARCH CHANGES KNOWLEDGE

Few sciences begin with no knowledge. People bring beliefs such as hunches, folk wisdom, common sense, prejudices, and the like to most topics. Thus the typical outcome of research is to change the state of knowledge, not to create knowledge where before there was none. Yet not all research shows that our hunches were wrong. Some research shows that what we always believed is in fact true. The first example below illustrates this type of research.

*Type 1: Reproducing Outcome.* "In groups containing both women and men, the men are likely to talk more and to be more influential than the women." Currently hundreds of studies in a great variety of settings have documented patterns of male interaction advantage in groups (see, for example, Wagner and Berger 1993). Thus we have considerable confidence in a knowledge claim that this phenomenon occurs. If one more study documents it again, our belief in the pattern increases slightly. However, if a new study appears to show women and men interacting as perfect equals, we do not immediately discard all the previous evidence and conclude that the gender difference has disappeared. To do that would be to commit the "I know a person who" fallacy. (Because of all the prior supporting evidence, we would look for design flaws in the new study to see whether the data actually show what the investigator thinks they do.)

*Type 2: Rejecting Outcome.* This is simple: what we used to believe we now disbelieve. Definitive rejection is unusual because results seldom are clear-cut. To reject a knowledge claim requires balancing the evidence supporting it against newer evidence disconfirming it. Both "I know a person who" and "sophomoric sophistication" are dangers here.

The following statements once were accepted as true, and now are recognized to be false. "Certain body builds (or head shapes) predispose people to criminality" (Kamin 1986); "Committees usually act more cautiously than their individual members would alone" (Janis 1982).

*Type 3: Controversial Outcome.* This is common, particularly where implications of the knowledge claim have important applications. We have conflicting results, and it is difficult to imagine how both could be correct. Or else, we have several studies that are only partially applicable, but nevertheless we often want to believe them.

One way to approach controversy is to withhold a decision. Yet frequently these cases are so urgent that we are not willing to suspend judgment until more evidence appears. When evidence is not clear-cut, emotions can run high. Some people substitute standards of internal verification, rejecting evidence they find offensive. Proponents of the conflicting positions dispute strongly, sometimes invoking moral arguments to claim that any "decent" person would believe as they do. Sometimes disputing parties are motivated by their own interests. Even an apparently simple matter such as counting people—conducting a census—can become controversial if the numbers will be used to allocate government funds. Following are some statements for which evidence is contradictory:

> "Memories of childhood sexual abuse that are recovered during psychotherapy sessions in adulthood are generally accurate" (see Loftus 1993).

> "Corporate teams who interact through computer terminals function more effectively than teams interacting face-to-face" (see Pinsonneault and Kraemer 1989).

*Type 4: Qualified Outcome.* This is probably the most common situation, where we find that an idea once accepted is too simple to describe later findings. For instance, many people believed without much evidence that more communication would inevitably lead to more productive work groups. Yet research shows this is true only when the interdependent nature of the task requires good coordination among members. When the work requires largely independent efforts, more communication is either neutral or distracting and harmful (see Cohen and Zhou 1991).

This book contains examples of all four types of research results. They illustrate the point that scientific knowledge is never perfectly certain or definite. Intelligent people make informed judgments about what to believe, and revise their beliefs with new information and further thought.

## VARIABLES, CAUSATION, AND CONFOUNDING FACTORS

Most simply, a hypothesis is a statement, some of whose terms are observable, describing an instance of a derived consequence (or a theorem) from a theory. If evidence confirms the hypothesis, it also increases confidence in the theory. In conducting research, we move from the theoretical world, where the goals are to formulate precise definitions of concepts and to propose exact relationships among them, to the empirical world where definitions can be imprecise and linkages can be obscured by confounding complications. The variability of the empirical world contains many possibilities for error in interpreting results of research.

Research is the activity of testing hypotheses against observations. The elemental structure of all hypotheses is "x → y," read "if x, then y," or "if x is true, then y is true also." For instance, "If a person's mother wants him or her to attend college, that person is more likely to do so than if the mother is indifferent to education"; "If a juror is an expert in an area related to the case then he or she probably will talk more than another juror who is not an expert."

Most hypotheses invoke probabilities, as in the examples above. That fact does not change the structure of the hypothesis, but it does have implications for testing it. A deterministic hypothesis, such as "Every expert will talk more than every non-expert," can be *dis*confirmed by a single case; a probabilistic hypothesis, such as "On average, experts talk more than non-experts," cannot be disconfirmed so easily. No single case disproves a probabilistic hypothesis, and virtually all scientific hypotheses are probabilistic. The "I know a person who" fallacy comes from missing this point. (On the other hand, nobody could ever *confirm* a deterministic hypothesis, for that would require an infinite number of observations to be sure every possible case conformed to prediction.) Research is governed by a need to confront probabilistic hypotheses with evidence gathered in imperfect circumstances, to develop an understanding of the world.

When we confront a hypothesis with evidence, we measure or observe both its x and its y. In research, the x and y are, respectively, the "independent" and "dependent" variables. Dependent variables are "observations" or "data"; that is, they are what we measure to test the hypothesis. In the second hypothesis above, amount of talking is the dependent variable. We test the idea that amount of talking "depends on" an individual's expertise. An independent variable is a factor our theory leads us to believe affects the dependent variable. To test the hypothesis, one could identify experts and non-experts, using cues such as occupation and educational level. We could see whether, after classifying people on expertise, we can predict amount of talking. If so, we say the hypothesis was "confirmed," though of course it never could be "proved" without examining an infinite number of cases.

A common, though not exactly correct, translation of "if x then y" is "x causes y." It is not precisely correct because, as David Hume (1955 [1748]) noted over two centuries ago, we cannot observe causation. We only observe correlation; that is, that two events happen together. Correlation is not causation. Seeing the sun rise each morning does not prove that it will rise tomorrow. However, the regularity of observations does suggest that there might be a theoretical reason for the reliable correlation of morning and sunrise. Repeatedly observing correlation may lead an investigator to suspect that there is a reason for it; that is, that some theoretical principles are producing the regular correlation of events. In the example of expertise and talking, principles of status generalization cause experts to talk more in certain kinds of group situations. (See Chapter 6 for a discussion of this topic.)

Suppose we find a correlation between independent and dependent variables. We wish to conclude there is a reason for it, that x and y are reliably linked under certain conditions. Often that is what the correlation means: the hypothesis is correct. However, the correlation also could be misleading. X and y might have nothing to do with each other, though they accidentally both occurred in some situation under investigation. Misleading associations also occur if both x and y are caused by a third factor. Third factor problems are more likely than simple accident, if we find x and y associated repeatedly. In such cases, the connection may be "confounded" with other, often unanticipated, factors. This is a "spurious relationship." What we want to establish is just how much of the effects observed are caused by the x of interest, and how much by other factors.

Following are some common confounding factors in research designs. (See Campbell and Stanley 1966 for a more thorough discussion of this topic.) Any of these might occur with any design, including experiments. Some, such as history and maturation, only become significant when sufficient time passes during the research. However, experiments, like other types of designs, can take place over several days or even months.

1. *History*. Between occurrence of the independent and dependent variables, many unrelated changes occur. It is possible that one or more of those factors is responsible for what we measure as the dependent variable. For instance, a design in which a movie on ethnic relations is shown might be followed by measurement of level of hostility in inter-ethnic attitudes. A lowered level then might be attributed to viewing the movie. However, other changes occurring between showing the movie and measuring attitudes—community events, theater movies, television shows—might be responsible for the change in hostility. Any effect from the movie would be confounded with those events. In our jury example, experts might talk more because the judge had told them to speak up during pre-deliberation instructions.

2. *Maturation*. Individuals develop (mature) on their own, and maturation changes can confound those produced by an independent variable. For instance, measuring children's vocabularies before and after a training program to build vocabularies might show increases for most children. Increases might be due to the program, but they also might occur because the children were growing and, on their own, building larger vocabularies. In our jury example, if experts initially were tired or sick, they might show a striking increase in talking after they recuperated.

3. *Testing*. Measurement itself can produce changes. In a classic study of factors affecting production line output, Roethlisberger and Dickson (1939) increased factory lighting in stages. Each increase in brightness was followed by an increase in production. A less skillful researcher might conclude that more light increases output, and he or she would have been wrong. The investigators cleverly then reduced illumination in stages, and each decrease was followed by an increase in production. What happened? Further investigation revealed that workers were responding to the attention they received from the researchers, and the concern they thought it represented on the part of management for their working conditions. Setting up the research project itself, rather than any particular change in lighting, led to increased productivity.[2] In our jury example, if a person knows he or she is considered an expert at a topic, that fact by itself could compel the person to try to dominate the deliberation.

4. *Regression*. Almost any extreme score moves (''regresses'') toward the group mean if measured repeatedly. Thus, if you know someone scored 1600 (the highest possible score) on the Scholastic Aptitude Test (SAT), you would be wise to bet that person would score lower if he or she took the test a second time. Many

---

2. This interpretation is controversial; see Jones (1992).

social experiments are devised for people who have scored an extreme value on some measurement, and their results can be confounded with regression effects. For instance, a "reading readiness" program that is given only to children scoring in the bottom 10 percent of their classes will, because of regression effects alone, show some success. (If the same program were given to children in the top 10 percent, regression effects would produce a *drop* in their scores.) Interpreting those changes as effects of the program would be a mistake. Regression is unlikely in a typical jury because there is only one measure of talking, namely that occurring during deliberation. However in an experimental study, we might compose a jury including some highly verbal individuals, identified by measuring their propensity to talk beforehand. Then regression effects, decreasing selected individuals' levels of talking, would be a concern.

5. *Instrumentation*. Measurement instruments themselves change in accuracy. Often in social research, the instruments are human observers. They can tire and suffer other changes affecting accuracy. For instance, those who watch and record interaction in hour-long discussion groups often score fewer interactions in the final fifteen minutes than in the first fifteen minutes. Sometimes that accurately reflects what happened in a group, but sometimes it just means that the observers became tired and their attention wandered, so they missed some later interactions.

6. *Mortality*. When repeated measurements are taken, some cases recorded at the first occasion are missed at the second. Two decades ago, mental health experiments in the United States apparently showed that recovery was faster if people lived outside of mental hospitals. Those studies were the foundation for large-scale programs to "mainstream"—that is, to release—involuntarily committed patients. However, most of those studies suffered from high mortality rates; usually over half the patients released did not return regularly for medication or psychotherapy. Results of mainstreaming looked good for those who did return, but of course those were the most highly motivated and competent of the patients. In a jury, for a difficult trial where deliberations take place over many days, some jurors might be replaced by alternates, raising the concern that the replacements may have confounded measurement of the dependent variable.

7. *Selection*. This is the most significant threat to most experimental research in group processes, and we discuss it in detail below. Selection bias means that for some reason individuals were not assigned randomly to research groups. For our example, suppose the single jury we watched happened to include garrulous people who then were found also to be experts in the subject. Expertise would be confounded with whatever else made those people talkative, and an investigator might mistakenly conclude that talking rates were affected by expertise.

## WHAT IS AN EXPERIMENT?

Some people call every study an experiment; in fact, not every study is. Social scientists have a variety of methods at their command. These include experiments, surveys, structured and unstructured observation, content analysis, and archival research. An experiment is a design in which the investigator *regulates* the levels of the independent variable(s), and *afterwards* measures the dependent variable(s). Thus an experiment has two essential characteristics. First, the experimenter creates different levels of an independent variable (for instance, greater or lesser perceived expertise) to study its effects on the dependent variable (for instance, influence). Second, the experimenter measures the dependent variable *after* regulating the independent variable. A third characteristic of experiments is that usually they occur in simplified, controlled situations with deliberate attempts made to reduce or eliminate extraneous factors—those other than the independent and dependent variables of interest. Attempts to identify and eliminate confounding factors are not unique to experimental studies, so this third characteristic is not part of the definition of an experiment. However, I argue that extraneous factors usually are more successfully controlled with an experimental design than with other types of research design. Simplification and control are discussed below, under "confounding factors."

The two essential characteristics distinguish experiments from other research designs. A survey, the most common design in sociology, seldom fits either part of the definition. Suppose an investigator wanted to assess the hypothesis that, in the United States, residents of southeastern states are more likely to vote Democratic than residents of western states. The investigator might survey people in different regions, asking how they voted, and classify them as Republicans or Democrats on that basis. Party vote would be the dependent variable; residence the independent variable. Simply comparing the proportion voting for each party in each region would test the hypothesis.

If the design were an experiment, the investigator would have to move people—assign them to live in the Southeast or in the West. Also, in a survey we usually measure the dependent variable before examining the independent variable. In an experiment, only after people had been assigned to live in an area for a while would we ask their voting choice. In that way we could see the effect of region on political choice.

Experiments occur with different degrees of control. The most highly controlled, and the type most often reported in this book, is a laboratory experiment. (See, for examples, Dovidio et al., 1988; Nemeth and Wachtler 1974; and Wood and Karten 1986, discussed respectively in Chapters 5, 6, and 9 of this volume.) Laboratory experiments offer advantages of isolating processes of interest, and creating exactly the conditions required for testing the hypotheses.

Investigators also conduct experiments outside a laboratory, though usually with some loss of control over extraneous variables. Rossi and Freeman (1989) describe many experiments conducted in natural settings. One experiment (Rossi, Berk, and Lenihan 1980) studied effects of different levels of monetary support upon prison recidivism. Released convicts received different amounts of income for varying periods after leaving prison. Amount of income and length of support were independent variables, and rate of new arrests was a dependent variable.

This experiment tested the hypothesis that higher levels of support reduce the likelihood of further crime, and results confirmed that hypothesis.

Another natural setting experiment (Hannan, Tuma, and Groeneveld 1977; see also Groeneveld, Hannan, and Tuma 1980; and Hannan and Tuma 1990) varied the level of welfare payments to poor families. The independent variable again was income level, and the (intended) dependent variable was likelihood of taking a job. This experiment tested the hypothesis that high welfare payments are a disincentive to look for work. Data disconfirmed the hypothesis: they show no disincentive effect of high welfare payments. However, an unanticipated finding was that higher levels of payment were associated with higher levels of marital breakup. The effect appears for black and white couples, but not for Hispanics. While investigators did not design the experiment to test a hypothesis relating money to separation, results certainly invite further study. Perhaps some couples stay together because one member fears being unable to earn a living alone.

## TYPES OF EXPERIMENTAL AND QUASI-EXPERIMENTAL DESIGNS

Experimental research provides an unusually good opportunity to develop reliable knowledge. Of concern in all research is whether the change we observe actually results from the independent variable, or whether the change was spurious or confounded. How can a researcher rule out alternative explanations of evidence? Good experimental design minimizes the presence of confounding factors, or it provides a way to assess just how much effect they have so we can estimate effects of the independent variable(s) alone. (See Cohen 1989, Chapter 13, for elaboration of these points.)

The following discussion is based on Campbell and Stanley's (1966) classic examination of research designs. A convenient way to picture their structure uses "e" to denote an event (a value of an independent variable, or a treatment presumed to cause change) and "o" to denote an observation of another event (a value of a dependent variable). When e occurs before o, that is, an event takes place and then someone records the effect, this is indicated:

$$e \qquad o$$

This first design, sometimes called the "one-shot observation," is the simplest possible. An event occurs, either naturally or because of intervention, and afterward someone records a dependent variable. This design describes research on rare or unpredicted events, such as effects of natural disasters (hurricanes, earthquakes, floods), changes in laws (such as school integration or busing), or changes in economic or political conditions such as elections and wars.

Suppose a supervisor, worried about poor communication among workers in her office, notices that they talk and listen more to each other (o) in the week following a birthday party held at the office (e). Is improved work communication a result of the party? We want to rule out alternative explanations—confounding factors—for it. Let us agree that the supervisor is sophisticated, and accurately observes that workers are talking and listening more to each other, and that she hears fewer complaints about miscommunication. Our supervisor knows her subordinates might be talking more because the weather has improved and they feel better; because better lighting has been installed in the office; because they have found ways to improve their moods independent of work place changes; or because holidays are approaching and they are in better spirits. So, the data might be confounded by history and maturation.

Unfortunately, with that first design type we cannot rule out *any* alternative explanation. Any idea proposed to explain the observation is consistent with data from this design. Despite its scientific weaknesses, many use this design and often believe results from it.

Next consider a more complex design that rules out the most common alternative explanations.

$$o_1 \quad e \quad o_2$$

Using this design, we take a measurement ($o_1$), an event occurs (e), and we repeat the measurement ($o_2$). Perhaps we measured communication, and a few weeks later the party occurs. We come back, measure again, and find improved communication.

Confounded factors are less often a problem with this "before-and-after" design. However, factors other than the party still could be responsible for increased communication. The party might have been the reason, but so might approaching holidays, prominent news stories, a change in the stockmarket, and many other events.

Our third design uses two groups, as follows.

**Group 1:** $o_1 \quad e \quad o_2$

**Group 2:** $o_3 \qquad o_4$

Group 2 is a "control group," chosen because of similarity to the group of interest. Adding a control group is a significant improvement in research design, as it allows an investigator to rule out most common alternative explanations. We measure Groups 1 and 2 at the same time, an event e affects only Group 1, and then we repeat observations on both groups.

When Groups 1 and 2 are equivalent except for e, we may be confident that e's presence explains any differences between the groups. For instance, if workers in two nearby offices (Groups 1 and 2) show the same interaction levels at the first observation, we can rule out the idea that we have found a group of abnormally communicative or uncommunicative people (selection). Other events, such as approaching holidays (history) also would presumably affect the two groups similarly. In an experiment, if we measured both groups, introduced an event to one (such as giving them a party or taking them on a weekend retreat), and measured again, we could be confident that any differences between the groups came from that event.

We are only "confident," not "sure," because the two groups might not really be comparable, despite having the same interaction level. Workers in the first office, Group 1, may be friendlier, more gregarious people than those in the second office, Group 2. If, because of different scores at the second measurement, we conclude that the party had beneficial effects, we would be wrong. Increased interaction actually would be due to sociability differences in the two groups of workers. Even worse, it might be that holding a party works for gregarious people like those in our experimental group, but would not work (or might even hurt relationships) in other people such as those in the control group; that is, the true effect might interact with confounding factors.

Overall, control group designs are a strong method for ruling out alternative hypotheses. Because they use two groups and multiple measures, they increase costs of time and expense, though the scientific benefits outweigh the added costs. Control groups do not solve all problems, however.

The next two designs allow us to rule out every possible alternative explanation. They are "true experiments." True experiments solve *all seven* confounding problems, as well as others not discussed here, such as interaction between factors. The simplicity and power of true experiments depend upon *random assignment* of people to groups, shown as the r before the first event.

$$\text{Group 1: } r \quad e \quad o_1$$

$$\text{Group 2: } r \quad \quad o_2$$

A true experiment creates groups containing individuals who are identical, so far as research considerations go. Of course, we do not control what people are like. Rather, by assigning them to groups randomly, we equally distribute to both groups whatever differences exist. We thus make the groups equivalent.

For an experiment, random assignment means there is no reason a particular person should be in one condition or another. To assign people to groups randomly we could use a computer-generated list of random numbers (having absolutely no pattern to them) and give each person a number from that list. Then we could assign those with even numbers to Group 2, and those with odd numbers to Group 1. A good approximation of random assignment would be to use Social Security numbers in the United States, telephone numbers, or birth dates (odd or even) to allocate individuals to groups.

Randomization does not assure that all characteristics of participants will be *equal* in the two groups. Rather, it assures that we can estimate, using statistics, the distribution of extraneous characteristics. Thus, we can estimate the probability of making a mistake from results of the experiment. Inferential statistics enable us to tell how likely we are to be wrong if we accept an experimental hypothesis that should have been rejected (Type 1 error), and how likely we are to be wrong if we reject an experimental hypothesis that should have been accepted (Type 2 error). A true experiment permits inference from experimental results with known chances of making a mistake.

Statistical tests tell the dangers of erroneously accepting or rejecting a "null hypothesis," namely the logical opposite of the experimental hypothesis. In the design just above, an experimental hypothesis would be that the two groups differ; that is, $o_1 \neq o_2$. The null hypothesis would then be that no difference exists, or $o_1 = o_2$. A Type 1 error is rejecting the null hypothesis when in fact it is true. A Type 2 error is accepting the null hypothesis when in fact it is false. The usual outcome of successful experiments is to reject the null hypothesis—without making a Type 1 error. That does not "prove" the experimental hypothesis, however, for any alternative hypothesis except the null is consistent with the outcome of the experiment. For experiments testing derivation from a theory, we often are concerned with differences between treatment conditions, not with rejecting a null hypothesis. That is, often we believe that all experimental conditions will show *some* effect, and the question is which will show larger effects than others. Thus we use statistics primarily to assess the size of effects and tell how reliable they are likely to be in repeated experiments.

If an effect appears at $o_1$, but not at $o_2$, we can be sure it was an effect of e, because the only difference between Groups 1 and 2 is that members of Group 1 experienced event e. With randomization we can create any number of equivalent groups. Thus, we may have a two-condition experiment, as follows.

$$\textbf{Group 1: r} \quad e_1 \quad o_1$$

$$\textbf{Group 2: r} \quad e_2 \quad o_2$$

We might, for instance, give members of Group 1 a party and Group 2 a weekend retreat, to see whether $e_1$ or $e_2$ had a better effect on their communication patterns. With experiments, we create as many conditions as we need to test a theory, with groups differing from each other only in known independent variables. If conditions were to differ in other ways, the designs would be subject to alternative interpretation, as non-experimental and quasi-experimental designs are.

Campbell and Stanley (1966) present dramatic evidence for the importance of randomization in their discussion of research designs. They show that to draw reliable conclusions from a study without random assignment to conditions would require at least four different groups of subjects, each matched on as many variables as the investigator could think of. To allow for differences among groups which the investigator did not anticipate, participants in each group would have to receive four different treatments (e's), each group receiving the treatments in a different order. Measurements before and after each treatment would have to be recorded for each group. This "sixteen-ordered-observation" design entails extraordinary costs in time, money, and effort. Randomization thus is critical for strong evidence from practical designs.

Most research involves disturbing the situation under investigation, although many of the disturbances only have minor effects. In group processes research, a particular type of disturbance, "experimenter effects," become a concern. In the discussion of *testing* above, we saw how workers responded to the attention from investigators, rather than to increased illumination, in changing their productivity. That is one type of experimenter effect. Other experimenter effects involve *history* (such as how people participating in the research view social scientists) and *instrumentation* (such as changes in accuracy of observation as time passes).

Thus it is important to include the experimenter in conceptualizing the situation. His or her presence is a part of every experiment, resulting in additional independent variables to be controlled. For instance, the age, education, and sex of the experimenter might be significant factors in an experiment. Ridgeway (1988) argued that all-female groups of college students will, under certain conditions, activate gender as a status characteristic because they are working within a university setting, and in universities most of the power and authority are controlled by men. If the experimenter too is male, we would expect that effect to be intensified. What happens in those groups depends not only on the sex of participants, but also on the sex of the experimenter and the sex composition of the authority structure which he or she is seen to represent.

The most common problem in experimental research is that participants try too hard to be helpful. If they can figure out (even incorrectly) what the experimental hypothesis is, often they will try to act to confirm it. Experimental participants, that is, will create Type 1 errors unless the experimenter guards against them. This may be surprising to someone who thinks that the more likely actions would be perverse, i.e., would be actions trying to disconfirm the hypothesis. However, because most participants have volunteered, and expect to be well treated by the experimenter (see the discussion of ethics below), they actually are disposed to try to help. "Helping" here can lead to erroneous conclusions. This issue is often examined under the label of "demand characteristics"; see Adair (1986) and Hendrick and Jones (1972, Chapter 3) for useful discussions.

Dealing with experimenter effects requires several steps. The investigator must recognize that they may occur, and try to anticipate their likely effects. Those ideas can be tested with pre-tests of the experiment. The experimenter must be conceptualized as part of the experimental situation, and his or her effect must be estimated. So far as possible, experimenter effects should be standardized across conditions; for instance, a condition with only an observation should nevertheless include as much interaction with the experimenter as a second condition where both treatment and observation occur. Sometimes experimenters can be unaware of which condition they are running at a particular time, so that they are less likely to influence favorable results, as in "double-blind" drug trials, where neither the experimenter nor the patient knows which drug he or she is receiving. In making decisions about handling data, the investigator has an obligation to counteract experimenter effects; for instance, by not excluding data which "look strange" to the investigator who, presumably, believes the hypothesis. (For a fuller discussion of experimenter effects, see Webster 1975, Chapter 17; Rosenthal 1976.)

## CREATING AN EXPERIMENT

To make the preceding considerations more real, let us consider the tasks involved in creating one standardized experimental design. This experiment was developed to test and extend expectations states theory. Here I outline the theory sufficiently to explain why and how researchers created this experimental design. Chapters 5 and 6 describe development of the theory and present supporting evidence; those chapters also discuss design considerations. Those interested in details of the experiment may consult Webster and Sobieszek (1974, Appendix 1) and Berger et al. (1977, Chapter 5). First, I describe events as they happen in the experiment, and how they relate to the theory's abstract conditions and concepts. This leads to examination of abstract concerns in experiment creation: design issues, how to deal with them, and criteria for judging success.

Individuals make up a "task-oriented group" if solving some task is their main reason for meeting. Juries, sports teams, and students working on a problem set together are examples of task-oriented groups. In such a group, if participants begin with no obvious distinctions among them, they quickly develop certain behavioral inequalities. Some talk more than others, some exert more influence, some receive more positive evaluations. If an investigator asks people to estimate how much each of them helped to solve the group's problems, the following patterns appear. Usually, the higher a person gets ranked on helping solve problems, the more he or she has talked, the more influence he or she has exerted over others, and the more positive evaluations he or she has received. Rankings on these and other behavioral inequalities tend to correlate highly (Berger et al. 1977).

Investigators working within this theoretical tradition hypothesize that two processes are at work here. (See Fisek, Berger, and Norman 1991 for a recent presentation of these ideas.) At the very early stages of interaction, members behave quite equally, mainly offering suggestions about how to solve the group's tasks. These ideas usually require evaluation, so people know whether to follow a particular lead or to keep looking for better ideas. Evaluations of early contributions eventually spread into evaluations of the person making them. If someone offers many good suggestions, at some point others begin to believe he or she has high ability. Their thinking changes from "I think you're right" to "I think you know how to do this sort of task." An opposite result occurs for ideas the group rejects. We call this process "forming expectations for each group member's task ability."

After expectations form, a second process begins: expectation patterns organize group interaction. The higher the expectations held for an individual, the more likely that the person will receive chances to talk, the more likely that he or she will actually talk, and the more likely that others will accept ideas and influence from him or her. For low expectations, reverse results appear.

The first process, expectation formation, depends upon performance evaluations. Positive evaluations lead to high expectations for an individual; negative evaluations lead to low expectations. The second process, expectation control of interaction, determines observable behavior in the group. High expectations associated with a particular individual provide that person with several interaction advantages.

Of course, parts of any group meeting have nothing to do with expectation formation and control of interaction. People introduce themselves, tell jokes, flirt, daydream, persist in arguments even after they realize they were wrong. These behaviors, which are not task-oriented, are outside the scope of expectation states theory, which focuses on the performing and evaluating process, and the later effects of expectations on interaction.

For expectation formation to occur, people must perform (make suggestions) and receive evaluations of those performances. In the first part of the experiment, that is just what happens. Two people meet, work on a series of visual problems, and choose what they think are correct answers (either a or b) for each. After each person replies, they find out who was correct. An answer is either right or wrong, and the experimenter controls the independent variable; namely the positive and negative evaluations each person receives. The hypothesis is that positive evaluations will produce high expectations, and negative evaluations will produce low expectations.

In a second phase of the experiment, researchers measure the impact of expectations upon influence. To measure influence clearly, an experimenter asks the two people to work together on a second set of problems. First, they study each problem and make an "initial choice." Then they see each other's initial choice, reconsider, and make a "final decision." The experimenter controls one more crucial feature: whether individuals' initial choices agree. Only when people disagree can the investigator observe one person exert, and one accept, influence.[3]

---

3. It is helpful to distinguish between scope conditions and initial conditions. Task orientation is a *scope condition*, or statement specifying the range of applicability of a process. Disagreements about the correct answer constitute an *initial condition*, or specification of events which must exist at the beginning of interaction for such a process to be activated, or to take place.

Acceptance or rejection of influence—more precisely, the proportion of times each person accepts influence under these conditions—is a function of the evaluations received (and the resulting expectations). The full prediction for this simple situation is: a person who received positive evaluations in Phase 1 will be less likely than a person receiving negative evaluations to accept influence when disagreements occur in Phase 2.

This experiment has the following features, all of them characteristic of a well-designed experiment:

1. It simplifies a naturally occurring situation. That is, it incorporates only a few (theoretically relevant) elements of the situation.
2. It realizes the theory's conditions for expectation processes to have effect and to activate them. The theory states that only task-oriented interaction falls within its scope, and under initial conditions of disagreement, expectation states will determine influence.
3. It controls crucial independent variables (evaluations).
4. It permits clear observation and objective measurement of the dependent variable (influence).

This design provides a standardized setting whereby investigators may introduce a variety of status and performance information, and clearly observe their effects upon behavior. Another advantage is that operational issues such as how to introduce that information, how many disagreements are believable, and how to maintain participants' interest and motivation, have largely been solved in this design. Moreover, adjusting for subject population differences, results from different experiments are directly comparable, allowing, for instance, assessment of the relative effects of status and performance information upon expectation states. Whenever possible, researchers are wise to adopt and modify a standardized experiment rather than creating new, untested, and incomparable designs for every study. (For further discussion of the standardized setting, and its comparison to other settings, see Chapter 6; also see Balkwell et al. 1992.)

## ARTIFICIALITY IN EXPERIMENTAL RESEARCH

In expectation states experiments, participants often receive extraordinary scores (very high or very low) at a task previously unknown to them. Moreover, they must resolve numerous, virtually continual disagreements with someone they have never before met, at the same or another unfamiliar task. Those circumstances are strange, and many aspects of the situation are artificial. An experimental laboratory *is* an unusual place, unlike any encountered by a typical person on an average day.

Sometimes people contrast experimental settings to what they call "real life." That distinction usually is not helpful. Experiments are as real as any other situation. Anyone who has participated in an experiment or has watched one will attest to this. The experiment may be unusual, but it is often highly involving, and it is real for the people in it.

Artificiality is often discussed in terms of "external validity," or "generalizability" to situations beyond the experiment. This section addresses questions of external validity and generalizability as they apply to experimental studies of group processes. Brief answers are: (1) External validity is the wrong question to ask; (2) Experimental results never generalize directly to other situations; and (3) Experiments must become more, not less, artificial to be most useful in understanding everyday group processes. These points may seem surprising as stated, so they are elaborated below. (Please see Mook 1983 for a comparable view.)

One common error is to take a result from a laboratory experiment and extrapolate it directly to other contexts (to the "external world"), and a second is to believe that experimental data alone can describe something about other contexts. Consider a classic experimental situation devised to study conformity by Solomon Asch (Asch 1951). About 32 percent of answers individuals give in this experiment conform to answers they know are wrong, but answers the majority gives. However, to say that the experiment shows people conform to errors about one-third of the time in their daily lives is nonsense. Results from this experiment depend upon its specific and unusual conditions. Unless those exact conditions existed outside the laboratory, it makes no sense to expect to find the same levels of conformity in other contexts. (Of course, if all conditions of the experiment occur naturally, why go to the trouble to create them artificially?)

Where research questions are formulated in concrete terms, as contrasted with abstract theoretical terms, a degree of generalization often seems possible. Locke (1986) reviewed a series of laboratory and field studies in industrial organizations and found that comparable studies in both settings usually reported similar direction and magnitude of effect. However, researchers developing abstract general theory, such as the authors in this volume, have an even wider aim. Their goal is to understand interaction in situations defined in abstract terms, not only research settings or particular organizations. Abstract theories look for generally true hypotheses, not limited to particular times or places.

Recall the discussion from Chapter 1 of "general" and "particular" approaches to understanding. A general approach constructs theories of abstract social processes, or of general features of social structures. A theory explains only *certain aspects* or certain facts of certain types of situations. Yet general theories apply to multiple cases. A good theory can help explain what happens in the laboratory, as it can help explain what happens outside. Ideally, a theorist constructs a sufficiently precise laboratory test of a theory to gain confidence in the theory before applying it to situations outside the laboratory.

A theory's scope conditions describe, in abstract terms, types of social situations to which the theory applies. If a particular situation meets the theory's scope conditions, the investigator can derive accurate predictions from the theory. This is how to assess empirical adequacy. A situation outside a theory's scope is irrelevant to testing that theory.

Experimental situations must be instances of scope conditions of the theory undergoing testing. Thus, when someone creates an experiment, the first design consideration is to be sure that the experiment fits the scope of the theory. Otherwise, results would be irrelevant to that theory. If the experiment meets the scope conditions, data from the experiment test the theory. Because of the control possible in an experiment, this setting offers an opportunity to test theory in a situation designed so that conditions for the theory's process definitely exist, and extraneous or confounding factors are minimal.

Experimental results show how much confidence to place in a theory. They do not directly show how people behave outside a laboratory. The investigator must have a theory to serve as a bridge between the laboratory and the outside world; that is, between artificial and naturally occurring situations. The theory predicts both inside and outside the laboratory, wherever situations meet the theory's scope conditions.

Anyone who hopes to generalize experimental results directly to any other concrete situation misunderstands this point. In laboratory experiments, we develop, test, and revise theories. Theories developed with the use of experiments help social scientists understand naturally occurring situations. A related error is to criticize experiments for being artificial. Experiments *are* artificial and, without a theory, they show only how people behave in an artificial situation that exists nowhere else. However, *with* a theory, experiments are unmatched as a means to assess and improve the theory.

In older disciplines where experiments are standard and familiar, the artificiality issue and the value of theory become clearer. A well-known physics experiment shows that, in a vacuum, a feather and a lead ball drop at the same rate; we conclude that a feather falls more slowly in natural settings because of air resistance.

Obviously, that experiment constitutes an unusual situation, existing nowhere on earth. We never encounter a place without air, unless we create it using a vacuum pump. The experiment is highly artificial, yet it is valuable for testing as well as demonstrating a derivation from Newton's theory regarding the acceleration of physical bodies. To assess Newton's theory properly, we must experimentally minimize the confounding factor of air resistance. The scope of this theory requires that other factors, such as air resistance, are lacking; that is, the theory predicts for a vacuum chamber, or for airless places such as the moon. To understand more complex situations on earth, we must also take air resistance into account.

Understanding the correct use of experiments implies that no one should undertake an experiment "to see what will happen." The experimenter must begin with a theory. When the scientist has a theory, the laboratory becomes a particularly good place to assess it. He or she can create exactly the conditions needed—scope conditions, initial conditions, and independent variables—to test the theory. The scientist also can design an experiment to permit clear observation of dependent variables, and accurate data collection. Because of their complexity and observational difficulties, natural settings seldom provide as good a place to test and develop theories as experiments do.

It should now be clear that group processes research needs *more* artificiality, not less, in two senses of the term. The first definition is "created by humans," and the second is "artful or ingenious." Experiments should be as highly controlled and as simple as possible, and they should reflect imaginative thought. Trying to recreate natural settings in the laboratory is a misdirection of effort and is sure to fail. Nobody could create an experiment approaching the complexity of a natural setting. An experiment is useful when we can see the operating theoretical forces in sharp relief. The simpler the experiment, the better it is for developing theory.

## ETHICAL EXPERIMENTS

Experiments have a bad reputation in some quarters, as some people view most of science with suspicion. Sometimes (fortunately, rarely) that suspicion is fully justified. Following are three contemporary examples of social science research that have created ethical controversy.

1. The National Institutes of Health, the agency of the United States Government that funds most research on physical and mental health, twice in recent years planned to support a survey of sexual behavior among high school students. It was argued that results would help track changing behavior patterns, estimate numbers of babies born to teenaged mothers in the future, and predict the spread of AIDS and other sexually transmitted diseases, among other benefits. Congress interceded the first time, and the Secretary of Health and Human Services blocked the project the second time. They objected that it would unduly invade privacy, might instigate undesirable practices, and could dilute parents' authority.
2. Some thirty years ago (Milgram 1963, 1965; see also Baumrind 1964, and Milgram 1964, for an exchange that followed on ethical issues), a social psychologist created a now-famous experiment to study limits of order-following. The experimenter told participants their job was to give increasingly severe electric shocks to another supposed subject to punish incorrect answers as the victim tried to learn a series of words. The learner/victim was a confederate of the experimenter, and did not actually receive any shocks. He did display considerable acting skill, simulating terrible suffering. Under the conditions of that experiment, most subjects were willing to give shocks that would have been lethal had they been real. Subjects pushed the buttons as the experimenter told them to, but many of them suffered painful distress. Some reported sleep-

less nights for days or weeks afterwards. Nobody could even begin such an experiment today, as stress on subjects far exceeds bounds permitted by the guidelines of professional societies, which I discuss below.

3. In another well-known experiment that could not be conducted today (Haney, Banks, and Zimbardo 1973; Zimbardo et al. 1973), student volunteers acted either as jailers or prisoners for a week. Jailers held prisoners in a simulated prison, and limited their freedoms in some of the ways that occur in actual jails. Investigators, to their credit, stopped the experiment when jailers began turning sadistic. However, a well established principle in social psychology is that the roles people play and their social situations shape their behavior and emotions. Investigators should have anticipated that people put into the jailer role and implicitly expected to treat prisoners badly would align their attitudes with their actions.

These are extreme examples, the last two particularly well-known ones. The vast majority of experiments do not present such problems. However, given that extreme cases have occurred, it is understandable that research involving human subjects now must include "informed consent." Experimenters must tell potential participants what treatments they will receive, what potential risks exist, and what alternatives there are. Next, individuals either consent to the research as described or experimenters may not accept them as subjects.

Informed consent marks a great advance in the ethical treatment of human beings. It is not, however, a complete solution for social science. First, informed consent sometimes is impossible. Some group interaction experiments necessarily involve deception, ranging from omitting a few details about the study to presenting a heavy proportion of false information. The experiment described earlier, in which expectation states affect influence, involves deception. Measuring influence between subjects is possible only when they disagree about answers. If they agree, there is nothing to measure. Thus the experiment includes artificially created disagreements. The communication equipment tells people they disagree far more often than they actually do. That permits efficient study of the process of interest, yet it also (temporarily) deceives people. The alternative, waiting for disagreements to occur naturally, is undesirable on practical and theoretical grounds.

The second reason informed consent is not a full answer lies in the psychological stress some situations place upon subjects, and their understanding of it. While a relatively low level of stress—causing people to resolve more disagreements than would normally occur, for instance—may sometimes be acceptable, great amounts of stress are always objectionable. We find the electric shock and the simulated prison experiments offensive because of the serious psychological stress they caused many of the participants. Moreover, often people are not good judges of whether a situation will be stressful to them, or of how stressful it will be. Most college students probably would say that they could handle the roles of jailer or prisoner in a simulated prison fairly easily. Yet we know from the actual case that it was dangerously stressful. As social psychologists, we should know better than a typical experimental subject whether a situation will be stressful, and if so, to what extent. To ask subjects to judge whether they can handle the stress abdicates our responsibility.

People err in the opposite direction as well. Many believe they could not survive failing grades in college, divorce, or death of a parent. Yet when those events occur, people survive. The point is, most of us do not know how we would respond in situations that we have never experienced. To rely upon informed consent to protect participants means relying upon their guesses of how they would respond to a situation they can only imagine.

Professional associations in which research involving humans occurs have developed codes of ethical conduct. For instance, the American Psychological Association (1990) has published principles for such research, and the American Sociological Association (1989) has adopted those standards in its code of ethics. Most scientists studying group interaction belong to professional societies such as these, which have the power to sanction members for violations. American Psychological Association standards state in part:

> The decision to undertake research rests upon a considered judgment by the individual psychologist about how best to contribute to psychological science and human welfare. . . . On the basis of this consideration, the psychologist carries out the investigation with respect and concern for the dignity and welfare of the people who participate and with cognizance of federal and state regulations and professional standards governing the conduct of research with human participants.

Specific rules (abridged from the American Psychological Association's "Ethical Principles of Psychologists" 1990) requires investigators to:

1. consider ethics in planning each study;
2. consider degree of psychological "risk" to participants;
3. retain ultimate responsibility for research assistants' behavior;
4. disclose as fully as possible all aspects of the study in obtaining informed consent, except as noted in 5;
5. when concealment or deception is unavoidable, explain those aspects fully as soon as possible afterwards;
6. inform participants that they may withdraw from the study at any time, without penalty of any sort;
7. protect participants from physical and mental discomfort;
8. provide full explanation, including answering any questions, as soon as possible after the study; and
9. detect and correct any negative consequences for any particular participant who may require such assistance.

These guidelines place responsibility upon the investigator to protect subjects. The investigator must: (1) anticipate possible dangers to participants from the research; (2)

eliminate or reduce dangers; (3) inform potential subjects as fully as possible before they agree to participate; (4) explain all details as soon as possible after completion of the research; and (5) watch for and treat any harmful effects.

Social psychologists know about past abuses of research subjects, and most wish to avoid transgressions. Many people are becoming more concerned with promoting ethical treatment of humans. In many countries, professional societies and the law can punish researchers who violate subjects' rights or welfare. Because of these developments, incidents of abuse have become, fortunately, rare.

One other matter requires comment. What about the effect of ethical procedures, including consent of participants, upon randomization? Does it not raise selection or mortality problems if some people decline to participate in one group, others decline another group, etc.? One consequence of ethical guidelines is that they have caused investigators to plan their research more carefully than they otherwise might, resulting in more pleasant, better designed experiments. Because of this, few potential subjects actually refuse to participate. The infrequent cases where individuals decline to take part usually have no pattern; that is, they distribute evenly across conditions.

Ethical experiments require planning, pretesting and monitoring, sensitivity to reactions of people in the situation, and taking any needed corrective measures afterwards. They require the experimenter to bear in mind that the research would be impossible without voluntary assistance of those who participate in the experiments, and treating those volunteers with the respect, concern, and appreciation they deserve.

## SUMMARY

Scientific understanding of group processes depends upon external verification of knowledge claims. Verification requires data from research. A primary concern in designing research is to avoid confounding factors that either misidentify or obscure effects of independent variables.

Laboratory experimentation, long the standard method in some sciences, is fairly new in the study of group processes. However, experiments provide the most reliable way to assess and improve theories of social processes. Without a theory, there is no reason to conduct an experiment. For testing a theory, there are strong reasons to prefer experimental methods.

Most of the experiment's advantages flow from its ability to produce data that clearly and unambiguously test hypotheses. If those hypotheses have a valid relationship to a theory, the experiment provides an excellent way to assess that theory. Theories, not experiments, explain aspects of group processes in natural settings.

Scientific knowledge, as contrasted with opinions, is scarce, yet infinitely more valuable. To build a structure of such knowledge, we must build theories of social processes and social structures, which, as Chapters 1 and 2 demonstrate, requires careful work. Devising experiments to test theories also demands effort. This chapter contains guidelines for profitably investing that effort. Our state of knowledge about group processes is the fruit of labor already invested in building theory and devising experiments. The pattern of prior success shows the way to create additional understanding.

## SUGGESTED READINGS

Aronson, Elliot, Marilynn Brewer, and J. Merrill Carlsmith. 1985. "Experimentation in Social Psychology." Chapter 8, pp. 441–86 in *The Handbook of Social Psychology*, vol. 1, 3rd ed., edited by G. Lindzey and E. Aronson. New York: Random House.

This article describes the uses of experimental methods, paying special attention to the concerns of psychologists. It does not fully explain the value of theory-guided research, but contains useful detail about confounding factors in experimental design, and also examines ethical issues.

Berger, Joseph. 1992. "Expectations, Theory, and Group Processes." *Social Psychology Quarterly* 55:3–11.

Berger reports how he and co-workers decided to pursue a strategy of developing abstract, general theory, resulting in the variety of contemporary theories of how status organizes group interaction. That tradition is referred to in several chapters of this book, and its origins and the considerations in the theorists' minds make for a fascinating study in the development of a research tradition.

Greenwood, John D. 1982. "The Relation Between Laboratory Experiments and Social Behaviour: Causal Explanation and Generalization." *Journal for the Theory of Social Behaviour* 12:225–50.

An excellent description of philosophical foundations of ideas in this chapter. Readers wishing to see most of the commonplace criticisms of experimentation, along with detailed analyses of their development, will find this chapter interesting.

Martin, Michael W. and Jane Sell. 1979. "The Role of the Experiment in the Social Sciences." *The Sociological Quarterly* 20:581–90.

The authors distinguish descriptive theory (of what are called "concrete phenomena" in this chapter) from abstract formal theory of general processes. They show why the artificiality objection applies only to the former type of activity.

Webster, Murray, Jr. and John B. Kervin. 1970. "Artificiality in Experimental Sociology." *Canadian Review of Sociology and Anthropology* 8:263–73.

This is an early examination of artificiality objections. It refutes critics who claim experiments have little to do with understanding natural settings, showing they misunderstand the purposes of experimentation.

Willer, David. 1987. *Theory and the Experimental Investigation of Social Structures*. New York: Gordon and Breach.

Chapter 1 gives a detailed explanation of reasons for conducting experiments, distinguishes deterministic theory from probabilistic hypotheses, and provides additional arguments on the artificiality issue. Chapter 2 analyzes three experimental studies of group processes, offering guidelines for avoiding mistakes.

Zelditch, Morris, Jr. 1969. "Can You Really Study an Army in the Laboratory?" Pp. 484–513 in *A Sociological Reader on Complex Organizations*, 2nd ed., edited by A. Etzioni. New York: Holt, Rinehart and Winston.

Zelditch introduces and explains the view of theory as bridge between the laboratory and natural settings. He shows how this view permits the study of *certain aspects* of an army as a type of formal organization.

# REFERENCES

Adair, John G. 1986. "Social Psychological Issues in Research." Pp. 5–13 in *Readings in Social Psychology: Classic and Canadian Contributions*, edited by B. Earn and S. Towson. Peterborough, Ont.: Broadview Press.

American Psychological Association. 1990. "Ethical Principles of Psychologists" (Amended June 2, 1989). *American Psychologist* 45:390–95.

American Sociological Association. 1989. *Code of Ethics*. Washington, DC: American Sociological Association.

Asch, Solomon E. 1951. "Effects of Group Pressure Upon the Modification and Distortion of Judgments." Pp. 177–90 in *Groups, Leadership, and Men*, edited by H. Guetzkow. Pittsburgh, PA: Carnegie Press.

Balkwell, James W., Joseph Berger, Murray Webster, Jr., Max Nelson-Kilger, and Jacqueline Cashen. 1992. "Processing Status Information: Some Tests of Competing Theoretical Arguments." Pp. 1–20 in *Advances in Group Processes: A Research Annual*, vol. 9, edited by E. J. Lawler, B. Markovsky, C. L. Ridgeway, and H. A. Walker. Greenwich, CT: JAI Press.

Baumrind, Diana. 1964. "Some Thoughts on Ethics of Research: After Reading Milgram's 'Behavioral Study of Obedience.' " *American Psychologist* 19:421–23.

Berger, Joseph, M. Hamit Fisek, Robert Z. Norman, and Morris Zelditch, Jr. 1977. *Status Characteristics and Social Interaction: An Expectation-States Approach*. New York: Elsevier.

Campbell, Donald T. and Julian C. Stanley. 1966. *Experimental and Quasi-Experimental Designs for Research*. Chicago: Rand McNally.

Cohen, Bernard P. 1989. *Developing Sociological Knowledge: Theory and Method*, 2nd ed. Chicago: Nelson-Hall.

Cohen, Bernard P. and Xueguang Zhou. 1991. "Status Processes in Enduring Work Groups." *American Sociological Review* 56:179–88.

Dovidio, John F., Clifford E. Brown, Karen Heltman, Steve L. Ellyson, and Caroline F. Keating. 1988. "Power Displays Between Women and Men in Discussions of Gender-Linked Tasks: A Multichannel Study." *Journal of Personality and Social Psychology* 55:580–87.

Fisek, M. Hamit, Joseph Berger, and Robert Z. Norman. 1991. "Participation in Heterogeneous and Homogeneous Groups: A Theoretical Integration." *American Journal of Sociology* 97:114–42.

Groeneveld, Lyle P., Michael T. Hannan, and Nancy B. Tuma. 1980. "The Effects of Negative Income Tax Experiments on Marital Stability." *Journal of Human Resources* 15:654–74.

Haney, Craig, W. Curtis Banks, and Philip G. Zimbardo. 1973. "Interpersonal Dynamics in a Simulated Prison." *International Journal of Criminology and Penology* 1:69–97.

Hannan, Michael T. and Nancy B. Tuma. 1990. "A Reassessment of the Effect of Income Maintenance on Marital Dissolution in the Seattle-Denver Experiment." *American Journal of Sociology* 95:1270–98.

Hannan, Michael T., Nancy B. Tuma, and Lyle P. Groeneveld. 1977. "Income and Marital Events: Evidence from an Income-Maintenance Experiment." *American Journal of Sociology* 82:1186–211.

Hendrick, Clyde and Russell A. Jones. 1972. *The Nature of Theory and Research in Social Psychology*. New York: Academic Press.

Hume, David. 1955. [1748]. *An Inquiry Concerning Human Understanding*. Indianapolis, IN: The Library of Liberal Arts (Bobbs-Merrill).

Janis, Irving L. 1982. *Victims of Groupthink*. Boston: Houghton-Mifflin.

Jones, Stephen R. G. 1992. "Was There a Hawthorne Effect?" *American Journal of Sociology* 98:451–68.

Kamin, Leon J. 1986. "Is Crime in the Genes? The Answer May Depend on Who Chooses What Evidence." *Scientific American* 254:22–27.

Locke, Edwin A. 1986. "Generalizing from Laboratory to Field: Ecological Validity or Abstraction of Essential Elements?" Pp. 3–9 in *Generalizing from Laboratory to Field Settings*, edited by E. A. Locke. Lexington, MA: D. C. Heath.

Loftus, Elizabeth F. 1993. "The Reality of Repressed Memories." *American Psychologist* 48:518–37.

Milgram, Stanley. 1963. "Behavioral Study of Obedience." *Journal of Abnormal and Social Psychology* 67:371–78.

_____. 1964. "Issues in the Study of Obedience: A Reply to Baumrind." *American Psychologist* 19:848–52.

_____. 1965. "Some Conditions of Obedience and Disobedience to Authority." *Human Relations* 18:57–76.

Mook, Douglas G. 1983. "In Defense of External Invalidity." *American Psychologist* 38: 379–87.

Nemeth, Charlan and Joel Wachtler. 1974. "Creating the Perceptions of Consistency and Confidence: A Necessary Condition for Minority Influence." *Sociometry* 37:529–40.

Pinsonneault, Alain and Kenneth L. Kraemer. 1989. "The Impact of Technological Support on Groups: An Assessment of the Empirical Research." *Decision Support Systems* 5:197–216.

Ridgeway, Cecilia L. 1988. "Gender Differences in Task Groups: A Status and Legitimacy Account." Pp. 188–206 and 495–97 in *Status Generalization: New Theory and Research*, edited by M. Webster, Jr. and M. Foschi. Stanford, CA: Stanford University Press.

Roethlisberger, Fritz J. and William J. Dickson. 1939. *Management and the Worker*. Cambridge, MA: Harvard University Press.

Rosenthal, Robert. 1976. *Experimenter Effects in Behavioral Research*, 2nd ed. New York: Appleton-Century-Crofts.

Rossi, Peter H., Richard A. Berk, and Kenneth J. Lenihan. 1980. *Money, Work, and Crime: Some Experimental Evidence*. New York: Academic Press.

Rossi, Peter H. and Howard E. Freeman. 1989. *Evaluation: A Systematic Approach*, 4th ed. Newbury Park, CA: Sage.

Wagner, David G. and Joseph Berger. 1993. ''Status Characteristics Theory: The Growth of a Program.'' Pp. 23–63 and 454–63 in *Theoretical Research Programs: Studies in the Growth of Theory*, edited by J. Berger and M. Zelditch, Jr. Stanford, CA: Stanford University Press.

Webster, Murray, Jr. 1975. *Actions and Actors: Principles of Social Psychology.* Cambridge, MA: Winthrop Publishers.

Webster, Murray, Jr. and Barbara Sobieszek. 1974. *Sources of Self-Evaluation: A Formal Theory of Significant Others and Social Influence.* New York: Wiley-Interscience.

Wood, Wendy and Steven J. Karten. 1986. ''Sex Differences in Interaction Style as a Product of Perceived Sex Differences in Competence.'' *Journal of Personality and Social Psychology* 50:341–47.

Zimbardo, Philip G., W. Curtis Banks, Craig Haney, and David Jaffe. 1973. ''A Pirandellian Prison.'' *New York Times Magazine*, April 8:38–60.

# PART II

# Basic Processes

# FOUR

# Social Perception

BARRY MARKOVSKY

## INTRODUCTION

Based only on relative velocities and locations, the typical automobile driver sometimes attributes deep and specific qualities to others whom he or she encounters on the road. This is especially so when the other seems to be traveling either significantly faster or significantly slower. When we pull up behind someone driving much slower than us we may think he or she seems dim-witted and oblivious to the outside world. When a fast driver comes up close behind us and tries to pass, he or she may seem callous and hostile. It is ironic how we fail to realize that our own driving is perceived in these ways by others and is therefore subject to the same critical reviews. At a particular time and place, the category into which *we* fall—dim-witted or hostile— then depends only on whether we happen to be driving slower or faster than the observer.

How do we translate perceptions of characteristics such as "relative driving speed" into evaluations of and attributions about people? At a very basic level, perceptions emerge from physical sensations. These sensations, marshaled through vision, hearing, taste, smell, and touch, establish our links to the world outside of our bodies. Our perceptions of this world—the ways we experience those raw physical sensations—emerge from an unconscious process of selective attention and reconstruction. When the sensations that our minds select and reconstruct involve people, *social perceptions* are the frequent result.

In turn, our perceptions of others' overt actions and characteristics, their inner qualities and likely responses, and the contexts in which perceptions are formed, all contribute to how we choose to act toward those others. For instance, consider Jill's simple statement "I think Jack is dangerous." In order to get to the point where she could make such a statement, Jill must have already accomplished a great deal of "social perceiving." She may have observed a sampling of Jack's actions and overt characteristics, or been told about Jack by a trusted friend. Based on information such as Jack's physical appearance, facial expressions, his behavior toward others, and what others have said about him, Jill has made some inferences about him that may or may not be correct. Jill may also have inferred something about Jack's inner qualities—his relative friendliness and assertiveness, his values and goals, etc. She may have even developed her evaluation of Jack by comparing his qualities and behaviors to her own. Based upon the outcomes of all of those inferences, Jill then may anticipate a strong negative reaction from Jack should their paths ever cross. If so, then she may alter her behavior so as to avoid the imagined confrontation. In response, Jack, who may not be a bad sort at all, may suffer diminished self-esteem and a variety of behavioral changes when he perceives Jill and her friends' avoidance. In turn, these may affect Jack's interaction with his friends. In short, social perceptions—and *misperceptions*—can have a cascading effect through intersecting social circles.

Analogous to the way that social perceptions develop from more primitive sensations, a general type of evaluation develops from specific social perceptions. For example, we may form the generalized social evaluation "Mary is a good person" based on the more specific social perceptions "She is modest, helpful, sincere, warm, and reliable." Or we may label Mary "bad" because she seems vain, pessimistic, superficial, and cold. Thus we can think of social perceptions as both comprised of "lower level" sensations and as comprising "higher level," more general evaluations.

As long as we are thinking about social perception as having multiple levels of operation, we need not stop at the three levels of sensation, perception, and general evaluation of individuals. Based on surprisingly little sensory information, we quite readily come to general conclusions about *groups* of people who share national origin, religion, race, or some other characteristic. When members of one group share such perceptions about members of other groups, there are often large-scale consequences. For example, racial segregation, patriotism, sex discrimination, political party affiliations, class structures, and many other phenomena owe at least part of their existence and maintenance to shared social perceptions.

The social psychological literature contains many different labels for theory and research on social perceptions and closely related topics. In general, though, "social cognition," "person perception," "social evaluation," "impression formation," "attribution," and other such designations, when distinguishable at all, point to different wrinkles on the same phenomena. Still, however, the field is vast and so this review is by necessity highly selective.

This chapter examines social perception by first discussing the more fundamental forms and structures of perception, and how they serve to organize perceptual experiences. Traditional approaches to social perception, i.e., self-, person- and group-perception, are then reviewed and placed in historical context. Following this, I consider a set of prevalent biases in social judgments and how they are manifested in and related to a variety of other group processes. Finally, a few of the large-scale phenomena that stem from and feed back into social perceptions are considered.

*Mis*perceptions and their many social consequences comprise an important focus of this chapter. From infancy our bodies place severe limitations on what properties of reality we may perceive. By necessity, our perceptions are selective and so, in a way, inaccurate. Through the study of perceptual biases and limitations we can learn a great deal about why we view the world the way we do, and why we make the world the way it is.

## FORMS AND STRUCTURES OF PERCEPTION

### The Senses

Elementary psychology teaches us that things "out there" in the world are often not as they appear. To illustrate this, basic textbooks frequently demonstrate several optical illusions. For instance, a small gray square on a black background will appear lighter than the same shade of gray on a white background, or the vertical line in an upside-down "T" will appear longer than the horizontal line even when they are of equal length. Such illusions demonstrate how our visual experiences are partially determined by such factors as backgrounds, reference points, and expectations. Somewhere between the *sensation* of light waves and the *perception* of the illusions, our brains imperfectly (but consistently) reconstruct the raw information that is received.

Illusions are not restricted to the visual realm. All of the senses are selective and attend to only certain aspects of complex stimuli (Goldstein 1989). All perceptions are built up from this selected information, and so all are at times subject to misinterpretation. The *contrast effect* (Helson and Kozaki 1968) is one very common source of misinterpretation. Most of us have noticed how the same sound (a ticking clock, for instance) will seem much louder in the still of a quiet night than in the din of daytime; or that a 50 degree day seems cold if preceded by an 85 degree day, and warm if the previous day was below freezing.

Perception is a complex process in which sensations are received, filtered, sorted, interpreted, labeled, and sometimes even consciously manipulated. In general, however, we have little or no access to this process as it operates within ourselves and others, but exceptions do sometimes occur. For example, surgery may provide sight to adults who have been blind since childhood or birth. Without fail, these people are at first unable to make much use of their newly acquired capability. They have great difficulty interpreting the onslaught of chaotic signals that they receive—an ability that most of us take for granted. As one patient wrote in his diary,

> My first visual impression after 27 years of blindness was vague and confused. I remember that I saw an indistinct shape moving back and forth, and I understood

later that it was the surgeon's hand and that a glimmering in this shape was a ring. The first nine months were quite disappointing: to me, the world was only a mosaic of meaningless patches. Then, little by little, I started improving (Valvo 1968).

Each of our senses serves as a "transducer," capable of transforming a particular form of energy into another form. For example, rod and cone cells in the eye's retinas are sensitive to electromagnetic waves within certain ranges of amplitude (size) and frequency (pulses per second). When these cells are stimulated above their thresholds, they send electrical impulses through the optic nerve to the brain's visual cortex where complex patterns of signals are transformed into neural representations virtually as they arrive. These representations may (or may not) reach the level of conscious awareness and constitute a perception. Analogous processes operate for hearing, touch, taste, and olfaction (Goldstein 1989).

## Organizing Experience

For those sensations that surpass sensory thresholds, survive filtering by our brains, and manage to break through into conscious awareness, subjective experiences of these sensations tend to exhibit three distinct qualities: *structure, stability,* and *meaning* (Schneider, Hastorf, and Ellsworth 1979). These are described in more detail below. If any of these qualities were lacking, reality as we know it would seem very different. As a consequence of how these tendencies operate under certain conditions, our perceptual experiences tend to be "packaged" in ways that can bias our impressions of the stimuli that produced them. Some of those resulting biases are discussed in a later section.

We experience the world as structured in the sense that we expect its elements to correspond to one another in patterned ways. When we walk into a house we are not surprised to see a ceiling over our heads and not a blue sky; corners generally appear as 90-degree angles; people enter rooms through doors and not through lighting fixtures. Violations of any of these features would arouse considerable confusion, even anxiety if the confusion could not be resolved. At times, though, what we perceive upon entering the house may be very different from what others perceive. This is not because reality is somehow altered, but rather because of differences in how our expectations structure our perceptions. For example, in the living room there is a 36-inch tall cabinet with a large glass door that contains electronic components. A woodworker may only notice its joinery and finish while an audiophile may only regard its contents. Each person imposes somewhat different perceptual structures on the same objective reality. Another example is the way dedicated fans view sporting events. Every fan *knows* that his or her favorite player or team is consistently the victim of more "bad calls" by the officials than the opponent. Of course, supporters of the opponent will disagree. We sometimes call this "seeing with our hearts" instead of with our eyes. In fact, what we "see" are slices of reality chosen so as to conform with our hopes and expectations.

Closely related to structure is the property of stability. Different sports fans may sometimes see different things, but they invariably agree on much more than they realize: the players they are watching do not melt into the playing field and pop up somewhere else; the ball does not change in size; the numbers on players' backs do not spontaneously change values; the sun does not rise and set during every time out. Despite the fact that a person moving toward or away from us casts images of varying sizes upon our retinas, we learn to perceive the person's size as stable and his or her distance from us as changing. In general, we actively process the sensations that we receive in order to impose the sense of stability on the world around us.

If structure and stability were the only properties of experience, then the world would appear as a succession of structured and stable objects and events passing us by without pattern or purpose. In fact, although we are sometimes faced with objects and events that fail to make sense, most of our perceptions are meaningful. Things we perceive seem to fit into larger patterns and appear to have significance, purpose, causes, and consequences. Much has been learned in the social sciences, however, by taking the position that the meanings we infer with regard to people, objects, and events are not necessarily correct. Just as optical illusions teach us about the operation and limitations of our powers of visual perception, "social illusions" may be thought of as false presumptions and meanings inferred in social contexts that provide insights into the operation and limitations of our powers of social perception.

## APPROACHES TO SOCIAL PERCEPTION

In his review of the history of social perception theory and research, Forgas (1981) identified several distinct disciplines in which the roots of today's research are found. In sociology, for instance, Max Weber's (1968 [1922]) analyses of culture and social relationships focused on the integration of thoughts and actions across individual social actors. Also, the work of George Herbert Mead (1934) explicitly called for a recognition of the role of behavioral gestures, symbols, and interpretations in the construction of social systems.

Psychologists such as Thomas (1937) and Lewin (1951) emphasized that social phenomena perceived by actors to be real are real in their consequences. In the middle of this century, Festinger's theory of cognitive dissonance (1957) and Kelly's (1955) construct theory had considerable influence on the field. Both relied upon cognitively evaluated social perceptions for their explanations of behavior in social situations.

Working within a phenomenological perspective, Berger and Luckmann

(1967) and Schutz (1970) describe how social actors constantly operate within socially constructed and subjectively interpreted worlds, employing stocks of social knowledge distilled from prior experiences. Furthermore, these subjective "life-worlds" are communicated among members of social groups, and it is through this sharing process—this recognition and understanding of the life-worlds of others—that phenomenologists believe social order is made possible.

The various threads that were spun in the early 1900s on up through the 1970s provide the foundation for more recent social perception research. Three large branches of this more recent work are evident, each identifiable by the object of perception with which it is concerned: self, person, or group.

## Self Perception

Self perception is social perception with the self as object. Through introspection and information from others, people develop beliefs about their many qualities—personality, physical appearance, behavioral proclivities, moral stature, athletic prowess, etc. One major branch of self-perception research focuses on inaccuracies in self knowledge; a second, on how information from others shapes the self concept. An excellent example of work in the first branch is Greenwald's (1980) review of evidence for three types of self-conceptual bias: (1) *egocentricity*—anchoring judgments, recollections, thought experiments, and attributions about others to the self; (2) *beneffectance*—perceiving the self as generally efficacious; and (3) *cognitive conservatism*—resisting cognitive change. Bem's (1972) self-perception theory asserts that under conditions of uncertainty, people use their own behavior as a guide to inferences about their inner selves.

The early insights of Cooley (1964 [1902]) and Mead (1934) exemplify the second branch of self-perception research: social origins of the self concept. Cooley coined the term "looking-glass self" to indicate our use of others' appraisals as mirrors of our "true" selves. Mead noted that people's self images are also affected by how they *imagine* significant others would respond to and evaluate them. More recently, social comparison theory (e.g., Festinger 1954; Suls and Miller 1977) deals with, among other issues, the choice and effects of our social referents. Social identification theory and research (Tajfel 1981; Hogg and Abrams 1988) focuses on how group characteristics become incorporated in members' self definitions and orient their subsequent behavior toward other members and toward non-members.

## Person Perception

Most work in the area of social perception deals with how people formulate impressions about the inner qualities and outward behaviors of others. For example, attribution theory—actually, a family of related theoretical insights—is concerned with how people form inferences about the causes of others' behaviors. Its basic question concerns the conditions under which another's behavior is attributed to either an internal disposition or aspects of the situation in which it occurred (Ross and Fletcher 1985). In fact, we exhibit a marked tendency to underestimate the impact of situational factors on others' behavior—the so-called *fundamental attribution error* (Ross 1977).

Some approaches to person perception focus on the integration of pieces of social information. For example, information integration theory (Anderson 1981) models how an observer forms an impression by employing weighted combinations of the other's traits. Psychophysics (Stevens 1975) applies a technology first developed for expressing judgments of physical properties (weight, brightness, pitch, etc.) to the scaling of judgments of personal or social properties (e.g., competence, fairness, attractiveness). Status characteristics theory (Berger, Wagner, and Zelditch 1985) explains the emergence of status and influence hierarchies in collective, task-performing groups on the basis of one's own and others' relative standings *vis-à-vis* combinations of salient characteristics—characteristics that can order interaction whether or not they are explicitly relevant to the task.

## Group Perception

The study of group perception is dominated by two approaches: reference group theories and social categorization theories. Reference group research is one of the first and, through its offshoots, one of the longest lived attempts in social psychology to understand how individuals choose groups and orient themselves toward those groups, and the consequences of their choices and orientations (Merton and Rossi 1968; Singer 1981). Attitude similarity, social inducements, and normative prescriptions have all been shown to affect referent choices in both field and laboratory settings. In turn, a variety of the consequences of such choices have also received study. For example, as the characteristics of reference group members come to be seen as normal, others having different characteristics risk being viewed as not only different but also abnormal, subnormal or deviant, depending on the importance attached to the particular characteristics involved. Self-esteem and feelings of injustice may also be tied to reference group choices. For instance, comparisons to advantaged others may lead one to feel less positive about oneself, or to believe that the situation stems from the enactment of a social injustice.

Social categorization approaches (Tajfel 1981; Wilder 1986) study the conditions for and effects of perceived membership in groups. Such perceptions are seen as part of a categorization process that is fundamental to survival. However, this process can have unintended social side effects, including one phenomenon at the heart of stereotyping: people tend to overestimate the differences between groups and to underestimate the differences among group members (Quattrone 1986). A now-classic finding in research on social identity theory (Tajfel 1981,

Chapter 13) demonstrated that arbitrary "we/they" distinctions created by random assignment to groups in a laboratory setting were sufficient to produce in-group favoritism and negative attributions regarding the out-group. Discrimination and prejudice are the too-frequent behavioral manifestations of perceptual stereotyping. Discrimination is the differential treatment of others based solely upon their group or categorical memberships, whereas prejudice refers to negative attitudes toward certain groups (or social categories) and their members. Race- and sex-based forms of discrimination and prejudice have received the most attention by social researchers (e.g., Dovidio and Gaertner 1986, and Eagly 1987, respectively). However, virtually any basis for categorization may serve as a basis for discrimination or prejudice.

## JUDGMENT BIASES

One of the most active areas of social perception research concerns biases in human judgments. As a consequence of the way we build experiences out of sensory information, we sometimes misattribute structure, stability, and meaning to the dispositions and characteristics of the people and groups that we observe. In recent years, a number of common perceptual biases have been catalogued, all of which are capable of generating such misattributions. Although some theories are capable of explaining limited subsets of these biases (e.g., Khaneman and Tversky 1979; Parducci 1965), the conditions under which each will and will not emerge are still not completely understood. Despite this lack of theoretical unification, each of the following sources of bias is worthy of closer examination.

### Imperfect Self-Knowledge

Earlier it was noted that we make attributions about people based on their relative driving speeds. To the degree that I am an unusually fast driver, my perceptions of other drivers will be biased toward the slow end of the spectrum. In general, comparative judgments are highly dependent on our ability to gauge our own behaviors and characteristics. At the same time, however, a great deal of research verifies that we have difficulty assessing our own qualities and properties in any definite, absolute way. For example, Bem and McConnell (1970) surveyed student opinions a week before and just after they wrote essays supporting a rather unpopular position. The post-essay survey not only showed a shift in attitudes toward the unpopular position, but also that students claimed to recall holding their current position all along, despite their earlier responses to the contrary.

We are also frequently unaware of factors that influence our attitudes and behavior, and sometimes go so far as to explain our behavior after the fact. This has been demonstrated in problem-solving experiments. For instance, Maier (1931) hung two strings from his laboratory ceiling far enough apart that they could not both be reached at the same time. The task was to tie the two strings together. Various objects were located in the room, and the trick was to tie an object to one of the strings, set it swinging, and grab it while holding the other string. A sizable proportion of subjects in a control group were unable to come up with the desired solution on their own. However, subjects in three experimental groups received subtle hints. In the first, the experimenter walked by the string several times, setting it swinging. Most of these subjects solved the problem, but denied that they were helped or influenced by the hint. In the second experimental group the experimenter tied a weight to the string and twirled it. Most of these subjects, however, still failed to solve the problem. In the third experimental group, the experimenter first twirled the string, then set it swinging. Most of these subjects solved the task, but reported that twirling—the "hint" that proved to be useless in another condition—was helpful, and that swinging—the useful hint— was not a factor in their discovery. It was clear that these subjects simply were not aware of the effect that the experimenter's hints were having on their thinking. In fact, we are frequently unaware or forgetful of the sources of our own beliefs, of the reasons for our actions, and of how our behaviors and characteristics are perceived by others.

## Preconceived Notions

All sensory inputs are sorted and filtered through preexisting categories, beliefs, and expectations. Such preconceived notions have a powerful influence on subsequent perceptions by determining the types of structures and meanings assigned to stimuli. We are all too familiar with the bigot who perceives only the most negative characteristics of a select few members of a group toward which he or she already holds a negative view, while exalting his or her own group by noting the accomplishments of only its elite members.

A side effect of preconceived notions is that once they are held, falsifying information is discounted, verifying information is accepted uncritically, and neutral information is interpreted in a manner favorable to the preconception. In a 1977 study, Rothbart and Birrell showed a photo of a rather neutral-looking man to subjects, offering one of two different pieces of information. In one case, subjects were told that the man was a Nazi Gestapo leader who committed atrocities on concentration camp inmates. In the second condition he was described as a leader in the anti-Nazi underground who saved thousands of lives. When asked to judge his facial expression, members of the first group described it as cruel and frowning. Members of the second group judged the same expression as warm and kindly.

This belief-maintaining effect is especially true when social support is available. For instance, through the centuries many groups have promoted claims that the world would come to an end on some specific date (see Festinger, Riecken, and Schachter 1956, for a description of one such group). Their members often make great sacrifices preparing for the end, relinquishing all of their possessions and severing all social ties with non-believers. As the specified doomsdays come and go without the world ending—a rather devastating piece of falsifying information, one would think—group members are usually able to collectively rationalize their failure and turn it into a success (see also Chapter 5 on this point). Members of end-of-the-world cults often conclude that it is their own purity and faith that staved off the predicted cataclysm. A non-event—the salvation of Earth from destruction—comes to be perceived as verification of the group's inherent value. Not only is the world spared, but also so are the group members' preconceived notions.

## Overestimating Abilities

The news gets worse: people are also generally unaware of the degree to which their judgments and perceptions are erroneous. We overestimate our abilities to determine correct answers to problems. In complex everyday situations it is often difficult to determine in retrospect whether or not a correct decision was made. This reinforces our overconfidence. We tend to selectively perceive the evidence or mentally reconstruct events after the fact so as to make our thoughts and actions appear to have been correct all along (Fischoff 1982). For example, if a personnel manager makes a bad hiring decision even after extensive interviews of the job candidate, the manager can always rationalize his or her way out of culpability by claiming that the employee was very clever at withholding relevant information. If the employee turns out to be excellent, managers pat themselves on the back and revel in their brilliance and insight.

## Reliance on Anecdotes

To the biases already discussed, we now add that people tend to employ useless, distracting, and unrepresentative information contained in anecdotes. The general rule is that people are slow to deduce particular instances from a general truth, but quick to infer general truth from a vivid instance (Nisbett and Ross 1980). Sometimes those vivid instances are highly unrepresentative, such as when we read in the newspapers of a terrible crime in a small town and conclude that there are no longer any safe places to live. We are also influenced to an unwarranted degree by individual testimonials. Media ads for weight loss, hair restoration, teeth whitening, and health-related products never tell you the percentage of users for whom the product worked as claimed. Instead, a few success stories are paraded before potential consumers and, unfortunately, they often have the desired effect on decisions to purchase. Political speeches are rife with anecdotes. A common and deceptive practice in negative election campaigns is for a candidate to point out a few very specific failures in the opponent's past record. Of course, the opponent is as likely as not to counter with the identical strategy rather than, say, to educate the public on the invalidity of unrepresentative information. Such is politics.

## *Illusory Relationships*

Were it not for our ability to detect cause-and-effect relationships between phenomena (such as the effects of our own actions in obtaining desired outcomes), we would quickly perish. It is probably for this reason that we are highly sensitive detectors of environmental contingencies—so sensitive, in fact, that we are sometimes prone to "detect" cause-and-effect relations that are not actually there. For example, Gmelch (1978) studied the superstitions of baseball players, observing that the more uncertainty involved in the skill (e.g., hitting compared to fielding), the greater the degree to which players felt that superstitions caused improvements in performance. Trumpy (1983) examined a more elaborate result of illusory correlation. Highly publicized claims by scientists at Maharishi International University (MIU) of Fairfield, Iowa asserted that by conducting group meditations, followers were able to induce positive effects on the weather. The claims were made after a winter during which cement was being poured for a construction project on campus. Above-freezing temperatures are needed to pour concrete, so on evenings before the cement company scheduled a pouring, the MIU community would perform Transcendental Meditation in a collective effort to produce warm weather the following day. When the data were analyzed, it was found that temperatures were significantly higher on days following meditation than on days that did not follow meditation. Trumpy proved that this correlation was entirely illusory, however. He found that prior to scheduling its visits to campus, the cement company would first check with the National Weather Service forecast for the Fairfield area, and only agree to pour the next day if the forecast was for temperatures above freezing. The accuracy of the National Weather Service's 24-hour forecasts is more than sufficient to account for the meditation-temperature coincidence. Unfortunately, MIU and other quasi-religious or cult-like organizations gain many followers and contributors by making similarly unfounded claims about their abilities to influence phenomena and cure the world's ills.

People often misperceive random events so as to confirm their decisions, beliefs, and abilities, and they treat anecdotal information about causal relationships as definitive. Effects can be seen in medicine and counseling. Most physical and psychological maladies improve on their own with time, at least to some degree and for some period. Thus, just about any benign treatment can be interpreted as having positive effects because the administration of the treatment is eventually followed by some form of improvement. In general, the mere coincidence of two unrelated events is capable of making us infer a causal relationship that simply is not there. Consequences may range from innocuous superstitions to harmful misjudgments.

## SOCIAL PERCEPTION IN GROUP CONTEXTS

In this section we consider some of the many ways that social perceptions and perceptual biases can affect each of the several types of group processes examined in this book. Most of these theoretical connections are speculative, however, because research that tests for judgment biases in interpersonal or group contexts is sorely lacking. Also, there is not sufficient space to relate each of the five classes of biases to all six of the other group processes covered in the book. Therefore, only selected biases are discussed in the context of each group process, and the reader is left to consider how the other types may come into play.

### *Performance Evaluation*

As described in Chapter 5 by Meeker, performance evaluations are judgments about the relative success of an actor at one or more tasks. A performance evaluation is a type of social perception. It entails forming beliefs about the quality of a person's task performance based upon perceptions of that person's activities. For many kinds of tasks, the evaluation of performance is a very straightforward process. For example, hockey games, spelling bees, and most mathematical tests are structured so that successful and unsuccessful outcomes are quite distinct and relatively easy to judge. Many situations are not so clear-cut, however. Frequently, in the realm of small groups, performance evaluations must be made under less than ideal conditions. When this is the case, perceptual biases such as those discussed previously are likely to come into play.

If you play a sport you know that it is often difficult to avoid evaluating the performance of yourself and others, even when nothing is at stake. To the degree that one does not know his or her own ability relative to a full range of other players, comparisons such as those between self and opponents are likely to be biased. I may conclude that I am good because my opponent looks worse, but we may both be near the bottom of the heap, and my conclusion would be severely biased as a result.

Preconceived notions are known to have a powerful effect on performance evaluations. An especially unfortunate manifestation of this effect involves teachers and their students. (See Rosenthal and Jacobson 1968. Tajfel 1981, 1982 and Hewstone 1989 provide more general discussions of how social position affects attributions.) For a variety of reasons, teachers often have preconceived notions about how particular students will perform in their class work. These reasons may be based on records of prior performance, reputation, anecdotal information from other teachers, or even racial, sexual, and other prejudices of the teacher.

Whatever the source of the preconceived notion, it has the potential to affect the way a student's performance is perceived by the teacher. Good performances may be attributed to skill or luck, bad performances to lack of ability or a bad day, depending upon the teacher's preconceptions. As a result, feedback to the student can be either encouraging or discouraging and thus affect subsequent performances.

## *Status*

Status organizing processes have the effect of ordering group members along a dimension of power and prestige. Members with higher status have more impact on group decisions than lower status members. They also receive more opportunities to contribute as well as more positive feedback from others. Although high status in task-focused groups can be achieved by demonstrating special skills useful for the task, this is not always the case. As Balkwell discusses in more detail in Chapter 6, certain characteristics of actors that are not related to task skills may nonetheless be used to infer those skills. In this way, perceptual biases involving social characteristics such as race, sex, age, education, occupation, or physical appearance can bias the status organizing process (Berger et al. 1985).

Status orders in small, informal, task-focused groups tend to form quickly—within the first minutes of task activity. Once formed, status orders are remarkably stable throughout the life of the group. Logically, a good deal of instability may be expected for extended periods of time as more information about members' capabilities is revealed. Once group members are initially "pigeonholed" into status positions, however, an overconfidence bias probably comes into play: group members overestimate their abilities to use social characteristics as cues to performance capabilities. Thus, initial status assignments are assumed to be correct, no matter how inaccurate they are in terms of actual task-related skills. Task contributions are then selectively invited from members already assumed to be of high status, and evaluations of those contributions are made in light of those positive preconceived notions. Thus social perceptual biases can maintain a status quo in the group, even when not in the group's best interest with respect to the problems it faces.

## *Power*

When used to denote social phenomena, the concept of "power" refers not so much to properties of certain individuals as it does to a property of social relationships. Simply put, having power means having the ability to get others to do your bidding, even against their wishes. By one view (discussed by Stolte in Chapter 7), the keys to social power are (1) having something that others value highly and/or (2) having alternative sources for the thing(s) you value highly. For example, employers are usually able to get employees to do work that they would rather not do. This is because employers have resources highly valued by employees—namely money—and employees usually have a severely limited number of alternative sources.

Power is affected by social perceptions in a number of ways. For instance, advertising may be viewed as an attempt to exert power over consumers. Manufacturers attempt to induce consumers to do something they generally prefer not to do—part with hard-earned wages—by selling them products that they do not really need. To accomplish this, many ads take an approach that tries to enhance the apparent value of the product in the eyes of the consumer. One way to do this is to create an illusory correlation between the product and the success of its users. We are bombarded with images of successful athletes, models, actors, or business leaders associating themselves with products claiming to make us healthier, more beautiful, popular, or prosperous. Manufacturers hope that we will mistake correlation for causation, and assume that the product *caused* the health, beauty, popularity, or prosperity. They also hope that we will perceive no other sources of gratification, so we will come to value the product highly. Advertising also relies heavily on the persuasive power of anecdotes. However biased they may be, a few testimonials are usually more convincing than statistical summaries. Needless to say, these tactics have a track record of success and consumers happily do manufacturers' bidding.

---

## Justice

Social psychologists rarely address philosophical questions concerning justice, such as what is the "true meaning" of justice, or what sort of distribution of resources across a society's members is the most just. Instead, as Hegtvedt affirms in Chapter 8, social psychologists are more concerned with how people arrive at fair reward estimates, how they come to perceive social exchanges as just or unjust, and the various consequences that follow from these perceptions. The broader philosophical questions are probably not answerable in any objective way. They involve fascinating but untestable value-laden judgments that fall outside the purview of scientific theory and research. In contrast, the social psychological questions are more amenable to testing and theoretical development.

Except in cases where an actor's social "inputs" are readily measured and reward standards are explicit and shared, justice evaluations are subject to perceptual bias. For example, the tendency to overestimate our own abilities may cause us to inflate the rewards we think we ought to receive. When actual rewards come up short of our inflated expectation, we perceive that an injustice has been done. We also tend to incorporate extraneous information into our justice perceptions.

In the same way that optical illusions demonstrate that *visual* backgrounds bias perceptions of foregrounds, perceptions of justice are biased by *informational* backgrounds. For example, one experiment (Markovsky 1988a) had subjects read fictitious descriptions of two hypothetical employees, one with a moderate "work quality index," and a second with either a very high or very low index, depending upon the condition to which the subject was assigned. All subjects took the role of personnel manager and estimated a fair hourly wage for the moderate-quality worker—after being informed that the other (high- or low-quality worker) was reassigned to a different division in the company. Still, subjects used this second worker as a comparison point. They judged a significantly higher level of pay to be fair for moderate workers when the poor worker was mentioned ($6.16/hour) than when the excellent worker was mentioned ($5.36/hour). It is difficult to ignore contexts when making judgments. You can imagine the profound effect that anecdotal information could have on reaching a "fair settlement" in actual salary negotiations.

## *Affect*

Most of us have witnessed how our own or others' judgments and perceptions can be clouded when in a highly emotional state, or how misperceptions of minor social incidents can explode into emotionally charged confrontations. Ridgeway's Chapter 9 examines some emotional concomitants of small group processes. Invariably, social perceptions play central roles in these processes.

Emotional expressions often affect others. How this occurs depends upon how those others perceive the expressed emotions. Given that people vary in their levels of emotional expressiveness, in their sensitivity to and awareness of their own emotional states, and to the emotional expressions of others, it is quite reasonable to expect that perceptions of emotions will at times be inaccurate. The implications of emotional ambiguity for newly forming relationships are well known. For example, if the emotions of the target of your affection are difficult to "read," you may be willing to rely upon cues of practically any sort—even anecdotal cues from third parties: "I heard that Mike heard that she told Marsha she likes you!" You may draw mistaken conclusions about her feelings toward you based on mere coincidences: she must like you because you keep running into her on the street, she often drives by where you live, and she sometimes smiles at you. Of course, none of these events necessarily indicate underlying emotional states. When trying to infer those states, however, such behaviors are readily misinterpretable in ways consistent with preconceived notions.

In more established relationships, problems arise when one party is overconfident in his or her ability to infer the other's feelings. A person may even mistakenly come to believe that he or she knows what the other feels more accurately than the other knows him or herself. Conflict may arise over what each is *really* feeling, and friends, therapists, or counselors may even encourage a variety of baseless interpretations for those ostensible feelings.

## Conflict and Bargaining

In many two-party bargaining situations, each side is interested in what the other has to offer, and each is motivated to get the most from the other while giving up as little as possible to obtain it. Conflicts may occur when neither party is willing to relinquish sufficient amounts of valued resources to the other. As Ford discusses in Chapter 10, these bargaining processes may be influenced in different ways depending upon the strategies adopted by the bargainers. Many of these strategies, in turn, are explicitly designed to manipulate social perceptions.

Social perceptions formed in bargaining contexts affect whether or not agreements are reached and, when they are reached, the exact nature of the agreement. Most bargaining situations have built-in ambiguities, primarily due to the fact that neither party is privy to the other's thoughts and plans. Neither knows just how much the other realistically hopes to obtain, or for how little the other is willing to settle. As a result, each bargainer is liable to overinterpret the other's behavior. For example, a concession by one party that is intended as a gesture of good faith may be interpreted by the other party as a trap to get him or her (or them) to concede. (See Bacharach and Lawler 1981 for a discussion of tactical concessions.) This effect would be amplified by preconceived ideas about the first party, such as a reputation for being ruthless and greedy. Another common strategy is to begin the bargaining with an extreme offer, even if both parties know it is unrealistic. A contrast effect can be exploited: the extreme initial offer makes subsequent offers seem less extreme than if no extreme initial offer was made. The result of this so-called "door-in-the-face" technique (Cialdini et al. 1975) is often a better deal than if a more "realistic" first offer had been made. Whether the bargaining is for a sombrero in Tijuana, the trade-in value of a used car, or nuclear arms reduction, success and failure often hinges on the ability to control social perceptions.

# LARGE-SCALE PHENOMENA

If everyone is vulnerable to misperceptions, and if certain types of misperceptions are relatively common, then the fact that multitudes hold a particular opinion does not rule out the possibility that they all misperceive relevant stimuli in similar ways. Small uncorrected *mis*perceptions, under the right conditions, become mass delusions. In *Extraordinary Popular Delusions and the Madness of Crowds,* Mackay (1980 [1841]) documented numerous historical cases of witch hunts, bank runs, religious crusades, consumer fads, and much more. More contemporary episodes have included rumors of devil worship and ritual sacrifice, fueled by "clues" such as road-killed animals, media hype, and "satan-hunters" out to make money by holding seminars (Hicks 1990). The social costs of these and other such unfounded rumors can be very high. Law enforcement resources are diverted, social mistrust is fostered, and needless anxiety is created among community members.

The small group processes covered in this volume have corresponding phenomena occurring at larger scales (Lawler, Ridgeway, and Markovsky 1993), although there is little systematic theorizing and research addressing actual linkages. To the extent that social perceptions determine the course of small group processes, they can also determine the course of large scale processes. In the case of status, for example, some of the same perceptions that affect power and esteem in the small task group may serve to maintain the stratification systems of larger societies (Della Fave 1986). Those in lower echelons of a social system are often perceived as deserving their lot, and such perceptions are supported through "evidence" construed through the lenses of preconceived notions. So are racist, sexist, elitist, and other attitudes, along with their broad social effects, maintained (Markovsky 1988b).

Social power at larger scales often refers to the ability of one group or organization to determine the resources or behaviors of others. A political organization's power, for instance, is based upon its ability to gather resources, influence public opinion, and manipulate voting patterns in elections. Some organizations are even imbued with the power, formally or informally, to establish criteria for determining what is and is not fair. Labor unions, legislative and judicial bodies, police departments, collection agencies, and many other formal organizations provide various functions in service of large-scale social justice concerns. Perhaps it is at this scale that perceptual ambiguities regarding the nature of justice become most evident. A labor union may denounce working conditions and salary scales deemed adequate by employers. It often does so not by reference to established and absolute standards of justice, but through interpreted perceptions of its members' worth, by comparisons to prior standards for the same workers, and by comparisons to workers with comparable skills and working conditions in other industries. Similarly, law enforcement and judicial agencies often respond to public perceptions about crime frequency, severity, and perpetrators, yet these perceptions can be easily biased or exaggerated by media reporting (Warr, Meier, and Erickson 1983; Parenti 1986).

Social conflict is often steeped in misperception. We are far more accepting and supportive of large-scale conflicts such as economic boycotts and wars when the targets have been successfully stereotyped as inferior, irrational, and generally less worthy than us of living good and prosperous lives. Yet public opinions regarding other nations can cycle from bitter hatred to benign disregard to devoted allegiance. Often in the span of a single generation—a virtual blink of an eye in the broader scope of history—collective perceptions and sentiments regarding other countries can swing from one extreme to the other.

Emotions have large-scale consequences that sometimes change the course of history. For such consequences to occur, however, there must be means for communicating and coordinating the emotional states of numerous people. Again, structured organizations and communication networks provide such functions. Turning once again to the labor union example, if in the course of negotiations, management is portrayed to members as unfeeling or antagonistic toward the rank-and-file, then members may react with anger and bitterness and be far less likely to vote in support of concessions to management. The same holds true from management's perspective. Similarly, broader-based social revolutions seem to require not only the perception by many individuals that an entire class of people is subjugated, but also that members of that class perceive that other members share those same feelings. The feedback effect resulting from this perception of shared emotional states can, under the right conditions, range from explosions of negative collective sentiment and violent social action to positive sentiments and social changes of a more peaceful sort.

## SUMMARY

Beginning with a discussion of how the human organism captures and processes raw physical sensations, we have trodden a path from physical to social perception, common forms of misperception and perceptual bias, some consequences of these biases for a number of small group processes and phenomena and, finally, some consequences of social perception and misperception at the larger organizational and societal scale. One goal has been to show the important link that group processes supply between individual and larger-scale phenomena. Theoretical integration and rigorous empirical testing in this area are lacking, however, and so many of the linkages suggested in this chapter must remain conjectural for now. Needed are programmatic efforts to pursue, on a long-term basis, the many good ideas and pieces of evidence found under the ''social perception'' heading.

By adopting a somewhat non-standard approach focusing on connections between these different scales of analysis, a second goal was served in this chapter: to illustrate how misperceptions and biases at the individual level become amplified and manifested in important ways at other levels. Most of our little social perceptual errors are harmless and of no cause for concern. On the other hand, when social perceptions become institutionalized in a school system, an industry, a class system, or in any other form of social organization, we are as likely to be the victim as the purveyor of harmful misperceptions. If there is a moral to this story, it is that we owe it to ourselves to take great care in formulating social perceptions. We should think about their sources and how they are socially influenced, and we should always regard them with a skeptical eye. We are human and prone to make serious mistakes, but we are uniquely endowed with the capacity to correct them.

## SUGGESTED READINGS

Forgas, Joseph P. 1981. "What Is it About Social Cognition?" Pp. 1–26 in *Social Cognition: Perspectives on Everyday Understanding,* edited by J.P. Forgas. New York: Academic Press.

This chapter provides a useful overview of the field of social cognition, including its intellectual history, problem foci, and research methods.

Jones, Edward E. 1990. *Interpersonal Perception.* New York: W. H. Freeman.

Jones offers a thorough accounting of social perception phenomena, with particular attention paid to interpersonal processes. The overarching issue that he addresses is how people develop methods for making sense of one another.

Myers, David G. 1990. *Social Psychology,* 3d ed. New York: McGraw-Hill.

A major section of Myers' introductory text focuses on "social thinking," or how people think about one another. Within this section are chapters on the formation of attitudes, attributions, and beliefs in social contexts.

Ross, Michael and Garth J.O. Fletcher. 1985. "Attribution and Social Perception." Pp. 73–122 in *The Handbook of Social Psychology,* vol. 2, 3rd ed., edited by G. Lindzey and E. Aronson. New York: Random House.

In a literature review both broad and deep, Ross and Fletcher emphasize attribution over social perception, providing a nice complement to the present chapter.

Sherman, Steven J. 1984. "Cognitive Heuristics." Pp. 189–286 in *Handbook of Social Cognition,* vol. 1, edited by R.S. Wyer, Jr. and T.K. Srull. Hillsdale, NJ: Erlbaum.

"Heuristics" are rules-of-thumb or convenient shortcuts for solving problems. Perhaps unique among the social perception subdisciplines, research on judgment heuristics combines a relatively high level of theoretical and methodological development with a wide variety of interesting everyday applications. Sherman provides a thorough review of heuristic principles, a general framework for understanding them, and an attempt to specify the conditions for their use.

## REFERENCES

Anderson, Norman H. 1981. *Foundations of Information Integration Theory.* New York: Academic Press.

Bacharach, Samuel B. and Edward J. Lawler. 1981. *Bargaining: Power, Tactics and Outcomes.* San Francisco: Jossey-Bass.

Bem, Daryl. 1972. "Self-Perception Theory." Pp. 1–62 in *Advances in Experimental Social Psychology,* vol. 6, edited by L. Berkowitz. New York: Academic Press.

Bem, Daryl and H. Keith McConnell. 1970. "Testing the Self-Perception Explanation of

Dissonance Phenomena: On the Salience of Premanipulation Attitudes." *Journal of Personality and Social Psychology* 14:23–31.

Berger, Joseph, David G. Wagner, and Morris Zelditch, Jr. 1985. "Expectation States Theory: Review and Assessment." Pp. 1–72 in *Status, Rewards, and Influence*, edited by J. Berger and M. Zelditch, Jr. San Francisco: Jossey-Bass.

Berger, Peter L. and Thomas Luckmann. 1967. *The Social Construction of Reality*. London, England: Allen Lane.

Cialdini, Robert B., Joyce E. Vincent, Stephen K. Lewis, José Catalan, Diane Wheeler, and Betty Lee Darby. 1975. "Reciprocal Concessions Procedure for Inducing Compliance: The Door-in-the-Face Technique." *Journal of Personality and Social Psychology* 31:206–15.

Cooley, Charles Horton. 1964 [1902]. *Human Nature and the Social Order*. New York: Schocken.

Della Fave, L. Richard. 1986. "Toward an Explication of the Legitimation Process." *Social Forces* 65:476–500.

Dovidio, John F. and Samuel L. Gaertner, eds. 1986. *Prejudice, Discrimination, and Racism: Theory and Research*. Orlando, FL: Academic Press.

Eagly, Alice H. 1987. *Sex Differences in Social Behavior: A Social-Role Interpretation*. Hillsdale, NJ: Erlbaum.

Festinger, Leon. 1954. "A Theory of Social Comparison Processes." *Human Relations* 7:117–40.

———. 1957. *A Theory of Cognitive Dissonance*. Stanford, CA: Stanford University Press.

Festinger, Leon, Henry W. Riecken, and Stanley Schachter. 1956. *When Prophesy Fails*. Minneapolis, MN: University of Minnesota Press.

Fischoff, Baruch. 1982. "For Those Condemned to Study the Past: Heuristics and Biases in Hindsight." Pp. 335–51 in *Judgment Under Uncertainty: Heuristics and Biases*, edited by D. Khaneman, P. Slovic and A. Tversky. New York: Cambridge University Press.

Forgas, Joseph P. 1981. *Social Cognition: Perspectives on Everyday Understanding*. New York: Academic Press.

Gmelch, George. 1978. "Baseball Magic." *Human Nature* 1:32–39.

Goldstein, E. Bruce. 1989. *Sensation and Perception*, 3rd ed. Belmont, CA: Wadsworth.

Greenwald, Anthony G. 1980. "The Totalitarian Ego: Fabrication and Revision of Personal History." *American Psychologist* 35:603–18.

Helson, Harry and A. Kozaki. 1968. "Anchor Effects Using Numerical Estimates of Simple Dot Patterns." *Perception and Psychophysics* 4:163–64.

Hewstone, Miles. 1989. *Causal Attribution: From Cognitive Processes to Collective Beliefs*. Oxford, England: Basil Blackwell.

Hicks, Robert D. 1990. "The Spread of Satanic Cult Rumors." *Skeptical Inquirer* 14: 287–91.

Hogg, Michael A. and Dominic Abrams. 1988. *Social Identifications*. London, England: Routledge.

Kelly, George A. 1955. *A Theory of Personality: The Psychology of Personal Constructs*. New York: Norton.

Khaneman, Daniel and Amos Tversky. 1979. "Prospect Theory: An Analysis of Decision Under Risk." *Econometrica* 47:263–91.

Lawler, Edward J., Cecilia Ridgeway, and Barry Markovsky. 1993. "Structural Social Psychology and The Micro-Macro Problem." *Sociological Theory* 11:286–90.

Lewin, Kurt. 1951. *Field Theory in Social Science*. New York: Harper.

Mackay, Charles. 1980 [1841]. *Extraordinary Popular Delusions and the Madness of Crowds*. New York: Bonanza. Originally published as *Memoirs of Extraordinary Popular Delusions*. London: Richard Bently Publishers.

Maier, Norman R.F. 1931. "Reasoning in Humans: II. The Solution of a Problem and Its Appearance in Consciousness." *Journal of Comparative Psychology* 12:181–94.

Markovsky, Barry. 1988a. "Anchoring Justice." *Social Psychology Quarterly* 51:213–224.

_____. 1988b. "From Expectation States to Macro Processes." In *Status Generalization: New Theory and Research*, edited by M. Webster, Jr., and M. Foschi. Stanford, CA: Stanford University Press.

Mead, George Herbert. 1934. *Mind, Self and Society*. Chicago: University of Chicago Press.

Merton, Robert K. and Alice S. Rossi. 1968. "Contributions to the Theory of Reference Group Behavior." Pp. 279–334 in *Social Theory and Social Structure,* enlarged ed., edited by R.K. Merton. New York: Free Press.

Nisbett, Richard and Lee Ross. 1980. *Human Inference: Strategies and Shortcomings of Social Judgments*. Englewood Cliffs, NJ: Prentice-Hall.

Parducci, Allen. 1965. "Category Judgment: A Range-Frequency Model." *Psychological Review* 72:407–18.

Parenti, Michael. 1986. *Inventing Reality: The Politics of the Mass Media*. New York: St. Martin's Press.

Quattrone, George A. 1986. "On the Perception of a Group's Variability." Pp. 25–48 in *Psychology of Intergroup Relations*, 2nd ed., edited by S. Worchel and W.G. Austin. Chicago: Nelson-Hall.

Rosenthal, Robert and Lenore Jacobson. 1968. *Pygmalion in the Classroom: Teacher Expectations and Pupils' Intellectual Development*. New York: Holt, Rinehart and Winston.

Ross, Lee. 1977. "The Intuitive Psychologist and His Shortcomings: Distortions in the Attribution Process." Pp. 174–220 in *Advances in Experimental Social Psychology*, vol. 10, edited by L. Berkowitz. New York: Academic Press.

Ross, Michael and Garth J.O. Fletcher. 1985. "Attribution and Social Perception." Pp. 73–122 in *The Handbook of Social Psychology*, vol. 2, 3rd ed., edited by G. Lindzey and E. Aronson. New York: Random House.

Rothbart, Myron and Pamela Birrell. 1977. "Attitude and the Perception of Faces." *Journal of Research in Personality* 11:209–15.

Schneider, David J., Albert H. Hastorf, and Phoebe C. Ellsworth. 1979. *Person Perception*, 2nd ed. Reading, MA: Addison-Wesley.

Schutz, Alfred. 1970. *On Phenomenology and Social Relations*. Chicago: University of Chicago Press.

Singer, Eleanor. 1981. "Reference Groups and Social Evaluations." Pp. 66–93 in *Social Psychology: Sociological Perspectives*, edited by M. Rosenberg and R.H. Turner. New York: Basic Books.

Stevens, Stanley S. 1975. *Psychophysics: Introduction to its Perceptual, Neural, and Social Prospects*. Beverly Hills, CA: Sage.

Suls, Jerry M. and Richard L. Miller, eds. 1977. *Social Comparison Processes*. Washington, DC: Halsted-Wiley.

Tajfel, Henri. 1981. *Human Groups and Social Categories*. Cambridge, England: Cambridge University Press.

———. 1982. *Social Identity and Intergroup Relations*. Cambridge, England: Cambridge University Press.

Thomas, William I. 1937. *Primitive Behavior*. New York: McGraw-Hill.

Trumpy, Franklin D. 1983. "An Investigation of the Reported Effect of Transcendental Meditation on the Weather." *Skeptical Inquirer* 8:143–48.

Valvo, Albert. 1968. "Behavior Patterns and Visual Rehabilitation After Early and Long Lasting Blindness." *American Journal of Ophthalmalogy* 65:19–23.

Warr, Mark, Robert F. Meier, and Maynard L. Erickson. 1983. "Norms, Theories of Punishment, and Publicly Preferred Penalties for Crimes." *Sociological Quarterly* 24: 75–91.

Weber, Max. 1968 [1922]. *Economy and Society*. New York: Bedmeister Press.

Wilder, David A. 1986. "Social Categorization: Implications for Creation and Reduction of Intergroup Bias." Pp. 291–355 in *Advances in Experimental Social Psychology*, vol. 19, edited by L. Berkowitz. New York: Academic Press.

# FIVE

# Performance Evaluation

BARBARA FOLEY MEEKER

## INTRODUCTION

A friend of mine designs, makes, and sells jewelry from a workshop in her home. For several years, she belonged to a small group of women who also sold hand-made jewelry. This group had a very simple structure; it met once a month, at a different member's home each time. At the meetings, members would work, exchange ideas for designs, trade materials, and encourage each other. Members also cooperated in buying supplies and loaning tools. There were no official leaders or officers, no dues, no files or minutes, no formal rules.

After several years, they decided to try a group show of their work in a local gallery and craft shop. They had the use of the shop for two weeks, and also the responsibility for setting up their displays, staffing the shop, and keeping accounts during their two weeks.

Just before the show opened, my friend complained to me: "Barbara, these just *aren't the same people I've known all these years!*" Why not? Well, all sorts of conflicts and disputes had arisen, new skills were demonstrated, the intensity of reactions had increased, people who had previously sat back and let others talk now were taking charge, and people who had seemed conscientious were now seen as shirking responsibility.

Had my friend's colleagues in fact suffered sudden personality changes? Of course not. After the show was over, everyone started behaving very much as they had before the show. What had happened was that the *group* had undertaken a set of activities that placed a different set of performance standards on the group and its members. For example: in setting up the display, only one design could finally be used. As differences of opinion arose as to the most attractive design, these conflicts had to be resolved, and some opinions won while others lost. Previously, any difference of opinion as to design could be tolerated; individuals made their own jewelry and each person could take or not take others' opinions into account as she wished. They all recognized that a gallery display in which each person did as she wished would have no unity, and would be poorly designed, but the group's previous structure left no guidelines for resolving an artistic dispute.

For another example: staffing the shop required a strict schedule, and that everyone take a turn at sitting in the gallery. Previously, the group's activities had required no more than one afternoon a month (although many members spent more time than that with each other on work-related activities). Now, differences in lifestyles, resources, occupations, and family responsibilities became important while previously they had not mattered in the relationships between the members. Members who felt that the personal cost of spending an evening out was great resented the demands of others to take a turn in the shop. On the other hand, those who found it easy to schedule a turn in the shop resented the claims of others that it was too costly for them. While they all wanted the show to succeed, the amount and type of effort each could contribute to this group goal was different, and also different from the amount and type of effort contributed in the past to the group when it met once a month.

If we agree that my friend's associates had not changed personalities, we need an explanation of the differences in behavior before, during, and after the group show that emphasizes group processes. Although the individuals had not changed, the group had; in particular, the tasks and goals of the group had changed. Notice that once the group had adopted a new goal, each action taken by each group member was evaluated by herself and by others in the group in relation to the group goal. They were also evaluated in relation to each individual's sense of what she deserved and could contribute.

For example, take the debate over the arrangement of the gallery. If Ellen wants the necklaces on the west wall, and Diane wants them on the east wall, Ellen and Diane, as well as all the other group members, have to ask themselves several questions. "Which arrangement will look best when someone walks in the door?" "Which will help us make the most profits from our show?" "Which will be the most artistic arrangement?" In addition to the questions related to the group's goal of a successful show, each individual has to ask herself questions about her own position in the group. For example, Ellen has to ask herself, "If I think the necklaces would really look best on the east wall, then I am saying that Diane's ideas are better than mine in this case. Is Diane really a better artist than I am?" And, of course, Diane has to ask herself the same question. If they resolve this in favor of Ellen's idea, the next dispute (for example, should we put the brochures to the right or the left of the cash register?) may be influenced by the resolution of the first. If this is defined as an artistic question, it may seem that, since Ellen was judged the better artist the first time, her idea will prevail this time. On the other hand, if this is judged a business question rather than an artistic question, and if Diane is seen as the better businessperson, then Diane's idea may prevail. It could also happen that, although Ellen's idea was the winner in the first case, this does not mean that she is judged the better artist, and Diane's idea may win the second time.

Another sort of dispute that needed to be resolved was the matter of staffing the gallery. If the group needed someone to be there every night, and if both Carla and Ann could only come on Monday, whose schedule should prevail? If Beth could come on any night, was she somehow more "devoted to" the group than Ann and Carla? Did the fact that Ann and Carla had other obligations that restricted their availability to this group, while Beth did not, make them more valuable, or did it make Beth more valuable? If Beth agreed to substitute for Ann, did that mean that she "deserved" more say in the arrangement of the display, or a larger portion of the profits?

## BALES' RESEARCH ON DISCUSSION GROUPS

Let us look at another example of group interaction: a type of group that has been extensively studied and written about by sociologists. This is a laboratory group, which consists of people who are initially strangers to each other, and who have volunteered to be in a study of "group decision making." These groups have no formal structure, and their membership is relatively homogeneous in status and abilities; that is, all the participants are the same age and sex, and all are students at the same university. They are invited to come to a "small groups laboratory" for an hour, given a topic to discuss, and told that they must reach consensus on their solution to the problem posed in the topic (typically, this involves some sort of problem concerning people getting along with each other in family, business, or professional relationships). This type of study has been extensively reported on by Bales (1950).

From behind a one-way window, a set of trained observers watches the discussion, recording each statement, question, or gesture in a coding system of twelve categories. This coding system, called by Bales "Interaction Process Analysis" (Bales 1950, 1965), requires the observer to note for each act who initiated it, to whom it was addressed (another member of the group or the group as a whole) and into which of twelve possible categories of acts it falls. The twelve categories use a set of theoretical distinctions that classify each act by the function it serves in advancing (or not advancing) the group's discussion. Although the full set of twelve categories has been useful in understanding small group interaction, they are not all necessary for a discussion of performance evaluation processes. What we need to know here are the distinctions Bales made between "task-oriented" and "expressive" acts and the distinctions between positive and negative reactions.

First, we need to make the distinction between task (instrumental, goal-directed) behavior and social (expressive, emotional) behavior. The idea that observable behavior and underlying processes in social interaction involve these two aspects is common in small group theory and research and indeed it seems to be rediscovered regularly (see, for example, the reviews of research on leadership in Fiedler 1967 and Hollander 1985). Thus, although central to Bales' theory, it is not unique to his work. Examples of task acts are suggestions about procedures, answers to factual questions, arguments as to why a solution will or will not work, and suggestions for "getting the job done." We are most concerned in this chapter with instrumental aspects of behavior in groups. Examples of social or expressive acts are laughter, statements of hostility or friendliness, agreeing or disagreeing with another's statement (but without saying why; a further elaboration on why would add a task act to a social act), and expressions of emotions such as satisfaction, boredom, or tension. The expressive aspect of an act is a reaction to the moment, while the instrumental or task aspect of an act has a reference to a future state, a "goal" that someone desires to achieve. An evaluation of "success" or "failure" can be attached to task aspects, while social aspects "just are" (although they can, of course, express negative feelings as well as positive feelings). As Bales originally formulated the theory, every act was either instrumental or expressive but no act could be both. Later research, including later work by Bales himself (1970) shows that acts can be both. An example might be an agreement, which both indicates a positive feeling and moves the task ahead.

The other distinction important to our discussion is that between questions and answers in task acts, and between positive and negative reactions among social acts. A positive social act or an answer moves the group forward, and affirms that group members think what is happening is satisfactory. A negative social act or a question, in contrast, does not move things forward; they are indications that someone thinks something needs to be different. In observing and recording a group discussion using Bales' scheme, any act produced by a group member can be coded as "question," "answer," "positive reaction," or "negative reaction." Questions and answers are task acts, and positive and negative reactions are social acts.

In a typical discussion lasting an hour, with a homogeneous group of strangers, on a complex topic such as a human relations case, and with a requirement to reach consensus, a profile of the interaction will usually show about 50 percent of the acts to be answers, 25 percent to be positive reactions, a little more than 10 percent to be negative reactions, and a little less than 10 percent to be questions. In other words, solutions outnumber questions, and positive reactions outnumber negative reactions (Bales 1950, p. 427).

Another typical finding of this research is that the group members do not all talk the same amount; in fact, if anything is known by sociologists, it is that the distribution of interaction in a face-to-face discussion group is almost always unequal. One person talks most regardless of how the amount of talking is observed. Furthermore, the most talkative group member not only talks much more than less talkative members, but also receives more acts from other group members, and is more likely to be named by the others as ''leader'' or ''person who contributed the best ideas'' on questionnaires answered after the discussion is over. It is also the case that in measures of influence (who won arguments by changing others' minds), power (who won arguments in other ways), and prestige (whose ideas are most respected), the more talkative group members usually have an advantage.

We thus have two related puzzles to solve; why is there almost always an unequal distribution of interaction in discussion groups, and why should this inequality be associated with power, influence, prestige, and perceived leadership? Although it does in some ways reflect common sense, is it really a scientific truth that being talkative leads to power? Another puzzle is how this relates to other types of groups. Is it just ''talking'' groups that show these patterns? What is associated with influence in groups such as the jewelry group described earlier, sports teams, mountain climbing expeditions, or string quartets, which have goals that are accomplished by activity other than talking?

## THE ELEMENTS OF INTERACTION IN GROUPS

One solution to this set of puzzles is expectations states theory, originated by Joseph Berger and his colleagues (Berger, Conner, and Fisek 1974; see also Berger et al. 1977). The following discussion is adapted from Meeker (1981). Berger's theory begins with an examination of the ways in which elements of group structure are related to each other. We can see the structure of a group as being made up of two sorts of elements: first, those that everyone in the group shares, and second, those that some people have more of (or do better) than others.

### Shared Features of Group Structure

In the first set of elements, those that characterize all members of a group, are included: (1) beliefs about the existence and characteristics of physical and social objects, and the nature of cause and effect; and (2) goals or values, that is, statements about what is desirable and how to evaluate what is happening.

In the case of the discussion groups, examples of beliefs about the world of facts include the recognition that the group is in a laboratory setting, that the group members have been assigned a topic, and that the experimenter will decide how well they have done at solving the problem they have been given. These groups also have a set of beliefs about ''human nature'' and the organization of work and family that allow the participants to interpret the ''facts'' in the human relations case. In the case of the jewelry group, beliefs about the nature of the world include the group members' knowledge of techniques and materials of jewelry construction, the terms of the rental contract for the shop, their beliefs about marketing and about artistic principles for arranging a display.

In the second category of shared assumptions, goals and values, the discussion group members share the goals of reaching a consensus on a competent solution to their human relations problem, and of acting like mature, intelligent college students while doing it. The jewelry group has goals of running their show successfully, making a profit, and maintaining their friendships. The two categories of shared assumptions are closely related to each other because the beliefs about the nature of the world tell the group members how to evaluate whether a specific action will lead to a valued goal. For example, if group members believe that the most effective way to achieve consensus is by making sure everyone has expressed an opinion, then the suggestion of going around the table so that each person can express him or herself will be seen as a valuable action. However, if group members believe that the most effective way to achieve consensus is to minimize the number of different ideas brought up, then the *same* suggestion will be seen as a bothersome distraction.

In any actual group there are varying degrees of consensus on beliefs and values. The amount of consensus is an important intermediate step (an intervening variable) in the process of developing a group structure. There is also variation in beliefs and values across groups. For example, actual groups vary in the number and complexity of the goals or values they endorse. The discussion group has a very specific set of goals; its task is to meet for an hour, achieve consensus, and then disband. On the other hand, the jewelry group members have a set of long-term goals related to maintaining their friendships and working on their crafts as well as a set of short-term goals about setting up the display, keeping the shop open, etc. This group discovered that some of the long-term goals seemed to conflict with some of the short-term goals (for example, keeping harmony versus choosing the best arrangement).

In any case, an important aspect of the concept of "goal" is that it implies that there is a state defined by group members as "success" and another defined as "failure." It is assumed that group members want to achieve success and to avoid failure and regulate their behavior accordingly. The combination of goals and beliefs about cause and effect produce *valued behavior standards*. These are the standards by which group members assess how likely an act is to lead to success. For example, passing a test with a certain minimum score may be seen as evidence that a person is likely to be successful in that activity in the future. It is important to remember that these beliefs *are not necessarily empirically true;* what is important for their effect on group structure is that *group members agree in believing that they are true.* In fact, the beliefs of a group may be incorrect or may refer to matters that are not empirically testable such as issues of taste or faith. As the well-known "Thomas principle" (Thomas and Thomas 1928, p. 572) goes, if people "define situations as real, they are real in their consequences."

Valued performance standards apply to actions in the instrumental realm, since they result in assessments of the probability an action will lead to successful accomplishment of a goal. There also exist behavior standards in the expressive realm, where the reference for evaluation is not a future state of affairs (success or failure on a task) but immediate sentiments. Such standards as those that refer to loyalty, to being a good or moral person, to expressing solidarity, or to showing high morale are examples. Together, the valued performance standards for task behavior and the standards for expressive behavior constitute *group norms*. The formulation that follows in this chapter is concerned mostly with instrumental actions and with valued performance standards; however, expressive norms are also important to the understanding of group structures and processes (see Chapter 9 on Affect for a discussion of these norms).

## *Inequalities, Power, and Prestige*

As mentioned earlier, there is a second set of elements that contribute to the development of a group structure. In contrast with the elements discussed above, these elements are *not* equally distributed among members of a group. The second set of components are features that are scarce or unequally distributed. As we have noted, inequalities appear in all groups in the number and type of acts members initiate and receive and in the amount and type of respect members are accorded. (Remember that here we are talking about groups composed of more or less similar people, not groups in which hierarchies are introduced by formal organizational structure or by initial differences in status and/or abilities.)

We will refer to the distribution of *inequality* in a group as a *power and prestige order*. This second set of components, in turn, may be divided into two subsets. First, there is an unequal distribution of rights, privileges, and opportunities: some group members have more influence, are granted more rights to control the attention of others, use their time to initiate action for the group, make decisions that are binding on the group, and resolve disagreements among other group members. Second, there is an unequal distribution of social rewards, the positive feelings and their expression in action that are variously termed "esteem," "respect," "popularity," or "approval." Inequalities in these areas almost always develop in small groups, even when the members have equal formal status.

For good examples of the development and maintenance of a group structure, the following readings are recommended: Whyte's *Street Corner Society* (1943) or Homans' discussion of Whyte's book in *The Human Group* (1950). If you are interested in mountain climbing, Emerson's (1966) description of an Everest expedition is fascinating. For one of the classic descriptions of a group of women working in an office, see Homans' "Status Among Clerical Workers" (1953). In all of these we see an integration of the notion of a task to be performed with the idea of power and prestige structure of the group. For example, in Whyte's description of the group of young men he studied, he shows how a group responds unanimously and negatively to attempts by lower status members to behave like higher status members even when such behavior would ostensibly help achieve one of the group's goals, such as winning an athletic contest.

The two sets of elements of group structure—values and beliefs that are shared and rights and rewards that are unequally distributed—are related. According to current research on small groups, these two sets of components are associated as follows: (1) Groups develop shared beliefs about who occupies what place in the structure, and the maintenance of the structure of inequality can become one of the group goals; and (2) Other things being equal, an individual's position in a power and prestige structure is a function of his or her performance in relation to valued behavior standards of the group. The more other group members think that the individual's actions will lead to success in a group goal, the higher the individual's position in the power and prestige structure.

The "other things that are equal" include the existence of a group consensus on at least some beliefs and goals and the ability of the group to establish its own internal standards for behavior. Under these conditions, the development of differentiated power and prestige structures is a product of the group members' *shared* aspirations to achieve success on a goal and their beliefs about what actions—and particularly whose actions—will lead to success.

## EXPECTATION STATES THEORY

### Basic Concepts

Expectation states theory explains the development and maintenance of power and prestige structures as a result of the development and maintenance of differentiated performance expectations that group members hold for each other.

Several of the basic concepts have been introduced in the discussion above. These include "actors" (the group members); a "task" (something the group works on that can have future states of success and failure); "behavior" (acts performed by group members); and "valued behavior standards." In addition to these, the theory requires three concepts that refer to observable behaviors, two concepts that refer to outcomes of behaviors, and two that refer to unobservable mental states.

The three observable behaviors are derived from the Bales Interaction Process Analysis coding categories. They are: (1) *action opportunities* (any chance to perform granted by one group member to another, including verbal acts such as questions and also nonverbal acts such as questioning looks and momentary silences); (2) *performance outputs* (any act by one group member that is an attempt to contribute to success in the task); and (3) *positive/negative reactions* (expressions of approval or disapproval).

The two concepts that refer to outcomes of behaviors are "disagreement" and "influence." Disagreement occurs when two group members produce conflicting performance outputs or when one tries to get the group to reject a performance output presented by another. A disagreement is distinguished from a simple negative reaction in that it requires a resolution in favor of one person and against another. Negative reactions often lead to disagreements, but not always, for groups sometimes try to avoid having to resolve a conflict and simply ignore or redefine the issue. "Influence" is defined as the direction of the resolution of a disagreement; the person whose idea is accepted is said to have influenced the one who accepts it. The term "influence" is in this sense *not* synonymous with "control"; a person whose performance output is accepted without challenge has exercised control over the group, but since there was no disagreement, influence has not occurred.

Two basic concepts in this theory refer to unobservable mental states. The first is "performance expectation." This is defined as a prediction about the quality of a performance output produced by a group member. A member of a group may have a performance expectation for his or her own act (a "self" expectation) and a performance expectation for the behavior of another group member (an "other" expectation). A performance expectation may be "high" (a prediction that the behavior will lead toward success) or "low" (a prediction that the behavior will lead toward failure).

Combining these basic concepts, we can arrive at the concept of a "performance expectation state." This is defined as a set of performance expectations for two (or more) persons relative to each other. A performance expectation state for person p (self) in which p thinks he or she is more likely than o (the other person) to perform well is called a High-Low expectation state and is denoted [+ −]. By convention, the expectation state for self is always written first. High-Low or [+ −] thus means that p expects him or herself to do better at a task than other, and Low-High or [− +] means that p expects him or herself to do more poorly than other.

In terms of our examples, in the jewelry group, if Ellen thinks she is a better businessperson than Carla, then Ellen will be in a High-Low or [+ −] state when she and Carla face a decision about finances. If Carla agrees with Ellen's assessment of their relative business abilities, then Carla will be in a Low-High or [− +] performance expectation state when she and Ellen are faced with a finance decision. Notice, however, that if Carla and Ellen think that Carla is better at artistic matters than Ellen, when faced with a decision involving artistic standards they will be in the reverse performance expectation states (i.e., Ellen in [− +] and Carla in [+ −]).

A performance expectation state in which p expects both self and other to do well would be a High-High or [+ +] and one in which p expects both self and other to do poorly would be a Low-Low or [− −]. A state in which expectations are undefined may also be recognized, and denoted [00].

A performance expectation state exists before a performance output occurs, and is a prediction about what the consequences of an act will be toward group success or group failure. "Performance expectation" is the first concept referring to an unobservable mental state; the second is that of "unit evaluation." A unit evaluation is p's evaluation of the quality of a performance output immediately after it has occurred. Such evaluations are called "unit" evaluations because they apply only to a single performance output. For example, Carla may decide that Ellen's idea about a particular arrangement is better than her own, even if in general she (Carla) believes her own ideas are better than Ellen's. Even the smartest person can have a poor idea, or the poorest worker can have a good day. (For a discussion of the relationship between performance expectations and unit evaluations that incorporates these ideas, see Foschi 1972.)

## The Fundamental Sequence of Interaction

These concepts furnish the basis for a complete description of the features of social interaction that are relevant to power and prestige structures. To tie them all together, Berger and associates have adapted one of the elements of Bales' theory, the idea of an action cycle or fundamental sequence of behavior (Berger and Conner 1974; Fisek 1974). A "full fundamental sequence of interaction" is a sequence composed of: action opportunity → performance output → reaction. In this sequence, a positive reaction closes the sequence but a negative reaction leads to possible disagreement and possible resolution by rejection of influence. After an attempted influence introduced by the negative reaction has been either accepted or rejected, the cycle returns to the starting point with an action opportunity. An individual's position in a power and prestige structure is described by the number of action opportunities received, the number of performance outputs accepted without disagreement, and the number of influence attempts (that is, initial negative reactions to performance outputs) resolved by rejection of the other's influence attempts. Persons at the top of a power and prestige structure score high on these variables, receiving many action opportunities, providing many performance outputs, and winning many disagreements (having much influence), while those persons at the bottom of a power and prestige structure score low on these variables.

Action opportunities, performance outputs, reactions, disagreements, and influence are all observable acts. We have also defined two types of unobservable mental states, the performance expectation state and the unit evaluation. In this theory of the fundamental sequence of interaction, the two types of unobservable states enter at different points in the interaction sequence and help direct the outcome of the sequence. Performance expectations enter before, and unit evaluations after, a performance output.

The fundamental sequence of interaction can be diagrammed as shown in the following figure from Meeker 1981, p. 298 (adapted from Berger and Conner 1974; Fisek 1974).

Although this figure begins with an action opportunity (for example, self may

**Figure 5.1.** **Diagram of the Full Fundamental Sequence of Behavior**

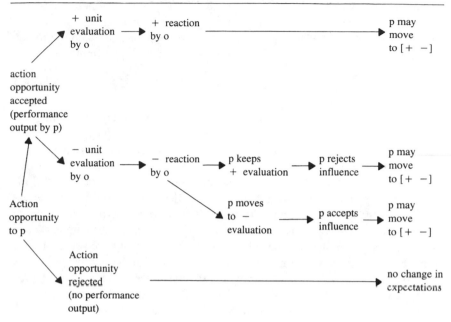

ask other a question) the sequence may also begin with a performance output that is not preceded by an action opportunity. (Recall that Bales found that discussion groups had many more suggestions than questions.)

This diagram incorporates the following assumptions:

1. Positive unit evaluations (which we do not observe) produce positive reactions (which we do observe), and negative unit evaluations likewise produce negative reactions.
2. Performance expectation states affect both action opportunities and performance outputs.
3. Performance expectation states affect unit evaluations.

The latter two assumptions represent a complicated process, and can be elaborated as follows. Assumption 2 consists of two parts:

2a. If a performance expectation state is "undifferentiated" (that is, p thinks self and other are of equal ability, or does not know what their relative abilities are), then self and other are equally likely to receive action opportunities, provide performance outputs if given an action opportunity, and provide performance outputs without being given an action opportunity.

2b. However, if there is a differentiated performance expectation state, that is, either [+ −] or [− +], then the group member for whom there are higher performance expectations is more likely to receive an action opportunity, to provide a performance output if given an action opportunity, and to provide a performance output without being given an action opportunity.

Assumption 2 thus seems intuitively sensible. If you and I are working together on a task on which we both want to do as well as possible, if I think you are better at the task, I will listen to you. In other words, those who think they have something worthwhile to contribute will speak up while those who think they don't, won't.

Assumption 3, about the effect of performance expectations on unit evaluations, is less intuitive. Here, we are assuming that the expectation (which exists *before* the performance output) affects the unit evaluation (which occurs *after* the performance output). This is another example of the operation of the Thomas principle; if people expect someone's contribution to be worthwhile, they are likely to evaluate it as worthwhile. Early studies of group structure in fact found evidence that group members actually overestimate the quality of acts by higher status or more active group members and underestimate the quality of acts by lower status or less active members (for example, Sherif, White, and Harvey 1955; Harvey 1953; Marak 1964; Riecken 1958). Although the theory does not state that this *always* happens, it happens often enough to be a substantial force in the development of group power and prestige structures, and indeed to be a hindrance to effective group problem solving in some cases (see, for example, Janis 1972). We have pointed out that valued behavior standards refer to the perceived usefulness of actions in achieving future goals, and that these beliefs need not be immediately testable to be effective. Many beliefs about behavior standards are hard to test, and the relationship between an action and some valued future goal is often very ambiguous.

Finally, there is a last step in the fundamental sequence of interaction that may produce change in the group power and prestige structure by (possibly) producing change in performance expectation states as a result of the resolution of disagreements. When a disagreement is resolved in favor of a person for whom there is a high performance expectation, this indicates a unit evaluation consistent with the performance expectation state, and no change will occur. However, if a disagreement is resolved in favor of a person for whom there has been a low performance expectation, the group members may reassess their expectations ("He was right this time, maybe he's not so incompetent").

Thus, the fourth and final assumption is as follows:

4. Following a unit evaluation that is consistent with a performance expectation state, no change in the expectations occurs. Following a unit evaluation that contradicts a performance expectation state, there may (or may not) be a change in expectations.

The early steps in the model describe the "interaction advantages" of a person with the high value of either a [+ −] or [− +] expectation state, showing how such a person is likely to get more action opportunities, produce more performance outputs, and win more arguments. In other words, the person for whom there are higher expectations is likely to talk more and have more influence. Once a differentiated performance expectation state exists, it has some of the force of a self-fulfilling prophecy, with the actions of both self and other tending to perpetuate it. Any features of the persons, tasks, or interaction settings that make people think one person may be better than another at doing something can set off a differentiated performance expectation state and hence an unequal power and prestige structure. In the discussion in this book about status generalization (Chapter 6 on Status), we see how many different kinds of characteristics can become associated with expectations of different levels of ability, even when there is in fact no connection between the characteristic and the task.

The final step, Assumption 4, gives the process its dynamic elements by showing how performance expectations are formed and either maintained or changed. The dynamic elements are introduced by the assumption that the long-term performance expectations are influenced by the short-term actions (unit evaluations and acceptance or rejection of influence). At any given moment, any factor that causes one actor to receive a positive unit evaluation when another actor does not can create the beginning of a differentiated performance expectation state, which may then become self-perpetuating. Thus, there are seemingly "accidental" features that affect group interaction.

One example is seating position: a person at the head of a table gets more action opportunities than those occupying the other seats (see, for example, Nemeth and Wachtler 1974). Other physical arrangements may also produce a power and prestige difference. For instance, the person whose desk is in the middle of the office talks to more people than those in the periphery (see, for example, the studies on communication networks; an early work is Bavelas 1948, a recent review can be found in Shaw 1978). Differences in the initial opportunity to contribute to a group product may also result from a variety of personality traits that may make one person speak earlier than another, or from etiquette dictating speaking order, or from anything else that affects the first stages of an interaction.

## Scope Conditions

This theoretical model is formulated for situations that meet the following scope conditions.

1. *The group is small, without formal structure, and homogeneous in the background characteristics of its members (for example, the Bales discussion groups).* Theory and research on situations in which there *are* background differences have also been pursued, as described in Chapter 6.

2. *The group is task-oriented.* This means that the members do share a definition of "task orientation" that includes the possibility of future success or failure and a desire to achieve the former and avoid the latter. This condition is important in linking the unit evaluations to the acceptance or rejection of influence; it is precisely because the members want the best possible task contributions that they accept the actions they think are most likely to lead to success. Although not all groups at all times care primarily about task success, all groups must meet some minimum standards or dissolve (for example, even a group with the sole purpose of having fun must at least decide where and when to meet and what to do).

When applying this theory, it is important to keep in mind that any given group may or may not accept the goals and tasks assigned to it by a supervisor or an experimenter. It is the task that the group members want to accomplish (which may involve deceiving their supervisor as to what they are doing) that activates the fundamental sequence of interaction. The research literature on work groups in industry is full of examples of groups of workers who enforce norms of limiting productivity (see, for example, Homans' (1950) discussion of the "fair day's work" norm in the Western Electric studies, originally published by Roethlisberger and Dickson 1939). In one of the classic early experimental studies of group dynamics, Schachter (1951) assigned half of the groups a task they were not interested in and half a task they were interested in. As Schachter had predicted and as our present model would suggest, it was only in the groups that were interested in their task that disruptive behavior of a deviant group member resulted in that member's low position in a power and prestige structure. In the groups that were assigned a task they thought was irrelevant to their goals, the apparent value of individuals' contributions was less related to the status structure of the group at the end of the discussion.

3. *The standards for evaluating success and failure are at least partly under the control of the group members.* (Technically, this is referred to as an "intrasystemic" task, one in which the outcome is evaluated within the same system of persons comprising the group). Whether a group can set its own standards or not is obviously related to the members' joint acceptance of a task, but it may be that the way an outcome is evaluated is not under their control. For example, an outsider such as a supervisor, teacher, or experimenter may be in charge of saying "you did well" or "you failed."

A substantial body of research exists on the characteristics of group tasks. (For a good review of some of this literature, see McGrath 1984 and Forsyth 1990, Chapters 9 and 10.) Our discussion so far has relied heavily on the Thomas principle that what people believe affects what they do, and therefore if a group believes an action has been valuable or successful, so it is. However, not all tasks allow for this flexible interpretation. In some cases the outcome of a contest (team sports, for example, or elections), a natural event (the crop fails, the patient dies), the internal logic of the task (the theorem cannot be proved, the checkbook does not balance), or the reaction of an outside evaluator (your work group is fired, your group's term paper only gets a C), does not allow group members to decide for themselves what has worked well and what has not. When the norms by which performances are evaluated are not developed by the group itself, the link in the model between performance expectation and unit evaluation is broken; that is, the group cannot assume that the person they think is the best worker actually made the best contribution.

Having made this restriction, however, it is also important to point out that groups can be very resourceful about redefining standards for evaluating performances and outcomes, even in the face of external and objective standards. Such statements as "We lost, but we played a good game," "She did all any doctor could for the patient," or "We learned a valuable lesson," not to mention "He just had a lucky day," "We're not really interested in that task after all," or "That teacher/supervisor is unreasonable and unfair," allow individuals and groups to redefine failure and success. To the extent that a group can do this, even tasks with external or objective performance standards can be included within the scope of this model.

In social psychology, the study of how people explain their own and others' successes and failures is addressed under the topic of "attributions" (most current introductory social psychology textbooks include a description of attribution theory; also, for reviews see Crittenden 1983; Ross and Fletcher 1985). Attributions are explanations people give for why and how an outcome has occurred. Research indicates that individuals do try to provide explanations for events including outcomes of task success and failure. The study of these explanations is much more developed for individuals than for groups, however. The ways in which individual attributions are related to the formation and change of *group* norms about performance evaluations is not well understood, but anecdotal evidence certainly exists that shows groups using attributions to preserve a status structure (see, for example, Whyte 1943).

4. *The fourth scope condition suggested by the originators of expectation states theory is that the group has a "collective orientation."* The idea of being "collectively" as opposed to "individualistically" oriented dates to Parsons' "pattern variables" (1951). Parsons, in analyzing social roles, theorized that every such role has attached to it a set of expectations for behavior on five dimensions: ascription/achievement, specificity/diffuseness, affectivity/affective neutrality, universalism/particularism, and individual/collective orientation. The concept of "individual versus collective orientation" refers to how people expect decisions to be made; in an individual orientation, role occupants are supposed to act on behalf of themselves only, while under a collective orientation, role occupants are supposed to act for the good of some larger set of people. For example, in most classroom settings, students are supposed to "do their own work" and helping another person with an examination is cheating; this is an individualistic orientation. On the other hand, members of a basketball team are supposed to help the team make the highest score rather than score as many points as they can as individuals; this is a collective orientation. This concept is applied

to small group interaction by noting that in a collectively-oriented group there are two components. First, the group members recognize that they are interdependent; that is, they need to take into account other members' actions. Second, members recognize that it is *legitimate* to seek and give advice, to help and to be influenced by others. In an individualistically-oriented relationship, it may be defined as cheating or demeaning to seek advice and help, or to be influenced.

The degree to which members are actually interdependent is one of the features of a task that can affect the relationship between performance expectations, actions, and evaluations. For example, in the jewelry group, before the members undertook to do the show, the group tasks were largely individual. Each person could do her own work independently. However, when setting up the show the group members had to mutually adjust their activities in order to succeed, including coordinating on arranging the display, scheduling time in the shop, and so on (see Steiner 1972 for a typology of tasks based on degree and type of interdependence). It is also possible for a group to define a situation as competitive or conflictual rather than either collective or individualistic. (Deutsch 1973 presents a set of theoretical distinctions along these lines.) We may note that a collective orientation is not precisely the same as a "cooperative" situation; there can be elements of competition in a collective orientation, as for example the competition for time and attention imposed by the demands of a discussion group to limit talking to one person at a time.

The scope condition of a collective orientation is important to the fundamental sequence of interaction because it means that group members can expect that others' contributions are well-intentioned (others are not trying to deceive or trick them, for example) and that it is legitimate to accept influence, thus making the final link between unit evaluations and resolution of disagreements in favor of the (supposedly) better contribution plausible.

## EMPIRICAL RESEARCH

We have reviewed two types of empirical research so far in this chapter; first, the studies documenting the unequal distribution of interaction in most face-to-face small groups associated with inequalities in influence and prestige (that is, the power and prestige structures that expectation states theory seeks to explain). Second, in the discussion of scope conditions, a variety of related research from other approaches to small groups was mentioned briefly (research on the characteristics and demands of tasks, on group norms, on group acceptance of goals, on attributions, and on conflict). In this last section of the chapter, we review some of the research developed from expectation states theory and designed explicitly to test predictions derived from it. We also examine the question of how multiple standards for performance evaluation develop and are integrated into valued performance standards.

A number of empirical studies of expectation states use a variant of a standardized experimental setting (see also Chapters 3 and 6 of this volume). This setting is designed to control for extraneous sources of expectations and also to incorporate the theoretically important features specified by both the scope conditions and the assumptions of the model. Looking at the model of the fundamental interaction sequence, we can easily see that it is the presence and resolution of *disagreements* that creates the links between the elements of the sequence. If there are no disagreements, no influence is exerted. If our interest is in the processes of differentiation, we must somehow produce disagreements, force their resolution, and yet hold constant other features of inequality.

In the standardized experimental procedure, therefore, subjects are drawn from homogeneous populations and assigned to two-person groups whose members do not previously know each other. They are told that they will be given a test of a newly discovered ability (in fact, hypothetical) and that the test consists of a set of slides on each of which both subjects must give an estimate, either a or b. Examples of tasks include deciding whether there is more black or white on a slide composed of approximately equal and randomly arranged rectangles of black or white, or deciding which of two "foreign" words has the same meaning as an English word.

In Phase I of the standardized experiment, subjects are told their "scores" on the first test, either high or low (in fact, randomly assigned). In the second part, Phase II, they are told they will work together on a similar task and will exchange with each other a preliminary answer to a slide similar to the ones they have just seen. After looking at the preliminary answers, they will each make a "final choice," which will count toward a group score. The experimenter arranges the exchange of preliminary choices so that both subjects believe the partner has disagreed with them on the first answer. Thus, to make a "final choice" each must decide whether to accept or reject the choice of the other. The independent variable in this experiment is the expectation state (on the first test self either did well or poorly compared to other) and the dependent variable is acceptance or rejection of influence in the second test. The proportion of times on the second test the subject *changed* his or her answer to agree with the answer of the (supposed) other is the measure of acceptance of influence. A high proportion of "self" or "stay" (stick with your own, don't change and accept influence) responses in Phase II indicates that the subject is assigning higher unit evaluations to his or her own choices than to the competing choices of other. A low proportion of stay responses indicates a high degree of acceptance of influence.

Studies using this setting have found that the proportion of stay responses for subjects assigned to a [+ +] expectation state (both made high scores on the test in Phase I) *and* of subjects assigned a [− −] state (both did poorly on the first test) is around 64 to 67 percent (Berger and Conner 1969; Camilleri, Berger, and Conner 1972), while the proportion of stay responses for a subject assigned to a [+ −] state (self did well on the first test, other did poorly) is slightly more than 75 percent.

In experimental research, the effects of independent variables are assessed in comparison to a control condition in which no manipulation is performed. In the expectation states literature, Moore (1969, pp. 154–55) reports a control condition where subjects with undefined expectation states did not see any of the partner's choices but did have a chance to rethink and change their initial answers. The proportion of stay responses for such subjects was also about 75 percent. This implies that subjects who have a [+ −] expectation state change their minds under conditions of disagreement about as often as subjects who do not have to take any other opinion into account. In other words, there is no evidence of acceptance of influence for [+ −] subjects.

The remaining possibility is the subject assigned low ability in a [− +] state (doing poorly on the first test while the partner did well). These subjects have a proportion of stay responses of about 40 percent, much lower than the others. It is worth noting that it is not so much whether the subject has done well or poorly on the first test, but *how* well or poorly the person performed relative to the partner that affects behavior on the second task. The people who did poorly with partners who also did poorly accept influence only about as often as those who did well with partners who did well. It is when subjects did poorly *and* had a partner who did well that the acceptance of influence is high. Other studies that show similar results include Conner (1977, 1985) and Berger, Conner, and McKeown (1969). Conner's studies also showed that people who respond *faster* seem to have an expectation advantage. These studies and also Berger and Conner (1974) and Foschi and Foschi (1979) examine how decisions made on unit trials (one decision at a time) can generalize into expectation states for performance.

The issue of the resistance to change of such expectations is addressed in Foschi (1971). In that study, subjects received what they considered to be unbiased evaluations of their performances. The first part of the task served to form expectations, and the second, to contradict them either totally or partially. Results point to the resilience of expectation states even under such conditions. Further theoretical development of the concept of expectation states, relating performance expectations to other types of social structures, is presented by Fararo (1973, pp. 393–422) and by Fararo and Skvoretz (1986). For example, the article by Fararo and Skvoretz applies the theory to changes in the structure of dominance relations among a small group of animals.

We have already noted that most groups have more than one task to work on; also, people usually have more than one source of information about each other's abilities. A series of experiments by Berger, Fisek, and Freese (1976), Freese (1976), and Berger and Fisek (1970) showed that in general, people will use information about one ability to predict performance on another; the more directly relevant the first ability is to the other tasks, the more effect it will have, and in cases where information about several abilities is inconsistent, people seem to combine the information they have.

Another set of questions concerns the possible sources of evaluations. In the experimental setting described earlier, the experimenter uses the inherent authority of his or her position to assign "test scores"; in everyday situations, many other sources of information may be available. Which of these do people use as sources of valued performance standards, and as sources of information about performance? One series of studies (summarized in Webster and Sobieszek 1974) shows that subjects will take into account information from other persons like themselves who have been assigned the right to evaluate their performance (see also Crundall and Foddy 1981; Foddy 1988). The ways in which objective standards of performance and the opinions of other persons are combined have been investigated by Foschi, Warriner, and Hart (1985) and Foschi and Foddy (1988); the effects of "second-order performance expectations" (the expectations held by third parties for themselves on the formation of expectations for self and other) have been studied by Moore (1985). Moore's work examined the issue of possible disagreement between self and other about their relative expectations. For example, if Diane thinks she is a better artist than Ellen, but becomes aware that Ellen does not share this view, how are disagreements resolved, and what effect does this have on subsequent expectations? Also, Moore examined the question of whether people form expectations after resolving disagreements not because they think they are right, but because their social role requires them to "stand firm." For example, if Ann thinks Beth will give in to her arguments because Beth is insecure but actually Beth is the better artist, will the need to have a single opinion make Ann stick to her own opinion? And if she does, will the resolution of a disagreement in her own favor eventually convince Ann that she is a better artist than Beth? Moore's research suggests that the answers to both questions are yes; the need to coordinate resources under such conditions may cause a person to act in a way that contradicts his or her own expectation state, and such role behavior may, in turn, result in changes in expectations.

## SUMMARY

Numerous observations of small groups have shown that groups develop differentiated power and prestige structures. That is, group members have different rates of participating, different amounts of influence on each other, and different degrees of prestige. These differences arise out of the process of cooperation on a group task and the need to resolve disagreements. If a group adopts as a goal a task requiring coordinated effort, then those members who are expected to contribute more to success are given more chances to contribute, their efforts are evaluated more positively, and they win arguments more often. Their acts have more influence on the group's final product, and they are given more respect by other members.

Expectation states theory expresses this process in formal terms, and specifies how and under what conditions it operates. The observable variables of action opportunities, performance outputs, positive and negative reactions, and resolution of disagreements (influence) reflect structures of the unobservable variables of performance expectation states and unit evaluations. Under conditions of task orientation, collective orientation and intra-systemic task evaluation, people allocate action opportunities, and produce and accept performance outputs in a manner consistent with their relative performance expectations. Empirical research examining various specific predictions derived from this theory have shown that performance expectations do affect acceptance or rejection of influence, and that in turn this can affect the underlying expectation states. These processes are also related to the existence of formal status structures, to the effects of different kinds of tasks on group structures, and to the mutual effects of instrumental and affective processes in groups.

We started with two related puzzles: the unequal distribution of interaction in small face-to-face groups, and the emergence of power and prestige structures in groups. Considering both those features of groups that are equally shared (beliefs, values, and goals) and those that are either equally or unequally distributed (task competence), expectation states theory shows how the acts of persons trying to reach a group solution to a collective task produce inequalities of power and prestige. Although task groups differ from each other in many ways, they almost all have differentiated power and prestige structures, arising out of a collective orientation to the task. In this chapter we have seen how such structures develop in groups that are initially homogeneous in background characteristics.

## SUGGESTED READINGS

Bales, Robert F. 1950. *Interaction Process Analysis: A Method for the Study of Small Groups.* Cambridge, MA: Addison-Wesley.

This book explains the twelve-category coding system and its theoretical background, and presents results of some of the early studies based on this system.

Berger, Joseph and Thomas L. Conner. 1974. "Performance Expectations and Behavior in Small Groups: A Revised Formulation." Pp. 85–109 in *Expectation States Theory: A Theoretical Research Program,* edited by J. Berger, T. L. Conner, and M. H. Fisek. Cambridge, MA: Winthrop.

This chapter provides an outline of the fundamental sequence of interaction and the theory behind it.

Homans, George C. 1950. *The Human Group.* New York: Harcourt, Brace and World.

Homans gives a classic description of group norms and status structures, and the twin processes of conformity and differentiation, using several famous examples of observational studies of groups. See especially Chapters 1 through 3.

Janis, Irving L. 1972. *Victims of Groupthink.* Boston: Houghton Mifflin.

Beginning with an analysis of the decision of President John F. Kennedy and his advisors to launch the Bay of Pigs invasion, Janis shows how groups of even the "best and the brightest'' can, by trying to avoid recognizing and resolving disagreements, make inadequate decisions.

McGrath, Joseph E. 1984. *Groups: Interaction and Performance.* Englewood Cliffs, NJ: Prentice-Hall.

Chapters 5 through 11 give an excellent review of research and theory on the nature of group tasks and the demands tasks impose on the structures of groups.

# REFERENCES

Bales, Robert F. 1950. *Interaction Process Analysis: A Method for the Study of Small Groups.* Cambridge, MA: Addison-Wesley.

_____. 1965. ''The Equilibrium Problem in Small Groups.'' Pp. 444–76 in *Small Groups: Studies in Social Interaction,* rev. ed., edited by A. P. Hare, E. F. Borgatta, and R. F. Bales. New York: Knopf.

_____. 1970. *Personality and Interpersonal Behavior.* New York: Holt, Rinehart and Winston.

Bavelas, Alex. 1948. ''A Mathematical Model for Group Structure.'' *Applied Anthropology* 7:16–30.

Berger, Joseph and Thomas L. Conner. 1969. ''Performance Expectations in Small Groups.'' *Acta Sociologica* 12:186–97.

_____. 1974. ''Performance Expectations and Behavior in Small Groups: A Revised Formulation.'' Pp. 85–109 in *Expectation States Theory: A Theoretical Research Program,* edited by J. Berger, T. L. Conner, and M. H. Fisek. Cambridge, MA: Winthrop.

Berger, Joseph, Thomas L. Conner, and M. Hamit Fisek. 1974. *Expectation States Theory: A Theoretical Research Program.* Cambridge, MA: Winthrop.

Berger, Joseph, Thomas L. Conner, and William L. McKeown. 1969. ''Evaluations and the Formation and Maintenance of Performance Expectations.'' *Human Relations* 22: 481–501.

Berger, Joseph and M. Hamit Fisek. 1970. ''Consistent and Inconsistent Status Characteristics and the Determination of Power and Prestige Orders.'' *Sociometry* 33:287–304.

Berger, Joseph, M. Hamit Fisek, and Lee Freese. 1976. ''Paths of Relevance and the Determination of Power and Prestige Orders.'' *Pacific Sociological Review* 19:45–62.

Berger, Joseph, M. Hamit Fisek, Robert Z. Norman, and Morris Zelditch, Jr. 1977. *Status Characteristics and Social Interaction: An Expectation-States Approach.* New York: Elsevier.

Camilleri, Santo F., Joseph Berger, and Thomas L. Conner. 1972. ''A Formal Theory of Decision-Making.'' Pp. 21–37 in *Sociological Theories in Progress,* vol. 2, edited by J. Berger, M. Zelditch, Jr., and B. Anderson. Boston: Houghton Mifflin.

Conner, Thomas L. 1977. ''Performance Expectations and the Initiation of Problem Solving Attempts.'' *Journal of Mathematical Sociology* 5:187–98.

_____. 1985. ''Response Latencies, Performance Expectations, and Interaction Patterns.'' Pp. 189–214 in *Status, Rewards, and Influence,* edited by J. Berger and M. Zelditch, Jr. San Francisco: Jossey-Bass.

Crittenden, Kathleen S. 1983. ''Sociological Aspects of Attribution.'' *Annual Review of Sociology* 9:425–46.

Crundall, Ian and Margaret Foddy. 1981. "Vicarious Exposure to a Task as a Basis of Evaluative Competence." *Social Psychology Quarterly* 44:331–38.

Deutsch, Morton. 1973. *The Resolution of Conflict: Constructive and Destructive Processes.* New Haven: Yale University Press.

Emerson, Richard M. 1966. "Mount Everest: A Case Study of Communication Feedback and Sustained Group Goal-Striving." *Sociometry* 29:213–27.

Fararo, Thomas. 1973. *Mathematical Sociology: An Introduction to Fundamentals.* New York: Wiley-Interscience.

Fararo, Thomas and John V. Skvoretz. 1986. "E-State Structuralism: A Theoretical Model." *American Sociological Review* 51:591–602.

Fiedler, Fred. 1967. *A Theory of Leadership Effectiveness.* New York: McGraw-Hill.

Fisek, M. Hamit. 1974. "A Model for the Evolution of Status Structures in Task-Oriented Discussion Groups." Pp. 53–83 in *Expectation States Theory: A Theoretical Research Program,* edited by J. Berger, T. L. Conner, and M. H. Fisek. Cambridge, MA: Winthrop.

Foddy, Margaret. 1988. "Paths of Relevance and Evaluative Competence." Pp. 232–47 and 501 in *Status Generalization: New Theory and Research,* edited by M. Webster, Jr. and M. Foschi. Stanford, CA: Stanford University Press.

Forsyth, Donelson R. 1990. *Group Dynamics,* 2nd ed. Belmont, CA: Brooks-Cole.

Foschi, Martha. 1971. "Contradiction and Change of Performance Expectations." *Canadian Review of Sociology and Anthropology* 8:205–22.

——. 1972. "On the Concept of 'Expectations'." *Acta Sociologica* 15:124–31.

Foschi, Martha and Margaret Foddy. 1988. "Standards, Performances, and the Formation of Self-Other Expectations." Pp. 248–60 and 501–503 in *Status Generalization: New Theory and Research,* edited by M. Webster, Jr., and M. Foschi. Stanford, CA: Stanford University Press.

Foschi, Martha and Ricardo Foschi. 1979. "A Bayesian Model for Performance Expectations: Extension and Simulation." *Social Psychology Quarterly* 42:232–41.

Foschi, Martha, G. Keith Warriner, and Stephen D. Hart. 1985. "Standards, Expectations, and Interpersonal Influence." *Social Psychology Quarterly* 48:108–17.

Freese, Lee. 1976. "The Generalization of Specific Performance Expectations." *Sociometry* 36:194–200.

Harvey, O. J. 1953. "An Experimental Approach to the Study of Status Reactions in Small Groups." *American Sociological Review* 18:357–67.

Hollander, Edwin P. 1985. "Leadership and Power." Pp. 485–538 in *The Handbook of Social Psychology,* 3rd ed., vol. 2, edited by G. Lindzey and E. Aronson. New York: Random House.

Homans, George C. 1950. *The Human Group.* New York: Harcourt, Brace and World.

——. 1953. "Status Among Clerical Workers." *Human Organization* 12:5–10.

Janis, Irving L. 1972. *Victims of Groupthink.* Boston: Houghton Mifflin.

Marak, George E. 1964. "The Evolution of Leadership Structure." *Sociometry* 27:174–82.

McGrath, Joseph E. 1984. *Groups: Interaction and Performance.* Englewood Cliffs, NJ: Prentice-Hall.

Meeker, Barbara F. 1981. "Expectation States and Interpersonal Behavior." Pp. 290–319 in *Social Psychology: Sociological Perspectives,* edited by M. Rosenberg and R. Turner. New York: Basic Books.

Moore, James C., Jr. 1969. "Social Status and Social Influence: Process Considerations." *Sociometry* 32:145–68.

———. 1985. "Role Enactment and Self-Identity: An Expectation States Approach." Pp. 262–316 in *Status, Rewards and Influence,* edited by J. Berger and M. Zelditch, Jr. San Francisco: Jossey-Bass.

Nemeth, Charlan and Joel Wachtler. 1974. "Creating the Perceptions of Consistency and Confidence: A Necessary Condition for Minority Influence." *Sociometry* 37:529–40.

Parsons, Talcott. 1951. *The Social System.* Glencoe, IL: The Free Press.

Riecken, Henry W. 1958. "The Effect of Talkativeness on Ability to Influence Group Solutions to Problems." *Sociometry* 21:309–21.

Roethlisberger, Fritz J. and William J. Dickson. 1939. *Management and the Worker.* Cambridge, MA: Harvard University Press.

Ross, Michael and Garth J. O. Fletcher. 1985. "Attribution and Social Perception." Pp. 73–122 in *The Handbook of Social Psychology,* vol. 2, 3rd ed., edited by G. Lindzey and E. Aronson. New York: Random House.

Schachter, Stanley. 1951. "Deviation, Rejection and Communication." *Journal of Abnormal and Social Psychology* 46:190–207.

Shaw, Marvin E. 1978. "Communication Networks Fourteen Years Later." Pp. 351–61 in *Group Processes,* edited by L. Berkowitz. New York: Academic Press.

Sherif, Muzafer, B. Jack White, and O. J. Harvey. 1955. "Status in Experimentally Produced Groups." *American Journal of Sociology* 66:370–79.

Steiner, Ivan D. 1972. *Group Process and Productivity.* New York: Academic Press.

Thomas, William I. and Dorothy S. Thomas. 1928. *The Child in America* New York: Knopf.

Webster, Murray, Jr. and Barbara Sobieszek. 1974. *Sources of Self-Evaluation: A Formal Theory of Significant Others and Social Influence.* New York: Wiley-Interscience.

Whyte, William Foote. 1943. *Street Corner Society.* Chicago: University of Chicago Press.

# SIX

# Status[1]

## JAMES W. BALKWELL

## INTRODUCTION

In a densely populated residential section of Boston, there is a neighborhood that for almost two hundred years has been home to the newest wave of American immigrants. First came the Irish, beginning in the early 1800s, continuing in significant numbers through about 1880. Then came the earliest of at least two waves of Italian newcomers, mostly from northern Italy at the start, then mainly from the southern Italian peninsula and Sicily. By the 1930s, "Cornerville" (as this neighborhood subsequently became dubbed) was inhabited primarily by first- and second-generation southern Italian immigrants. William F. Whyte's sociological classic, *Street Corner Society* (1943), describes the structure and functioning of Cornerville as an anthropologist might describe life on some distant Pacific island.

As you might anticipate, Cornerville had its clubs, political organizations, places of employment, schools, churches, and so on. To some extent, these gave structure to life in the community. But to a considerable degree the social fabric of Cornerville was (and remains today) a fabric of *small groups*, collections of friends who associated regularly and depended on each other for companionship, amusement, and emotional support. To the several generations of sociology students who read *Street Corner Society*, perhaps the most lasting impressions were those of a group that hung out on Norton Street, referred to by Whyte as "the Nortons," or "Doc's gang."

The Nortons were a group of young men with about a dozen regular members, plus several marginal participants who associated with the others on an occasional

---

1. I am indebted to Joseph Berger and Dawn T. Robinson for helpful comments and suggestions on previous drafts of this chapter.

basis. Doc was their acknowledged leader. He was reputedly the toughest fighter, the best card player, the most dangerous baseball player (especially in a clutch), the guy who gained the most favorable attention from attractive women, and so forth. A notch beneath Doc were Mike and Danny. Below them, in turn, were Nutsy, Angelo, Fred, and Frank. Carl, Lou, and others were further down; and at the bottom were Tommy and Alec. Among the Nortons, this "status ranking" could be detected in almost every activity in which the group engaged.

Common sense suggests that people's various natural and acquired talents are far from perfectly correlated. The physically strongest men are not necessarily the most socially adept, nor are they necessarily the top players in games of skill or contests of wits. It follows that either the monolithic status structure seen in the Nortons was an enormous coincidence, or else social processes of some kind must have brought it about. A basic premise of this chapter is the latter: social processes operate in groups to create perceptible patterns of interaction.

Many of the groups in which people participate develop status rankings that affect practically all activities carried out within them. These rankings describe not only observable interactions but also the norms that guide them and the lenses through which they are interpreted after they have occurred.

When any member's performance departs too noticeably from what is expected on the basis of the established status ranking, other members commonly interpret that departure, contrary to what common sense might suggest, as *support* for the established order, not as disconfirmation. The old adage, "the exceptions prove the rule," finds much application in groups, whose members indeed frequently are quite ingenious in construing whatever happens as support for their prior beliefs (see also Chapters 4 and 5 on this point). In the Nortons, for instance, were Alec to beat Doc at bowling, that would be discounted, probably chalked up to incredible luck. Were Doc to beat Alec, however, that would be viewed as a confirmation of what everyone already knew. More generally, anyone in the Nortons who performed too far out of line with his position in the group was subjected to pressures to modify his performance. These usually took the form of "friendly razzing," which almost always had the effect (perhaps by influencing the uncompliant member's confidence level) of bringing his performance back into line with what the group regarded as normal. This kind of interpersonal process, so clearly revealed by Whyte's insightful observations, may be only dimly recognized by the group members themselves as they carry on their activities.

This chapter, in common with the previous one, takes as problematic the emergence of a "power and prestige order" as a group strives to attain its goals. As argued in Chapter 5, such orders can emerge through sequences of interaction involving successive evaluations of group members' performances. The special concern of this chapter is how initial differences among group members in recognized status or ability modify the operation of the processes discussed in the earlier chapter. *It is the effects of externally established status upon status within the group that constitutes our distinctive concern.* These effects surely are among the most fundamental connections between macrosociology and the sociology of small groups.

## What Kinds of Groups?

In chemistry, it is customary to divide the basic chemical elements into subsets having certain common properties (e.g., into metals and nonmetals). Although chemistry undeniably differs from the social sciences in many respects, this strategy of classifying and theorizing separately about distinctive categories is as useful in the study of sociology as in the study of chemistry. The Nortons and other groups like them are best thought of as *one type* of group having certain distinctive sociological and social psychological properties. Some of these properties are fairly obvious: members of the Nortons shared both purposes and standards for evaluating their success or failure in achieving those purposes. There were social ties among the Nortons that carried rights and obligations (although these were not written down anywhere and many not have been explicitly recognized by the Nortons themselves). Both imperatives of efficiency and norms of legitimacy constrained conduct within this group. And members could (and did) bring social pressures to bear upon one another. In the language of the group processes pioneer Leon Festinger (1950), the Nortons were a "cohesive" group.

A rigorous definition of "cohesiveness" is notoriously difficult to formulate. (See Cartwright 1968 for one notable but not wholly satisfactory attempt to arrive at a definition.) Whatever the difficulties in rigorously defining it, this concept does refer to something important. Roughly speaking, a cohesive group is one whose members, for whatever reason, want to be in this group more than they want to be out of it. They may find the other members attractive or pleasing in some way; they may believe strongly in the group's purposes or goals; or they may think the group provides them with important benefits they could not easily obtain elsewhere (see Festinger 1950; Festinger, Schachter, and Back 1950; Back 1951; Schachter 1951; Cartwright 1968). Even without seeing research evidence, you would probably tend to agree that, compared with a weakly cohesive group, a strongly cohesive one would be more stable, would have greater control over its members' behavior, would generate higher levels of participation and loyalty, and would better serve its members' psychological needs for security and self-esteem. All of these claims appear to be correct (Cartwright 1968).

In choosing to concentrate upon cohesive groups, a group processes theorist excludes from further consideration collections of people that do not adequately fit the description of such groups. Particularly notable among these, the theorist excludes groups whose members are pitted against one another in some way, such as groups divided into factions with different goals. A group of management and labor representatives meeting to bargain over a contract would fall into this category, as would any group in which all the members' interests were not substantially aligned (see Bacharach and Lawler 1980). By making this choice, a theorist also excludes groups that are very tenuous, with few pressures on members to remain in the group.

Paradoxically, the scope condition of cohesiveness also includes groups a theorist may not originally have had in mind. While friendship groups like the Nortons are cohesive, so (in most cases) are the four-man crews of M-1 tanks, or the three-man crews of B-26 bombers (Torrance 1954). So, too, are all but the most ineffective trial juries (Strodtbeck and Mann 1956; Strodtbeck, James, and Hawkins 1957). Regarding the latter, when twelve people are formed into a trial jury to make a decision on the guilt or innocence of a criminal defendant, they almost invariably view the group's purpose as important and accept it as their own. They have what sociologists call a "collective orientation" as opposed to an "individual orientation." (See also Chapter 5 on this point.) Since a jury's verdict requires everyone's agreement, it is both necessary and proper that everyone's assessments of the evidence and legal arguments be weighed, debated, and ultimately formed into a single judgment (a verdict of "guilty as charged" or "not guilty"). There is substantial research evidence that, in jury deliberations, status processes operate much as they do in groups such as the Nortons (see, for example, Strodtbeck et al. 1957).

Another very ubiquitous kind of group satisfying this scope condition is the *committee*, that staple of all modern societies. Complex organizations such as businesses, educational institutions, and government agencies carry out much of what they do through committees. As John Kenneth Galbraith noted in his book, *The New Industrial State*: "One can do worse than think of a business organization as a hierarchy of committees" (1967, p. 64). In fact, one can think of almost any modern organization as an interlocking structure of committees. As is true of most juries, most committees exist to accomplish recognized purposes; their members typically accept the group's purposes as important; and it ordinarily is considered legitimate and necessary for the group to take everyone's contributions into account as its members work towards achieving their common purposes. Experimentally created groups patterned after committees have been carefully studied by social scientists, and the evidence is very convincing that such groups develop status structures and show regularities like those found in juries and in the Nortons (see Bales 1950, 1953, 1970; Bales et al. 1951; Heinecke and Bales 1953; Bales and Slater 1955).

With what kinds of groups, then, will we be concerned in this chapter? To codify and refine the distinctions I have been suggesting, we will concentrate in the sections that follow upon groups satisfying the following *scope conditions*: (1) the group is small enough for face-to-face interaction to occur among all its members; (2) the group convenes for the purpose of accomplishing shared and well-defined goals; (3) there are shared standards for success and failure in achieving those goals; and (4) group members consider it both necessary and proper to take each other's contributions into account as they pursue their objectives. These scope conditions are narrower than would be implied by some definitions of "cohesiveness." As a strategy, however, I think it best to be conservative in stipulating scope conditions—it is always possible to relax them in the future if research shows them to be more restrictive than necessary.

## Power and Prestige as Elements of a Process

The preceding remarks suggest regularities in the ways groups function that are much the same in several (but not all) kinds of groups. Before we proceed further, I want to point out a potential pitfall theorists must avoid if their efforts are to be fruitful. This is the fallacy of circular argument. If a group's power and prestige order is defined by patterns of participation and influence observable among its members, a theorist cannot legitimately explain those very patterns as consequences of this order. That would be like defining a happy person as someone who dances and sings, and then explaining that Sandra dances and sings because she is happy!

Such circularity can be avoided by conceptualizing the power and prestige order of a group as a part of an ongoing process. That process involves: (1) cues stemming from appearance and demeanor, (2) performance expectations, and (3) behaviors. For our purposes in this chapter, a useful schematic representation of this process is given in Figure 6.1, in which c denotes cues, e denotes expectations for performance, b denotes behaviors, and subscripts refer to identifiable segments of time:

**Figure 6.1. Cues, Expectations, and Behaviors as Parts of an Ongoing Process**

$$\{c_1 \to e_1 \to b_1\} \to \{c_2 \to e_2 \to b_2\} \to \ldots \to \{c_n \to e_n \to b_n\}$$

This diagram is intended to suggest that within a selected segment of time, cues lead to performance expectations, which in turn lead to certain kinds of actions or behaviors. Actions at a given time, however, may produce cues that modify performance expectations, and thus actions, at a subsequent time. Each of the portions of this process enclosed in braces could be further elaborated in terms of what in Chapter 5 is called "the full fundamental sequence of behavior." But let me explicate further the distinctive focus of the present chapter: cues stem in part from group members' differences in external status, not merely from their previous verbal and nonverbal behavior within the group in question. From the very beginning, therefore, some members of a group are given more action opportunities than others and more benefit of the doubt in evaluations of their performances, increasing their likelihood of achieving relatively high positions in the group's power and prestige order. With this additional understanding, the power and prestige process when group members initially differ in status can be understood in exactly the same terms as those discussed in the previous chapter.

To summarize, the most important points are: (1) the group's power and prestige order is an unobservable set of differential performance expectations for its members, (2) the antecedents of this order are cues stemming from the appearances and demeanors of group members, and (3) the consequences of this order are differential rates of certain kinds of behavior.[2] But as the diagram above indicates, behavior at a given time is one source of cues that may modify performance expectations, and thus actions, at a later time.

With scope conditions now specified, and some essential concepts now at our disposal, let us consider a theory about how and why external status organizes many of the interactions within small goal-oriented groups.

## STATUS CHARACTERISTICS THEORY

Currently, the most comprehensive account of status processes in groups is provided by status characteristics theory, first proposed by Berger, Cohen, and Zelditch (1966, 1972). This theory (which is part of the larger "expectation states theory" program) is rooted in, and serves to organize, a large volume of previous empirical research (e.g., Hurwitz, Zander, and Hymovitch 1953; Torrance 1954; Zander and Cohen 1955; Strodtbeck and Mann 1956; Strodtbeck et al. 1957; Caudill 1958; Katz and Benjamin 1960). The principle that unifies this work is that ". . . external status differences among members of a task group determine the distribution of power and prestige within the group" (Berger et al. 1966, p. 43). Let us now consider the underlying ideas upon which this principle rests.

### Status Characteristics

A status characteristic is defined as any attribute possessed by members of a group whose culturally specified meaning is such as to make it potentially relevant to performance at the group's task. (I emphasize *potentially* relevant because, as we will see, a potentially relevant characteristic may not actually operate in a particular group.) Socially recognized distinctions such as age, sex, or race satisfy this definition. These are referred to as *diffuse* status characteristics because, in most societies (including Canada and the United States), most people believe them to have wide-ranging connotations for performance. For instance, gender stereo-

---

2. Some authors use language that seems to equate the power and prestige order with observable behavior. Thus one may encounter the phrase "observable power and prestige order" (for instance, in Berger, Cohen, and Zelditch 1966, pp. 39–42). The important requirement is that the theorist maintain a clear distinction between the unobservable distribution of performance expectations and the observable distribution of participation and influence. The second is best thought of as a joint consequence of (1) the first and (2) the vagaries of chance.

types include all sorts of ideas about what men can do better than women, and vice versa. On the other hand, distinctions in such things as skill at bridge, talent for sketching, or ability at algebra are referred to as *specific* status characteristics, because most people believe these to have relatively restricted connotations for performance. Skill at bridge, for instance, has few implications for anything except playing bridge.

Status characteristics reflect cultural beliefs that may or may not be objectively true. The theory says absolutely nothing about whether the entailed cultural beliefs are true. In the theory, it merely is assumed that if people believe something is true, they will act as if it were true, and thus it will tend to be true in its consequences. This assumption is often called the "Thomas theorem," having originally been set forth by William I. Thomas (1923, pp. 41–50).

## Four Basic Postulates

The theory consists of four postulates or general hypotheses, from which a variety of specific hypotheses can be logically derived.[3] The theory's postulates are its basic assumptions about how status processes operate.

Postulate 1 (the *salience* hypothesis) tells us when a status characteristic will be operative. According to this postulate, if a characteristic discriminates among the actors in a situation, it ordinarily will become salient (that is, operative or activated). An exception occurs when there is a collective belief (cultural or idiosyncratic to the group in question) that a particular attribute is *not* relevant to a particular task. On the other hand, if a characteristic equates the actors in a situation, it ordinarily will *not* become salient. An exception occurs when there is a collective belief (cultural or idiosyncratic to the group in question) that a particular attribute *is* relevant to a particular task. In sum, simple differentiation among the members of a group, or lack of such, is the most fundamental factor in making a characteristic salient or not salient; strong collective beliefs, if such exist, may override this factor.[4]

Postulate 2 (the *burden of proof* hypothesis) asserts that any salient status characteristic will come to link its possessor to the possible outcomes of the group's task. The linkages themselves are called "paths of relevance," which can be represented in diagrams, and understood as connections between an actor

---

3. Some presentations of the theory discuss five basic postulates rather than four (see, for example, Berger et al. 1977; Balkwell 1991a). Often these are referred to as Assumption 1, Assumption 2, and so forth. For our purposes, it will suffice to consider only the four original highest-level hypotheses (Berger, Cohen, and Zelditch 1966).

4. This statement of Postulate 1 accurately reflects Berger et al. (1977) and most other explications of status characteristics theory; however, recent research by Foschi and Freeman (1991) suggests that a characteristic may also become salient if group members make implicit comparisons between themselves and outside sources of evaluation (see also Ridgeway 1988). This might occur, for instance, if a group of female secretaries were to meet within a predominantly male organization.

and the possible results of striving to accomplish the task (success or failure). In an actor's initial structuring of a situation, a characteristic may not be task-linked, but it will come to be task-linked through a structure-completion process (ordinarily not a conscious process). According to the theory, individuals behave as if the burden of proof were on a characteristic's *irrelevance* to the group's task, rather than on its relevance. As a consequence, any salient status characteristic will contribute to the structuring of social interaction *unless* its inapplicability is clearly established.

Suppose, to illustrate, that two high school students were working together on a homework problem for a class in algebra. Let us call the two persons p (self, or the focal actor) and o (other). Imagine that in a biology class the previous semester, p received an A, whereas o received a C. Logically, the students' prior performances in biology, considered by themselves, imply nothing at all about their present abilities to solve an algebra problem; yet in forming his or her definition of the present situation, p is likely to make the tacit assumption that these abilities are indeed associated. That such inductions occur is the essence of Postulate 2.

Postulate 3 (the *aggregation* hypothesis) describes how group members combine status information on multiple characteristics to form aggregated (or overall) performance expectations for themselves and others. According to the theory, all salient status information is processed to arrive at performance expectations for each group member. These performance expectations are single quantities. If there were five group members, for example, each possessing multiple specific and/or diffuse status characteristics, Postulate 3 implies that all this information would be processed by p, the result being a collection of five aggregated performance expectations held by p, one for each group member. It is assumed that, in small cohesive groups, each actor arrives at essentially the same set of aggregated performance expectations as each other actor. That is, if John and Sandra constitute the group under consideration, and if they are a cohesive group, then John's aggregated performance expectations for John and Sandra are assumed to be the same as Sandra's aggregated performance expectations for John and Sandra. (If different group members have different definitions of the situation, this makes social interactions much more problematic. Such cases nonetheless do occur. The theoretical implications of such cases are dealt with more fully in Ridgeway (1991) and Ridgeway and Balkwell (1992).

Postulate 4 (the *translation* hypothesis) asserts that an actor's production of certain specifiable behaviors (e.g., performance outputs) is a direct monotonic function of the aggregated performance expectations held for him or her relative to those held for other group members. Suppose p and o are any two members of the group in question. Let $e_p$ and $e_o$ denote their *aggregated performance expectations*, $b_p$ and $b_o$ their *expected rates of behavior*. (By "rate" I mean amount per unit of time.) Postulate 4 asserts: If $e_p > e_o$, then $b_p > b_o$. It is important to note that the postulate concerns *expected* rates of behavior. The *actual* rates of behavior we could observe in a particular group for a particular time period generally would differ from these expected values, which are best thought of as "long run average" values.

## Graphic Representations of Situations

It is often helpful in applying Postulates 1 and 2 to represent an actor's completed definition of the situation as a diagram. Such a diagram portrays paths of relevance connecting each group member to the possible outcomes of the group's task. The actors and task outcomes are mediated by status characteristics and sometimes also by "induced elements" related to status characteristics. (We will consider one example of a purely induced element in a later section.) For purposes of illustration, consider again the two students working on an algebra problem who had previously been in a biology class together (p receiving a high grade, o a low grade). Let $C_1$ (+) and $C_1$ (−) denote high and low states of "biology ability," $C^*$ (+) and $C^*$ (−) high and low states of "algebra ability," and T (+) and T (−) success and failure in solving the problem (task) in question. Based on Postulates 1 and 2, the paths of relevance we would expect to develop are given in Figure 6.2.

**Figure 6.2. Paths of Relevance for the Algebra Problem Illustration**

$$p \xrightarrow{\ +\ } C_1 (+) \xrightarrow{\ +\ } C^* (+) \xrightarrow{\ +\ } T (+)$$
$$\Big| -$$
$$o \xrightarrow{\ +\ } C_1 (-) \xrightarrow{\ +\ } C^* (-) \xrightarrow{\ +\ } T (-)$$

Paths of relevance may be positive (producing expectations for good performance at the task) or negative (producing expectations for poor performance at the task). In general, each actor in a social situation has both positive and negative paths linking him or her to the possible task outcomes. The signs, plus or minus, located along the path segments, signify "possession" (plus), "association" (plus), or "opposition" (minus).

Regarding "opposition," lines representing this relation are included *only* for characteristics known to be *possessed* by actors in the situation. Thus, $C_1$ (+) and $C_1$ (−), known to be possessed by p and o respectively, are joined by a line; but $C^*$ (+) and $C^*$ (−), induced by a burden of proof process, are *not* joined by a line.

In this illustration, p is connected to the possible task outcomes by two positive paths of lengths 3 and 4 respectively. These can be described as follows: (1) p *possesses* high "biology ability," which is *associated* with high "algebra ability," which is *associated* with likely success at the task at hand; and (2) p *possesses* high "biology ability," which is the opposite of low "biology ability," which is *associated* with low "algebra ability," which is *associated* with likely failure at the task at hand. If we multiply the signs of the path segments together with the sign of the potential task outcome, using a rule analogous to that for multiplying numbers, we find $(+) (+) (+) (+) = (+)$, and $(+) (-) (+) (+) (-) = (+)$. Thus, p's paths of relevance are both positive. In this example, o is connected to the possible task outcomes by negative paths of lengths 3 and 4.

## Measurement of Performance Expectations

Measurement issues are beyond the confines of a general discussion such as this one; however, for later reference, we should note the following points. Well-developed procedures exist for finding numerical values for aggregated performance expectations. The most widely used of these is based on diagrams such as that of our example (which derive from Postulates 1 and 2), along with two measurement assumptions and a mathematical interpretation of Postulate 3 (for details, see Berger et al. 1977, pp. 122–29). When this procedure is applied to our example, the results are:

$$e_p = +0.495$$

$$e_o = -0.495$$

In this instance, the two actors' aggregated performance expectations are equal in absolute value, but opposite in sign. This is a consequence of the symmetry of the diagram. Such a situation is not always the case; not all diagrams are symmetrical. By this measurement procedure, aggregated performance expectations necessarily fall somewhere between $-1$ and $+1$. Closely related to aggregated performance expectations is an actor's "expectation advantage" over a second actor. This is defined as his or her aggregated performance expectations minus the other person's. Continuing our example, the expectation advantage of p over o equals $+0.990$. (That of o over p is $-0.990$, the minus sign indicating an expectation *disadvantage*.) When you encounter references to these quantities in later sections of this chapter, one important thing to remember is that they were (or can be) computed from a measurement formula.

## ELEMENTARY STATUS SITUATIONS

More than three dozen status characteristics experiments have been carried out in a standardized experimental setting designed by Berger and his associates at Stanford University in the early 1960s (Berger et al. 1977, pp. 43–48; see also Chapters 3 and 5 in this volume). I now want to describe a study by Moore (1968), conducted in this setting, that helped to establish what seemed to many researchers at that time to be a very implausible premise: the burden of proof hypothesis.

Postulate 2 of status characteristics theory implies that when people lack adequate information to act they will mentally construct linkages among the elements in their situation so as to make it intelligible. Moore's research addressed an important application of this principle.

The subjects who participated in his study were female volunteers from a junior college in California. They were scheduled in pairs to take part in the experiment. After a pair of subjects arrived at the Stanford Laboratory for Social Research, they were taken to separate booths and asked to fill out a short questionnaire, which requested background information including education. Although the subjects were in the same room, they could not see each other because of a screen erected between their booths. When the subjects had completed their questionnaires, the experimenter collected them and skimmed through them as he began his instructions.

Differences among the experimental conditions were created by giving different information to the subjects. In Conditions 1 and 3, the experimenter addressed the two subjects, identifying one of them as a woman from California High School and the other as a woman from California Junior College.[5] In fact, both subjects were students at California Junior College, so each person could reasonably conclude from this remark that the other person was a high school student. This would induce each subject to believe that she herself was above the other in educational status. In Conditions 2 and 4, in contrast, the experimenter identified one subject as a student from California Junior College and the other as a student from Stanford University. This would induce each person to believe that she herself was below the other in educational status. These remarks constituted the *status manipulation* of the experiment.

The experiment also involved a *relevance manipulation*. In Condition 1 (but *not* in Condition 3), the experimenter added: "One of the interesting things we have found [about this ability] is that Stanford University students consistently do much better than California Junior College students." In Condition 2 (but *not* in Condition 4), the experimenter added: "One of the interesting things we have found [about this ability] is that California Junior College students consistently do much better than California High School students." From this each subject in Conditions 1 and 2 could reasonably conclude that not only did she *differ* from the other subject in educational status, but that this difference was *highly relevant* to the task to be undertaken in this experiment.

Following the status and relevance manipulations, the experimenter explained that the task was to consist of a series of binary choices. Before each choice, the experimenter would present a pattern on an overhead screen. Each pattern consisted of small black and white rectangles; the subject's job would be to judge

---

5. These two names are pseudonyms for the actual junior college and high school near Stanford University referred to in the experiment.

whether the total pattern was predominantly black or predominantly white. In fact, all the patterns contained close to 50 percent of each color, making them very ambiguous. This task was referred to as a test of "spatial judgment ability."

The experimenter explained that on each slide (1) each subject would have five seconds to make an *initial choice*, (2) each would then receive information on her panel on what the other person had chosen, and (3) each would then have five seconds to restudy the slide if she wished and make a *final choice*. The primary goal, the experimenter emphasized, should be to make as many joint correct *final choices* as possible. (The purpose of this last instruction was to create a collective orientation.)

There were 44 trials. Each subject's feedback indicated that she and her partner disagreed on their initial choices on 28 of these, and agreed on the remaining 16. When they disagreed, each subject had to decide whether to stay with her initial choice or change to the other subject's initial choice. Since there were 28 disagreement trials, a subject's number of "stays" (or "self-responses") could be anywhere between 0 and 28, her number of changes equalling 28 minus her number of stays.

The question at issue was whether "educational status," as indicated by school affiliation, generalizes to create differentiated performance expectations for "spatial judgment ability," a special talent not logically related to a person's school affiliation. To answer this question, Moore created a dependent variable whose operational definition was a subject's proportion of stay responses, p (s). A subject who stayed 20 times out of the possible 28, for instance, would have a p (s) value of .714. Moore's basic findings were presented as average p (s) values, computed separately for each of his four experimental conditions.

It is important to understand exactly how Moore's experimental conditions relate to status characteristics theory. In Condition 1, each subject had *high* diffuse status, and had been informed by the experimenter that most persons in her category have *high* spatial judgment ability. A graphic representation of her situation would show her to be connected to the possible task outcomes by *positive* paths of lengths 3 and 4. In Condition 2, each subject had *low* diffuse status, and had been informed that most persons in her category have *low* spatial judgment ability. She would be connected to the possible task outcomes by *negative* paths of lengths 3 and 4. Little status generalization would be required in these two "explicit relevance" conditions. In Condition 3, each subject had *high* diffuse status, but this was *not* initially linked to high spatial judgment ability. Similarly, in Condition 4, each subject had *low* diffuse status, but this was *not* initially linked to low spatial judgment ability. Status characteristics theory's Postulate 2 implies that even in situations such as Conditions 3 and 4 diffuse status would become connected to the possible task outcomes. In our earlier discussion, I did not explain how this happens in cases where no obvious association exists. According to the theory, in a situation like that of Condition 3, diffuse status becomes associated with a new "mental element" referred to as "generalized ability." In the graphic

**Table 6.1. Observed and Predicted Proportions of Stay Responses**

| Condition | Observed | Predicted | |Error| |
|---|---|---|---|
| High Status, High Relevance | 0.693 | 0.709 | 0.016 |
| Low Status, High Relevance | 0.591 | 0.599 | 0.008 |
| High Status, Low Relevance | 0.699 | 0.677 | 0.022 |
| Low Status, Low Relevance | 0.634 | 0.634 | 0.000 |

representations described earlier, high and low states of generalized ability are denoted $\Gamma$ (+) and $\Gamma$ (−), respectively. This *induced element* is, in turn, posited to become associated with the task ability, in this case spatial judgment ability. This induced element mediating diffuse status and the task ability increases all paths by one segment. Thus, each subject in Condition 3 would be connected to the possible task outcomes by *positive* paths of lengths 4 and 5. Similarly, each subject in Condition 4 would be connected to the possible task outcomes by *negative* paths of lengths 4 and 5. Since the paths of relevance of Conditions 3 and 4 are increased in length, they produce weaker aggregated performance expectations than do the shorter paths of Conditions 1 and 2.

Using the method for measuring aggregated performance expectations referred to in the preceding section of this chapter, together with a standard statistical procedure (logistic regression), a researcher can compute predicted p(s) values and then compare those with the observed p(s) values for the four experiment conditions (for more details, see Balkwell 1991a, pp. 358–60). A summary of Moore's results is presented in Table 6.1.

Note that the observed and predicted p(s) values are nearly the same. The largest prediction error is 0.022; the average error is 0.012. Moreover, as the theory predicts, status generalization evidently did occur. Subjects in Condition 3 stayed with their own initial choices about 70 percent of the time, whereas those in Condition 4 stayed with their initial choices about 63 percent of the time. Moore (1968, p. 56) reports that this difference is statistically significant; these results thus support Postulate 2 of the theory.

Examining these findings more closely, however, we might note that status characteristics theory also implies a strict rank-ordering among the four conditions: $p_1(s) > p_3(s) > p_4(s) > p_2(s)$. Contrary to this predicted rank-ordering, the observed p(s) for Condition 1 is slightly less than that for Condition 3. How concerned about this should we be? That is a difficult question to answer. Good researchers are concerned about *any* discrepancy, but the fact remains that the observed and predicted p(s) values agree tolerably well, being easily within a margin of error attributable to chance alone.

The significance of this latter observation becomes more clear if one examines subsequent research. Berger, Cohen, and Zelditch (1972) obtained comparable results, but without the discrepancy, using air force rank as their diffuse status characteristic. In addition, Berger and Conner (1969) reported comparable results, again without this discrepancy, using a specific status characteristic ("meaning insight ability"), which they manipulated by means of a pretest.

Until now we have considered only the most elementary kind of status situations. In Moore's research, the subjects were differentiated by merely *one* diffuse status characteristic. We might wonder: How is the power and prestige process modified if the actors in a task-oriented group are differentiated by *two* characteristics? Or *several*? In fact, most of the status characteristics research carried out over the last two decades has been addressed to the many questions that can be asked about status processes in such "multicharacteristic status situations." It is to some of these questions that we now turn.

## MULTICHARACTERISTIC STATUS SITUATIONS

Imagine a situation in which two persons are differentiated simultaneously by two specific status characteristics, $C_1$ and $C_2$. Suppose that p were *high* on $C_1$ but *low* on $C_2$, and o were *low* on $C_1$ but *high* on $C_2$. How would this status inconsistency be reflected in the distribution of participation and influence in the group?

Let $b_p$ and $b_o$ denote p's and o's rates of some kind of power and prestige behavior (e.g., performance outputs). It is conceivable that the two actors would attend only to their differences on $C_1$, ignoring their differences on $C_2$, in which case we should find $b_p > b_o$. But it also is conceivable that they would attend only to their differences on $C_2$, ignoring their differences on $C_1$, in which case we should find $b_p < b_o$. Or they could attend to both equally, in which case we should find $b_p = b_o$. Were either of the first two conjectures found to be correct, the obvious next question would be: What principle is used for deciding which characteristic will be considered and which will be ignored?

Analogous questions could be asked about a situation in which the actors were differentiated simultaneously on two *diffuse* status characteristics, $D_1$ and $D_2$. Similarly, one in which they were differentiated simultaneously by one *specific* and one *diffuse* status characteristic, $C_1$ and $D_1$. More complex situations involving three or more specific and/or diffuse status characteristics would raise additional questions, as would situations in which two or more status characteristics were *consistently* allocated. We could imagine the need for an incredibly complex theory to provide answers to all of these questions.

It would be useful to find a general principle that would remove as much of this complexity as possible. Consider the following two candidates for such a principle: (1) Actors attend to *all salient status characteristics equally* and the resulting power and prestige order is an average of those orders that would follow from each of the characteristics by itself. (2) Actors attend to *only the strongest status characteristic* and the resulting power and prestige order is that which would follow from *this characteristic by itself*. The first alternative can be called the "combining hypothesis," the second, the "selection hypothesis." (Many authors have used the term "balancing" instead of "selection." See, for example, Berger et al. 1977.) The latter, it should be noted, presupposes general criteria for identifying the strongest characteristic. But either candidate would eliminate the need for a catalog of special theories, and would thus be very attractive.

From the late 1960s through the early 1980s, much research was addressed to choosing between these two alternatives (see, for example, Berger and Fisek 1970; Tress 1971; Freese and Cohen 1973; Webster and Driskell 1978; and Zelditch, Lauderdale, and Stublarec 1980). Related investigations redefined the problem as a search for scope conditions under which each alternative applies, raising the possibility that both principles might sometimes be activated, one principle applying to some group members, the second to others (see, for example, Martin and Sell 1980, 1985; Hembroff, Martin, and Sell 1981; Hembroff 1982; and Sell and Freese 1984). This research led to distinctive variants of status characteristics theory, most notably a combining variant and a selection variant.

Adherents of the combining variant seem to have won the battle (see Balkwell 1991b) but this victory, I think, has been mainly at the level of vocabulary. What few seem to full understand is that Postulates 2 and 3 presented earlier incorporate the central ideas of the selection hypothesis, albeit in modified form. Postulate 2 incorporates the important insight that some status characteristics are stronger than others in their effects; Postulate 3 (and its associated measurement procedure) posits a "combining" principle that does not even approximate simple averaging, the original connotation of the combining hypothesis. Thus, while status characteristics theory as described in this chapter is usually identified with the combining hypothesis (e.g., Hembroff 1982, pp. 184–85, 195), it could just as accurately be identified with a modified selection hypothesis. It is a *hybrid* theory incorporating the most important insights of both these hypotheses. You will see the truth of this point shortly, as we examine some pertinent research conducted by Zelditch, Lauderdale, and Stublarec (1980).

In this study, there were six experimental conditions defined by the focal actor's status characteristics: (1) high specific status;(2) low specific status; (3) high diffuse status; (4) low diffuse status; (5) high specific status and low diffuse status; and (6) low specific status and high diffuse status. To operationalize *specific* status, Zelditch and his colleagues gave each appropriate subject a pretest on "contrast sensitivity" (the same fictitious ability used in Moore's study, though given a different name) during the manipulation phase. When this pretest was over, the subject was provided with a result showing that he/she scored very highly (Conditions 1 and 5) or very poorly (Conditions 2 and 6) in contrast sensitivity. To operationalize *diffuse* status, Zelditch and his colleagues used educational status, following a procedure similar to that used by Moore. Notice that Conditions 5 and 6 create status inconsistency.

Based on the information just given, the focal actor's expectation advantage

Table 6.2. Observed and Predicted Proportions of Stay Responses

| Condition | Observed | Predicted | \|Error\| |
|---|---|---|---|
| High Specific | 0.850 | 0.831 | 0.019 |
| Low Specific | 0.360 | 0.343 | 0.017 |
| High Diffuse | 0.670 | 0.672 | 0.002 |
| Low Diffuse | 0.535 | 0.557 | 0.022 |
| High Specific, Low Diffuse | 0.785 | 0.794 | 0.009 |
| Low Specific, High Diffuse | 0.393 | 0.400 | 0.007 |

can be computed for each experimental condition; then the predicted p(s) values can be obtained. A summary of the observed and predicted values is given in Table 6.2.

Looking at this table, you can see that the largest discrepancy between the observed and predicted p(s) values is 0.022; the average discrepancy is 0.013. The empirical evidence and the theoretical predictions thus agree extremely well.

But now consider the following question: Is either the pure combining principle or the pure selection principle, as they were described earlier, supported by these results? According to the first, the p(s) value for Condition 5 should be equal to a simple average of the p(s) values for Conditions 1 and 4, and the p(s) value for Condition 6 should be equal to a simple average of the p(s) values for Conditions 2 and 3. According to the second, the p(s) values of Conditions 1 and 5 should be equal, as should those of Conditions 2 and 6. (By any reasonable assessment, the specific status characteristic is the stronger one.) In fact, the observed p(s) values fall between the *combining* and *selection* predictions. But so too do the values predicted by status characteristics theory, which demonstrates that this theory, to some degree, is actually a selection theory in disguise.

While the Zelditch et al. (1980) research supports status characteristics theory, a skeptic might argue that it involves incomplete comparisons. That is, multicharacteristic inconsistent status situations are compared with elementary status situations; but there are no comparisons of multicharacteristic *inconsistent* status situations with multicharacteristic *consistent* status situations. Thus the effects of inconsistency and those of complexity are yoked together. Let us consider a second multicharacteristic study that adds to the Zelditch et al. study by more fully isolating the effects of inconsistency.

Wagner, Ford, and Ford (1986) carried out a study that has both practical and theoretical significance. The title of their article, "Can Gender Inequalities Be Reduced?" suggests that the study is germane to contemporary efforts to eliminate gender discrimination. The study's theoretical importance stems from the fact that it involves two distinct status characteristics, one specific, the other diffuse, both consistently and inconsistently related. (For other discussions of reducing

**served and Predicted Proportions of Stay Responses**

| n | Observed | Predicted | |Error| |
|---|---|---|---|
| Baseline | 0.510 | 0.486 | 0.024 |
| Confirmation | 0.372 | 0.377 | 0.005 |
| Disconfirmation | 0.735 | 0.697 | 0.038 |
| seline | 0.719 | 0.718 | 0.001 |
| nfirmation | 0.779 | 0.800 | 0.021 |
| sconfirmation | 0.479 | 0.512 | 0.033 |

ation be likely to cause a change in our performance expectations
? Would it perhaps make our diffuse status irrelevant? Or would
mation perhaps simply be ignored? Referring to Table 6.3, notice
er did operate as a status characteristic. In the baseline conditions,
was 0.719, the female p(s) 0.510. When the expectation that men
igher contrast sensitivity was confirmed, the male p(s) increased to
e female p(s) decreased to 0.372. If we may generalize from these
uggest that when a stereotype is confirmed by other information,
c operates more strongly than it would otherwise. But when the
at men would have higher contrast sensitivity than women was
the male p(s) fell to 0.479, and the female p(s) increased to 0.735.
ations of these findings seem to me to be especially noteworthy. If
itial expectations for herself are *lower* than those she holds for a
e expectations become *disconfirmed* by performance information,
ops expectations for herself that are *higher* than those she holds for
arly, if a man's initial expectations for himself are *higher* than
s for a woman, and these expectations become *disconfirmed* by
nformation, then he develops expectations for himself that are *lower*
holds for a woman. Gender inequality is not just reduced but
sed when the expectations it activates are clearly contradicted by
nformation.

been several other studies carried out in this standardized setting
relationships between multiple diffuse and/or specific status charac-
sistance to social influence as measured by p(s). It would take too
present each of these studies in detail. However, data from studies
ek, and Crosbie (1970), Freese and Cohen (1973), Webster (1977),
riskell (1978), Martin and Sell (1980), Greenstein and Knottnerus
roff, Martin, and Sell (1981), Knottnerus and Greenstein (1981),
82), and Martin and Sell (1985) were reassessed by Balkwell
found substantial agreement between data and theory in each case.
mployed several different status characteristics in several different

gender inequality, using status characteristics
Wahrman 1983 and Carli 1991.)

In those conditions in which the focal acto:
and vice versa. The subjects were randomly a
(1) baseline; (2) confirmation; and (3) discont
women in each of these situations, there wer:
In this study the task ability was also contra

In the *baseline* conditions, the only experin
link sex and contrast sensitivity. After a pair
booths, the experimenter announced: "One
emerge from previous studies of contrast se
far more accurate at solving contrast sensit:
appears that contrast sensitivity may be a ge:
you have a high or low level of contrast sens
sex or gender" (Wagner, Ford, and Ford 198
could not possibly be true, for contrast sens
served a purpose absolutely crucial for the suc
that contrast sensitivity is a sex-linked abilit
average, surpass women. Without creating th
not have been able to study how confirming or
performance expectations deriving from ger

In the *confirmation* conditions, the subject
ity pretest. When this pretest was over, it w
subject had achieved 16 correct out of the
correct out of the possible 25. In the *disconfi*
manipulation was carried out; but for these (
male subject had obtained 9 correct, the fer

Analyzed in terms of status characteristic
tive paths of lengths 3 and 4, while being
lengths 3 and 4. In the conditions that had
performance generates positive paths of leng
ates negative paths of lengths 2 and 3. (For {
see Wagner et al. 1986, pp. 50, 56.) Usinj
*expectation advantage* can be computed for (
predicted p(s) values can then be obtained. .
Examining these results carefully, we find
0.038, the average discrepancy 0.020. Erro:
the range attributable to chance.

While these results support a general the
standably might wish to ask: What, if anytl
to the experiences I am likely to have in sm
the expectations for performance I or my ass
are confirmed or disconfirmed by other inf(

**Table 6.3.** O

| Condit: |
| --- |
| Women |
| Women |
| Women |
| Men, B |
| Men, C |
| Men, D |

or disconfir:
for each oth
the new info
first that gen
the male p(s)
would have k
0.779, and th
results, they
that stereoty;
expectation t
disconfirmec

The impli
a woman's i:
man, and the
then she deve
a man. Simi
those he hol.
performance
than those he
actually reve:
performance

There hav
to explore the
teristics and :
much space t
by Berger, Fi
Webster and
(1980), Hem
Hembroff (1
(1991b), wh(
These studies

combinations, so this finding adds to our confidence in the theory's general adequacy.

## TESTS IN OTHER SETTINGS

Each of the studies discussed so far has been carried out in the standardized experimental setting; in each case the dependent variable has been p(s). But this setting is by no means the only one in which status characteristics theory has been tested. Cohen and Roper (1972), Cohen (1982), and Entwisle and Webster (1974) applied the theory in elementary school classrooms; Webster and Driskell (1983) assessed ideas from the theory using a form of survey research; and Dovidio and his associates (1988) investigated some of the theory's key hypotheses using novel measures of power and prestige in an experimental setting quite different from the standardized setting with which we have been concerned. More recently, Ridgeway and Diekema (1989) tested ideas from the theory in open interaction discussion groups; Fisek, Berger, and Norman (1991) and Balkwell (1991a) have used models based on the theory to predict behavior in both initially homogenous and initially heterogeneous discussion groups; and Balkwell et al. (1992) have tested hypotheses from the theory using subjects' responses to vignettes (short imaginary stories).

Each of these investigations employed not only an alternative research situation, but also an alternative dependent variable. In this regard, it is important to understand that the dependent variable with which we have been primarily concerned, p(s), is neither a perfect reflection nor the only reflection of a group's power and prestige order. More generally: "The higher the performance expectation held for a [group] member relative to others, the more likely he or she is to (1) receive opportunities to contribute to the group's task efforts, (2) offer task contributions, (3) receive positive evaluations of these contributions, and (4) be influential in group decisions" (Ridgeway and Berger 1988, p. 210). The variable p(s) is linked to this fourth point in that it is necessary, though not sufficient, that a person resist others' opinions if he or she is to prevail when disagreements occur (i.e., be influential in group decisions).

Space limitations preclude me from describing in detail the range of settings and dependent variables that have been studied. Nevertheless, in this section I want to present two additional kinds of studies to give you some idea of the research that has been done.

### Positive Evaluations

One of the more consternating yet intriguing ideas of status characteristics theory is that people tend to evaluate ideas in terms of their sources rather than in terms of the logic and evidence that support them. Suppose p is listening to suggestions offered by two other actors, $o_1$ and $o_2$. If these suggestions are mutually exclusive, which will sometimes be the case, then a positive reaction to the first entails a negative reaction to the second, and vice versa. The question is, how does p choose between the suggestions of $o_1$ and $o_2$? Ideally, he or she would make this choice by evaluating the suggestions in terms of logic and evidence; but for a variety of reasons (lack of sufficient evidence, expertise, time, energy, and so forth) he or she is likely to choose between them on the basis of the performance expectations he or she holds for $o_1$ and $o_2$. Recent research by Balkwell et al. (1992) sought to test this hypothesis.

The participants were male and female students in freshman history classes at a large state university. Each subject was asked to fill out a questionnaire. There were ten different versions of the questionnaire (to be explained below), the version a subject received decided by random assignment. A cover sheet requested information on the respondent's background, interest in mathematics, and several other items. But the heart of each questionnaire was its vignette, followed by questions pertaining to that vignette. The following portion of the vignette was identical for all versions of the questionnaire:

> Imagine that you have studied late the night before you are to take an exam in algebra. Although you have studied hard, you still cannot figure out how to set up a certain kind of story problem you know will be on the exam. This is a real dilemma for you, because you know that 15 percent of the exam will be over this type of problem. You arrive in class 20 minutes early, and find two students (call them x and y) who are studying for the exam. You ask them for help. X and y offer *different* solutions. The question you face is: Whose method will you use on the exam? Both x and y are single, the same sex as you, and the same age as you.

All the vignettes were identical in the kind of setting and dilemma they described, but they differed in the combinations of characteristics attributed to person x and person y. In one of the ten versions, for example, the following information was given:

> You have talked with these students before, and you happen to know that: x received an A on the previous test in this class; x graduated in the lower third of his/her high school class; and x scored at the 82nd percentile (near the top) on the math part of the ACT test.[6] Y received a C on the previous test in this class; y graduated in the upper third of his/her high school class; and y scored at the 16th percentile (near the bottom) on the math part of the ACT test.

Other combinations of (1) previous test grade, (2) standing in high school class, and (3) performance on the ACT test defined the remaining nine experimental conditions. To control for primacy and recency effects, in each experimental condition the descriptions of persons x and y were reversed half of the time.

---

6. The ACT test is an aptitude test used by many colleges and universities as part of their basis for admitting new students.

**Table 6.4. Observed and Predicted Proportions of Subjects Choosing Person x and Person y**

| Condition | Observed | Predicted | |Error| |
|---|---|---|---|
| a — Person x | 0.971 | 0.984 | 0.013 |
| Person y | 0.029 | 0.016 | 0.013 |
| b — Person x | 0.861 | 0.862 | 0.001 |
| Person y | 0.139 | 0.138 | 0.001 |
| c — Person x | 0.683 | 0.680 | 0.003 |
| Person y | 0.317 | 0.320 | 0.003 |
| d — Person x | 0.568 | 0.600 | 0.032 |
| Person y | 0.432 | 0.400 | 0.032 |
| e — Person x | 1.000 | 0.994 | 0.006 |
| Person y | 0.000 | 0.006 | 0.006 |
| f — Person x | 0.946 | 0.947 | 0.001 |
| Person y | 0.054 | 0.053 | 0.001 |
| g — Person x | 0.842 | 0.858 | 0.016 |
| Person y | 0.158 | 0.142 | 0.016 |
| h — Person x | 0.838 | 0.810 | 0.028 |
| Person y | 0.162 | 0.190 | 0.028 |
| i — Person x | 0.972 | 0.966 | 0.006 |
| Person y | 0.028 | 0.034 | 0.006 |
| j — Person x | 0.750 | 0.747 | 0.003 |
| Person y | 0.250 | 0.253 | 0.003 |

(Primacy effects are people's tendencies to prefer the first item presented while recency effects reflect preferences for the most recent item presented, in both cases regardless of content.) In each of the ten conditions, labeled Condition a, Condition b, and so on, the three status characteristics differentiated x and y, making each characteristic salient according to Postulate 1 of the theory.

Each combination of status characteristics implies a paths of relevance diagram like the ones described earlier, there being a distinctive diagram for each experimental condition. From these diagrams, for each experimental condition, the investigators calculated performance expectations, $e_x$ and $e_y$, for persons x and y. Then they calculated the theoretical probabilities that p, the focal actor, would choose person x or person y. A comparison of the observed and predicted proportions is given in Table 6.4.

There is a very high degree of correspondence between the observed data and the theoretical predictions. For the twenty relevant comparisons (those for persons x and y in each of the ten experimental conditions), the average discrepancy between the observed and predicted proportions is only 0.011, an amount easily attributable to chance variations. These findings increase our confidence in status characteristics theory. While the p (s) measure and the standardized experimental setting have been very important, even indispensable, to the development and testing of the theory, the research just described demonstrates that it gives accurate predictions for a different dependent variable observed in a different kind of social setting.

## Participation in Discussion Groups

As a final illustration, I want to consider interactions among two or more persons in relatively uncontrolled settings. The problem is to account for amounts of participation in such groups, particularly how these differ from one group member to another. Probably we all have been in groups in which someone has tried to dominate the conversation, in spite of the fact that he or she seemed to have little of importance to say. Think about the last time you were in such a situation, and the way it made you feel. Did you wish that you could somehow stop this person's monopoly of the floor? If so, you have a good intuitive grasp of the insight upon which the research to be described rests: *Groups tend to allocate "floor time" (amount of talking) among their members in direct relation to how useful or informative they expect each member's contributions to be.* In other words, floor time tends to be a direct function of performance expectations. This is not a rule consciously held by group members; it simply is understood. Those who talk too much, relative to what others expect their contributions to be, are viewed by others as "floor hogs," and those who talk too little are viewed as not doing their share of the work. Social pressures motivated by these sentiments ordinarily prevent group members from talking too much or too little. Of course, as most of us know, such pressures occasionally fail to work.

Performance expectations in a small group may be thought of as being derived from the pattern of pair-wise performer-reactor relations in that group. To clarify what I mean by this, consider two group members, $p_1$ and $p_2$, and their typical pattern of interactions with each other. Suppose $p_1$ tends to give many suggestions, make direct eye contact while speaking, speak in a firm and confident voice, receive many positive evaluations, and prevail more often than not when disagreements occur. Suppose $p_2$, on the other hand, tends to react positively to $p_1$'s suggestions but offer few of his or her own, make eye contact mainly while listening, speak in a halting or tentative manner, and acquiesce more often than not when disagreements occur. We would say that $p_1$ is primarily the performer in this relation, and $p_2$ primarily the reactor. (In real groups, the indications usually are somewhat more subtle than my illustration suggests, but this does not alter the essential point.) We would symbolize this relation as $p_1 \rightarrow p_2$.

In almost any task-oriented group, there are likely to be some pairs of members having recognizable performer-reactor relations. Consider the hypothetical six-person group represented in Figure 6.3.

**Figure 6.3. Performer-Reactor Relations in a Hypothetical Six-Person Group**

| $p_1$ | | $p_2$ | $\rightarrow$ | $p_3$ |
|---|---|---|---|---|
| $\downarrow$ | $\searrow$ | $\uparrow$ | $\searrow$ | $\downarrow$ |
| $p_4$ | $\rightarrow$ | $p_5$ | | $p_6$ |

Depicted here is the pattern of performer-reactor relations in the group as a whole. Notice that there are some pairs of persons, such as persons 1 and 2, who do *not* have *direct* performer-reactor relations. Nevertheless, person 1 seems to have higher status than person 2, because of their *indirect links* through persons 4 and 5. (Person 1 is in the "superior" position relative to person 5, who in turn is in the "superior" position relative to person 2).

There exists a theoretical argument linking performer-reactor relations to paths of relevance connecting actors to possible task outcomes (see Fisek, Berger, and Norman 1991, pp. 124–25). I shall omit the details of this argument; its essential conclusion is that each "superior" position connects an actor to the possible task outcomes by two *positive* paths of lengths 4 and 5, while each "inferior" position connects an actor by two *negative* paths of lengths 4 and 5. The important point is that a researcher can construct paths of relevance diagrams and from those calculate performance expectations for each group member. Based on the resulting set of performance expectations, the investigator can calculate theoretical predictions of the proportion of times each group member will hold the floor, and compare these with the corresponding observed proportions (often operationalized as the proportion of "unit acts" initiated by each person).[7]

Robert F. Bales and his associates studied groups of two to eight persons (see Bales 1970; Chapter 5 of this volume). The subjects were previously unacquainted, male Harvard students. In each meeting, the group was asked to discuss and make recommendations on a human relations case involving a supervisor who was having some difficulties with his staff. Before each meeting, the experimenter provided summary sheets to the group members on the case to be discussed, which they had several minutes to read and think about. While each summary sheet contained roughly the same amount of information, each contained somewhat *different* information, giving each person relevant knowledge the others did not

---

7. Most of the results from the analyses described in the rest of this section were originally presented in Balkwell 1991a (pp. 360–67). For a more complete description of the procedures employed, particularly the more technical details, you might wish to consult this source.

have. The subjects were asked to view themselves as a committee formed to advise the supervisor on how to deal with this problem. Each group was given forty minutes to discuss its assigned case and arrive at a recommendation. Applying the model to Bales' data yields the results summarized in Table 6.5.

The accuracy of these predictions is quite remarkable. The largest discrepancy between any of the corresponding observed and predicted rates is only 0.041, the average discrepancy being only 0.013. Furthermore, the correlation between the observed and predicted rates is an extremely high +0.99.

More recently, a study of six-person discussion groups was conducted by Smith-Lovin, Skvoretz, and Hudson (1986). (See also Skvoretz 1988.) The participants in this study were college students, both male and female. Thus, unlike Bales, Smith-Lovin et al. experimentally manipulated sex composition of the group. This composition ranged from all male to all female, and included each of the five possible intermediate distributions (seven experimental conditions in all).

As I suggested at the beginning of this chapter, the power and prestige process is not essentially different when there are initial status differences from when there are not. When there are no initial status differences, as in Bales' research, the cues that give rise to performance expectations stem from patterns in the sequences of behavior within the group in question. When there also are initial status differences, however, as in Smith-Lovin et al.'s research, these cues stem *in part* from these externally anchored status differences. The implications for what we should find in empirical data are merely that the emergent power and prestige order should be detectably, though imperfectly, correlated with any salient status characteristics.

When the status characteristics model is applied to Smith-Lovin et al.'s data, the results are very similar to those reported in Table 6.5 for Bales' data. For this second study, there are 42 observed and predicted participation rates (seven distinct sex compositions, with six persons per group). The largest prediction error from the 42 is 0.049, the average prediction error being 0.014. The correlation between the observed and predicted participation rates is +0.98, once again very high.

Concerning the distinctive implication of status characteristics theory for mixed-sex as opposed to same-sex groups, Postulate 1 implies that sex is salient in the former but not in the latter. Therefore, rates of participation should be about the same in all-male and all-female groups, but in mixed-sex groups the male rate (on the average) should be increased, and the female rate (on the average) should be decreased. The Smith-Lovin et al. data show exactly the pattern predicted. In same-sex groups, the average participation frequency for men was 25.7 unit-acts (suggestions offered, etc.) while the average frequency for women was 26.8. In mixed-sex groups, the average male output was 31.4, the average female output 24.8. There can be little doubt that sex operated as a source of cues in this experiment, and that it operated as predicted by status characteristics theory. At

**Table 6.5.  Observed and Predicted Participation Rates in the Groups Studied by Bales (1970)**

| Group Size | Person Number | Observed Rate | Predicted Rate | \| Error \| |
|------------|---------------|---------------|----------------|-------------|
| 2 | 1 | .573 | .585 | .012 |
|   | 2 | .427 | .415 | .012 |
| 3 | 1 | .444 | .440 | .004 |
|   | 2 | .327 | .323 | .004 |
|   | 3 | .229 | .237 | .008 |
| 4 | 1 | .322 | .363 | .041 |
|   | 2 | .289 | .274 | .015 |
|   | 3 | .228 | .207 | .021 |
|   | 4 | .161 | .156 | .005 |
| 5 | 1 | .469 | .491 | .022 |
|   | 2 | .219 | .179 | .040 |
|   | 3 | .154 | .139 | .015 |
|   | 4 | .103 | .108 | .005 |
|   | 5 | .055 | .083 | .028 |
| 6 | 1 | .431 | .448 | .017 |
|   | 2 | .188 | .166 | .022 |
|   | 3 | .142 | .132 | .010 |
|   | 4 | .110 | .105 | .005 |
|   | 5 | .075 | .084 | .009 |
|   | 6 | .054 | .066 | .012 |
| 7 | 1 | .431 | .413 | .018 |
|   | 2 | .152 | .155 | .003 |
|   | 3 | .119 | .125 | .006 |
|   | 4 | .099 | .102 | .003 |
|   | 5 | .086 | .084 | .002 |
|   | 6 | .063 | .068 | .005 |
|   | 7 | .050 | .054 | .004 |
| 8 | 1 | .398 | .383 | .015 |
|   | 2 | .166 | .145 | .021 |
|   | 3 | .127 | .119 | .008 |
|   | 4 | .098 | .099 | .001 |
|   | 5 | .086 | .083 | .003 |
|   | 6 | .055 | .069 | .014 |
|   | 7 | .043 | .056 | .013 |
|   | 8 | .027 | .045 | .018 |

the same time, however, as we should anticipate based on the disconfirmation conditions in the Wagner et al. (1986) study described earlier, the effects of gender on the power and prestige order, though detectable, were not as large as those of performance evaluations.

## SUMMARY

Groups such as the Nortons, the friendship group so poignantly described in Whyte's *Street Corner Society*, have long fascinated sociologists, for the interactions occurring in such groups, across situations and over time, appear to reflect stable power and prestige orders. Not all groups, however, display such stable orders and their associated behavioral regularities. This has led group processes theorists to try to identify scope conditions for theories about power and prestige in groups, their antecedents, and their consequences. One especially notable formulation, status characteristics theory, applies to groups (1) small enough that each group member can interact face-to-face with the other members, (2) having implicit or explicit goals upon whose importance the group members agree, (3) sharing standards for success and failure in achieving those goals, and (4) having a collective orientation. In broad terms, status characteristics theory posits that cues stemming from appearance and demeanor, including markers of external status, lead to aggregated performance expectations for each group member. These in turn give structure to members' rates of offering suggestions, receiving positive and negative reactions from others, and influencing the group's decisions. Cues lead to performance expectations which in turn lead to rates of behavior. But the process is ongoing, with no unambiguously defined beginning or end. Current behaviors produce cues that may modify performance expectations, which in turn may modify subsequent behaviors.

Status characteristics theory attempts to capture and explain this process in terms of four postulates, which stipulate when characteristics will be salient or nonsalient, how logically nonrelevant information becomes behaviorally relevant, how multiple items of information are combined into aggregated performance expectations, and how the latter structure social interactions.

In the early 1960s, a standardized experimental setting was developed to isolate and rigorously assess hypotheses derived from the theory, focusing first upon elementary (single characteristic) status situations and later upon complex (multicharacteristic) status situations. The use of this standardized experimental setting is an important strength of the status characteristics (and, more generally, the expectations states) research program, because it has allowed social scientists to examine particular parts of the power and prestige process uncontaminated by the complexities of everyday realizations of this process.

During the last decade, investigators increasingly have focused their efforts on testing implications of the theory for interactions in settings more like those of everyday life, often using alternative indicators of power and prestige. While much important research remains to be done, the studies reviewed in this chapter give reason to believe that status characteristics theory will continue for many years to guide and organize the endeavors of theorists and researchers to achieve a fuller understanding of status in groups.

## SUGGESTED READINGS

Berger, Joseph, M. Hamit Fisek, Robert Z. Norman, and Morris Zelditch, Jr. 1977. *Status Characteristics and Social Interaction: An Expectation-States Approach*. New York: Elsevier.

This is the original and still the most complete statement of the graph-theoretic version of status characteristics theory. It is "must" reading for serious researchers.

Homans, George C. 1950. *The Human Group*. New York: Harcourt, Brace and World.

This is the first really insightful effort to develop a theory of group processes, viewing groups as systems of social interaction. Homans applies his theory to five different groups, ranging from a family on a South Sea island to a work group in an American factory.

Schwartz, Barry. 1981. *Vertical Classification*. Chicago: University of Chicago Press.

Why do people insist on classifying social objects, including themselves as they interact in groups, in hierarchical terms? Is this merely a cultural idiosyncracy, or does it represent something fundamental about human experience? Schwartz's work addresses this question, and in so doing provides a strong link with the core ideas of status characteristics theory.

Webster, Murray, Jr. and Martha Foschi, eds. 1988. *Status Generalization: New Theory and Research*. Stanford, CA: Stanford University Press.

Several of the papers in this collection deal with provocative extensions of status characteristics theory not covered in this chapter.

Whyte, William F. 1943. *Street Corner Society*. Chicago: University of Chicago Press.

For three and a half years Whyte lived in "Cornerville" and recorded his observations on its people's lives. This sociological classic is fascinating and surprisingly consonant with status characteristics theory.

## REFERENCES

Bacharach, Samuel B. and Edward J. Lawler. 1980. *Power and Politics in Organizations*. San Francisco: Jossey-Bass.

Back, Kurt W. 1951. "Influence Through Social Communication." *Journal of Abnormal and Social Psychology* 46:9–23.

Bales, Robert F. 1950. "A Set of Categories for the Analysis of Small Group Interactions." *American Sociological Review* 15:257–63.

———. 1953. "The Equilibrium Problem in Small Groups." Pp. 111–61 in *Working*

*Papers in the Theory of Action*, edited by T. Parsons, R. F. Bales, and E. A. Shils. Glencoe, IL: Free Press.

———. 1970. *Personality and Interpersonal Behavior*. New York: Holt, Rinehart and Winston.

Bales, Robert F. and Philip E. Slater. 1955. "Role Differentiation in Small Groups." Pp. 259–306 in *Family, Socialization, and Interaction Process*, edited by T. Parsons and R. F. Bales. Glencoe, IL: Free Press.

Bales, Robert F., Fred L. Strodtbeck, Theodore M. Mills, and Mary E. Roseborough. 1951. "Channels of Communication in Small Groups." *American Sociological Review* 16:461–68.

Balkwell, James W. 1991a. "From Expectations to Behavior: An Improved Postulate for Expectation States Theory." *American Sociological Review* 56:355–69.

———. 1991b. "Status Characteristics and Social Interaction: An Assessment of Theoretical Variants." Pp. 135–76 in *Advances in Group Processes: A Research Annual*, vol. 8, edited by E. J. Lawler, B. Markovsky, C. L. Ridgeway, and H. A. Walker. Greenwich, CT: JAI Press.

Balkwell, James W., Joseph Berger, Murray Webster, Jr., Max Nelson-Kilger, and Jacqueline Cashen. 1992. "Processing Status Information: Some Tests of Competing Theoretical Arguments." Pp. 1–20 in *Advances in Group Processes: A Research Annual*, vol. 9, edited by E. J. Lawler, B. Markovsky, C. L. Ridgeway, and H. A. Walker. Greenwich, CT: JAI Press.

Berger, Joseph, Bernard P. Cohen, and Morris Zelditch, Jr. 1966. "Status Characteristics and Expectation States." Pp. 29–46 in *Sociological Theories in Progress*, vol. 1, edited by J. Berger, M. Zelditch, Jr., and B. Anderson. Boston: Houghton Mifflin.

———. 1972. "Status Characteristics and Social Interaction." *American Sociological Review* 37:241–55.

Berger, Joseph and Thomas L. Conner. 1969. "Performance Expectations and Behavior in Small Groups." *Acta Sociologica* 12:186–97.

Berger, Joseph and M. Hamit Fisek. 1970. "Consistent and Inconsistent Status Characteristics and the Determination of Power and Prestige Orders." *Sociometry* 33:287–304.

Berger, Joseph, M. Hamit Fisek, and Paul V. Crosbie. 1970. "Multicharacteristic Status Situations and the Determination of Power and Prestige Orders." *Technical Report Number 35*. Laboratory for Social Research. Stanford University, Stanford, CA.

Berger, Joseph, M. Hamit Fisek, Robert Z. Norman, and Morris Zelditch, Jr. 1977. *Status Characteristics and Social Interaction: An Expectation-States Approach*. New York: Elsevier.

Carli, Linda L. 1991. "Gender, Status, and Influence." Pp. 89–113 in *Advances in Group Processes: A Research Annual*, vol. 8, edited by E. J. Lawler, B. Markovsky, C. L. Ridgeway, and H. A. Walker. Greenwich, CT: JAI Press.

Cartwright, Dorwin. 1968. "The Nature of Group Cohesiveness." Pp. 91–109 in *Group Dynamics: Research and Theory*, edited by D. Cartwright and A. Zander, 3rd ed. New York: Harper and Row.

Caudill, William. 1958. *The Psychiatric Hospital as a Small Society*. Cambridge, MA: Harvard University Press.

Cohen, Elizabeth G. 1982. "Expectation States and Interracial Interaction in School Settings." *Annual Review of Sociology* 8:209–35.

Cohen, Elizabeth G. and Susan S. Roper. 1972. "Modification of Interracial Interaction Disability." *American Sociological Review* 37:648–55.

Dovidio, John F., Clifford E. Brown, Karen Heltman, Steve L. Ellyson, and Caroline F. Keating. 1988. "Power Displays Between Women and Men in Discussions of Gender-Linked Tasks: A Multichannel Study." *Journal of Personality and Social Psychology* 55:580–87.

Entwisle, Doris R. and Murray Webster, Jr. 1974. "Expectations in Mixed Racial Groups." *Sociology of Education* 47:301–18.

Festinger, Leon. 1950. "Informal Social Communication." *Psychological Review* 57:271–82.

Festinger, Leon, Stanley Schachter, and Kurt Back. 1950. *Social Pressures in Informal Groups*. New York: Harper.

Fisek, M. Hamit, Joseph Berger, and Robert Z. Norman. 1991. "Participation in Heterogeneous and Homogeneous Groups: A Theoretical Integration." *American Journal of Sociology* 97:114–42.

Foschi, Martha and Sabrina Freeman. 1991. "Inferior Performance, Standards, and Influence in Same-Sex Dyads." *Canadian Journal of Behavioural Science* 23:99–113.

Freese, Lee and Bernard P. Cohen. 1973. "Eliminating Status Generalization." *Sociometry* 36:177–93.

Galbraith, John Kenneth. 1967. *The New Industrial State*. Boston: Houghton Mifflin.

Greenstein, Theodore N. and J. David Knottnerus. 1980. "The Effect of Differential Evaluations on Status Generalization." *Social Psychology Quarterly* 43:147–54.

Heinecke, Christoph and Robert F. Bales. 1953. "Developmental Trends in the Structure of Small Groups." *Sociometry* 16:7–38.

Hembroff, Larry A. 1982. "Resolving Status Inconsistency: An Expectation States Theory and Test." *Social Forces* 61:183–205.

Hembroff, Larry A., Michael W. Martin, and Jane Sell. 1981. "Total Performance Inconsistency and Status Generalization: An Expectation States Formulation." *Sociological Quarterly* 22:421–30.

Hurwitz, Jacob I., Alvin F. Zander, and Bernard Hymovitch. 1953. "Some Effects of Power on the Relations Among Group Members." Pp. 483–92 in *Group Dynamics: Research and Theory*, edited by D. Cartwright and A. F. Zander. Evanston, IL: Row, Peterson and Company.

Katz, Irwin and Lawrence Benjamin. 1960. "Effects of White Authoritarianism in Biracial Work Groups." *Journal of Abnormal and Social Psychology* 61:448–56.

Knotternus, J. David and Theodore N. Greenstein. 1981. "Status and Performance Characteristics in Social Interaction: A Theory of Status Validation." *Social Psychology Quarterly* 44:338–49.

Martin, Michael W. and Jane Sell. 1980. "The Marginal Utility of Information: Its Effect Upon Decision-Making." *Sociological Quarterly* 21:233–44.

———. 1985. "The Effect of Equating Status Characteristics on the Generalization Process." *Social Psychology Quarterly* 48:178–82.

Moore, James C., Jr. 1968. "Status and Influence in Small Group Interactions." *Sociometry* 31:47–63.

Pugh, M. D. and Ralph Wahrman. 1983. "Neutralizing Sexism in Mixed-Sex Groups: Do Women Have to Be Better than Men?" *American Journal of Sociology* 88:746–62.

Ridgeway, Cecilia L. 1988. "Gender Differences in Task Groups: A Status and Legitimacy Account." Pp. 188–206 and 495–97 in *Status Generalization: New Theory and Research*, edited by M. Webster, Jr. and M. Foschi. Stanford, CA: Stanford University Press.

————. 1991. "The Social Construction of Status Value: Gender and Other Nominal Characteristics." *Social Forces* 70:367–86.

Ridgeway, Cecilia L. and James W. Balkwell. 1992. "The Diffusion of Status-Value Beliefs in Society." Paper presented at the American Sociological Association Annual Meeting, Pittsburgh.

Ridgeway, Cecilia L. and Joseph Berger. 1988. "The Legitimation of Power and Prestige Orders in Task Groups." Pp. 207–31 and 497–501 in *Status Generalization: New Theory and Research*, edited by M. Webster, Jr. and M. Foschi. Stanford, CA: Stanford University Press.

Ridgeway, Cecilia L. and David Diekema. 1989. "Dominance and Collective Hierarchy Formation in Male and Female Task Groups." *American Sociological Review* 54:79–93.

Schachter, Stanley. 1951. "Deviation, Rejection, and Communication." *Journal of Abnormal and Social Psychology* 46:190–207.

Sell, Jane and Lee Freese. 1984. "The Process of Eliminating Status Generalization." *Social Forces* 63:538–54.

Skvoretz, John V. 1988. "Models of Participation in Status Differentiated Groups." *Social Psychology Quarterly* 51:43–57.

Smith-Lovin, Lynn, John V. Skvoretz, and Charlotte G. Hudson. 1986. "Status and Participation in Six-Person Groups: A Test of Skvoretz's Comparative Status Model." *Social Forces* 64:992–1005.

Strodtbeck, Fred L., Rita M. James, and Charles Hawkins. 1957. "Social Status in Jury Deliberations." *American Sociological Review* 22:713–19.

Strodtbeck, Fred L. and Richard D. Mann. 1956. "Sex Role Differentiation in Jury Deliberations." *Sociometry* 19:3–11.

Thomas, William I. 1923. *The Unadjusted Girl*. Boston: Little, Brown and Company.

Torrance, E. Paul. 1954. "Some Consequences of Power Differences in Decision Making in Permanent and Temporary Three-Man Groups." *Research Studies* (State College of Washington, Pullman) 22:130–40.

Tress, Paul H. 1971. "Inconsistent Status Characteristics and Influence Processes: A Replication and Reformulation." *Technical Report Number 6*. Department of Sociology. Michigan State University, East Lansing, MI.

Wagner, David G., Rebecca Ford, and Thomas W. Ford. 1986. "Can Gender Inequalities Be Reduced?" *American Sociological Review* 51:47–61.

Webster, Murray, Jr. 1977. "Equating Characteristics and Social Interaction: Two Experiments." *Sociometry* 40:41–50.

Webster, Murray, Jr. and James E. Driskell, Jr. 1978. "Status Generalization: A Review and Some New Data." *American Sociological Review* 43:220–36.

————. 1983. "Beauty as Status." *American Journal of Sociology* 89:140–65.

Whyte, William F. 1943. *Street Corner Society*. Chicago: University of Chicago Press.

Zander, Alvin F. and Arthur R. Cohen. 1955. "Attributed Social Power and Group Acceptance: A Classroom Experimental Demonstration." *Journal of Abnormal and Social Psychology* 51:490–92.

Zelditch, Morris, Jr., Patrick Lauderdale, and Steven Stublarec. 1980. "How Are Inconsistencies Between Status and Ability Resolved?" *Social Forces* 58:1025–43.

# SEVEN

# Power

## JOHN F. STOLTE

People influence one another in many ways. Parent and child, teacher and student, boss and worker, friend and friend influence one another continuously. This chapter examines one process of influence: social power. "The power of actor a over actor b is equal to the amount of resistance on the part of b that can be potentially overcome by a," according to Emerson (1962, 1972). To clarify this concept of power, three tasks are undertaken. First, some everyday social situations will be described to illustrate power processes concretely. Second, major approaches, some of which do not distinguish power from other forms of influence such as authority, persuasion, or leadership, will be reviewed as background. Third, social exchange theory of power, which does distinguish power from other forms, will be examined in depth as well as the main lines of research stimulated by this theory.

## HYPOTHETICAL SITUATIONS OF SOCIAL POWER IN EVERYDAY LIFE

Some social situations like those often observed in everyday life are portrayed in Figure 7.1. In the solid-lines box at the center of the figure is a husband-wife relationship between Jane and Jim. Each provides the other a variety of benefits— from emotional support and problem-solving through sexual satisfaction to a variety of everyday favors.

Suppose that on weekends Jane loves to go dancing, while Jim abhors dancing. Jim loves to attend the local professional football games, while Jane despises football. Across a series of weekends, the couple almost never goes dancing, but they usually attend the local football games. In decisions about the way recreational time will be spent, Jim can be said to have used social power over his wife, Jane.

Next, consider the portion of Figure 7.1 enclosed in dashed lines. Jim is a self-employed carpenter/building contractor. For each house to be built, Jim must negotiate subcontracts with each of various tradespersons: an electrician, a plumber, a drywaller, a roofer, and an excavator. The terms of each subcontract (e.g., the amount of pay Jim will provide, and the quality of labor and materials a tradesperson will provide) may vary from occasion to occasion.

Imagine that a new plumber has moved into the area and that he would like work. Because he is not yet known in the area, he is currently getting very few subcontracts. Jim contacts the plumber and negotiates a subcontract that is relatively more favorable to himself than the plumber (i.e., Jim pays relatively little, while the plumber provides superior work and materials). In setting the terms of the subcontract, Jim can be said to have used social power over the new plumber.

Finally, consider the part of Figure 7.1 enclosed in dotted lines. It portrays a network of relationships connecting Jim and Jane to their various friends: Sally and Al, Mary and Bill, Doris and Art, and Betty and Ralph.

Suppose that Mary and Bill have just moved into the neighborhood. Because of an extremely busy social calendar, Jim and Jane do not readily reciprocate friendly invitations, and when they do, the attention they show Mary and Bill is characterized by lower quality and quantity than that shown by Mary and Bill to them. With regard to friendship transactions, Jim and Jane can be said to have used social power over Mary and Bill.

To clarify what power is and how it operates, we now turn to some important theoretical material. The social situations depicted in Figure 7.1 will be used to provide concrete illustrations of key concepts and principles. The reader is invited to elaborate these illustrations and/or invent his or her own.

## BACKGROUND: MAJOR APPROACHES TO SOCIAL POWER

### Field Theory and Social Power

Given impetus by Lewin (1939), field theory is one of the classic approaches to the social psychology of group dynamics. Central to this approach is the notion of a person's "life-space." The "life-space" (also known as "the psychological field") is composed of static factors (e.g., a cognitive structure) and dynamic factors (e.g., tensions or motive forces). Lewin's approach has been used to analyze various aspects of psychological experience, including conflict, task motivation, and attitude change.

Field theory also has been used to understand social power, as Cartwright (1959) has shown. A "powerfield" is a field of forces that induce change in a person's life-space. Suppose Jane, Jim's wife, intensely wants Jim to stop smoking. If so, as an external agent, Jane might become the source of a powerfield for Jim regarding his smoking. Such a powerfield would be composed of (1) things she says and does to induce a change in Jim (to get him to quit smoking), and (2) the current state of Jim's psychological field, including the positive valence (i.e.,

**Figure 7.1.  Hypothetical Situations of Social Power**

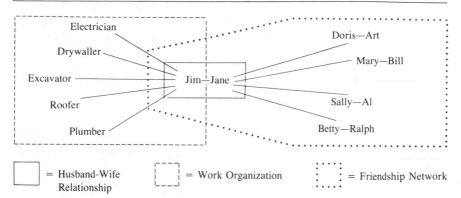

value) he attaches to smoking. The different acts Jane might use in order to get Jim to stop smoking have various kinds of significance for him, depending on which "motive base" they activate in him.

Building upon the idea of variable "motive bases" in a powerfield, French and Raven (1959) proposed a well-known typology of the bases of social power. These authors suggest that when one person (e.g., Jane) influences another person (e.g., Jim), any of the following "bases" may be used: (1) reward power, where Jane administers some condition or event that Jim values positively (e.g., she leaves work early to take him out to dinner) or Jane might remove some event that Jim values negatively (e.g., she reduces his anxiety about a problem at his job by letting him talk it out); (2) coercive power, where Jane administers some condition or event that Jim finds punishing (e.g., she presents him with a cold, stoic face, and treats him like a perfect stranger); (3) legitimate power, where Jane evokes Jim's compliance with formal authority (e.g., in some settings where smoking is officially prohibited, she might draw the rule against smoking to his attention); (4) referent power, where Jane attempts to serve as an attractive, non-smoking model, so that Jim will identify with her and thus stop smoking; and (5) expert power, where Jane demonstrates her competence and knowledge (e.g., she prepares for him an erudite, technical report on the hazards of smoking).

An elaboration of the French and Raven typology is found in Kipnis' (1974) analysis of why a "powerholder" draws from particular resources and uses particular means of influence to gain compliance from a target. He describes a sequential set of steps comprising "the power act." First is the emergence of a need in the powerholder that can be satisfied through actions undertaken by the target. Such a need motivates the powerholder to influence the target. Second is resistance displayed by the target. Third is the powerholder's choice of a resource base. For example, the powerholder might employ his or her own physical attributes (intelligence or beauty) or institutional resources (money, legal rights, or social role privileges). Fourth, the powerholder encounters inhibitions that limit influence. For example, certain cultural norms or low self-confidence might limit the powerholder's influence attempts. Fifth, within such limits, the powerholder will choose a specific means of influence through which resources are used to gain compliance from the target. The main means of influence include persuasion, threats, promises, rewards, force, or ecological change. Sixth, the target displays some response to the powerholder's influence attempt. For instance, the target might comply with the powerholder's request for a certain action, either willingly or unwillingly. Seventh, the power act results in some consequence for the powerholder, satisfaction if the motivating need is met, frustration if the influence attempt fails to overcome resistance in the target.

Kipnis' (1974) research has addressed the powerholder's decision making with regard to resource bases and means of influence. Given available alternatives, charm versus physical strength versus money versus role privileges, or persuasion versus threats versus rewards versus force, why does the powerholder select a particular resource and means? In general, his studies have shown that the powerholder actively analyzes the source of resistance in the target, attributes the resistance to various causes, and employs a resource and influence means that are predicted to be the most effective in producing compliance. To illustrate, suppose Jim notices that the roofs installed on the last several houses he and his tradespersons have built have had a number of problems—they leak and are of lower than average quality. Jim would probably become motivated to influence the roofer so as to obtain higher quality roofing. Jim would analyze the roofer and his behavior to try to determine why the quality of roofing has become poor. Depending on the perceived cause of the roofer's actions, Jim would select a resource and means of influence predicted to be most effective in changing the roofer's behavior. Jim might draw from his economic resources and use persuasion to influence the roofer. Or Jim might draw from the legal basis of his subcontract with the roofer and threaten legal action.

---

## A "Three-Process" Model

Suppose Jim loves football and watches it all the time on TV. However, Jane hates both football and what it does to her weekends. Her goal is to reduce the amount of time Jim spends on the weekends in front of the TV watching the game.

Kelman (1958) argues that Jane might successfully use any one of three alternative modes of influence to change Jim's attitude and behavior. First, she might use compliance based on her "means control" over Jim, meaning that she mediates important rewards or punishments for him (e.g., all the benefits he obtains from his marriage with her). She can manipulate such "means" to get Jim to change his attitude and behavior toward TV football. For example, imagine that Jim really enjoys playing chess with Jane. Her chess playing is a "means" she might manipulate, contingent on Jim's reducing the time he spends watching football. Second, Jane might use "identification" based on her "attractiveness" to Jim, implying that she provides a satisfying self-defining relationship for Jim, which she can use to get Jim to change his view of and actions toward TV football. To illustrate, suppose Jim seeks Jane's approval of the kind of person he is. Through words and deeds, Jane might let him know that she would be substantially more approving of a person who spends less time vegetating in front of the TV tube watching football. Third, Jane might use "internalization" based on her ability to deliver a "credible message" to Jim that fits into a reasonable interpretation and that results in Jim's changing his attitude and behavior. Suppose Jane knows that Jim is concerned about the impact of televised violence on children. She might put forward a reasoned message that TV football is a gross depiction of violence having deleterious effects on many youngsters, and therefore ought not be watched and supported by Jim.

Kelman describes "means control," "attractiveness," and "credibility" as different "bases of power." He argues that Jim will manifest the induced response (i.e., act in terms of a changed attitude toward TV football) differently, depending upon which power base (which process of influence) has been used. If Jane has used "compliance/means control," Jim will manifest a new attitude only under conditions of "high surveillance" by Jane (i.e., when Jane is directly present to monitor Jim's behavior). If Jane has used "identification/attractiveness," Jim will display in action the new attitude only when his relationship with his wife is "salient" (prominent in his awareness). If Jane uses "internalization/credibility," Jim will show in performance the modified attitude whenever such behavior is "relevant" (i.e., whenever a game is on TV), regardless of surveillance by or salience of Jane. Implications of the three-process theory have been supported by experimental evidence (Kelman 1958).

## A Decision Game Theory of Social Influence

Tedeschi, Schlenker, and Bonoma (1973) have developed a theory of social influence stressing the way persons weigh rewards and costs in deciding among alternative courses of action. It also emphasizes the way persons communicate to others so as to affect the way they perceive and weigh rewards and costs.

Imagine a relationship between a "source" person Jim and a "target" person Jane. Suppose there is a conflict of interest in the relationship: Jane loves to spend her time on the weekend shopping for antiques, an activity Jim despises. How can Jim act to influence Jane so that she will not spend as much time antique-hunting?

Tedeschi et al.'s theory predicts that Jim will attempt to deliver some kind of communication to Jane which will influence her choice between compliance and non-compliance with Jim's preferences. Jane's choice behavior will be subject to determinants studied in research on "decision game theory," a rational-economic model of individual and joint behavior. Jane's choice will be a function of the relative "subjective expected utility" of the options before her. Whichever option has the greatest value on this factor will be selected. Jane's calculation of the subjective expected utility of a given option will be the product of (1) the positive and/or negative value associated with that option multiplied by (2) the subjectively assessed probability of the occurrence of that option.

The essential properties of value and probability considered by Jane, and thus her choice, will be a function of Jim's characteristics, Jane's characteristics, and the particular mode of persuasive communication used by Jim in relation to Jane. Jim might deliver a "threat," a message predicting some harm or punishment Jim will deliver to Jane in the event that she fails to comply. Jim might deliver a "promise," a message predicting some benefit or reward he will provide to Jane in the event that she complies. Jim might deliver a "warning," a message that predicts that some harm or punishment not caused by Jim directly will befall Jane in the event that she fails to comply. Jim might deliver a "mendation," a message that predicts that some benefit or reward not caused by Jim directly will be experienced by Jane in the event she complies.

The effectiveness of these various modes of persuasive communication (threats, promises, warnings, mendations) will be conditioned by various characteristics of Jim. He might be more or less attractive to Jane, depending upon the history of interaction that has occurred between the two (e.g., the past experiences by Jane of rewards, promises, warnings, punishments, mendations, etc.), as well as the general attitude similarity between Jim and Jane. The more attracted Jane is to Jim, the more likely Jane is to find promises credible and threats noncredible. Jim might have greater or lesser prestige, depending upon his general economic, or political capabilities ("slack resources"). The higher Jim's prestige, the greater the credibility of his persuasive communications. Jim might have greater or lesser esteem, depending on the personal respect he commands on the basis of his expertise. The greater Jim's esteem, the more credible his communications will be for Jane. Jim may have greater or lesser status; that is, legitimate authority based in formal role expectations. The greater Jim's status, the more credible will be the persuasive communications he delivers to Jane. (Notice that this use of "status" differs from that in Chapter 6 of this volume.)

Finally, the effectiveness of Jim's persuasive communications will be conditioned by certain of Jane's characteristics, which will create variation in Jane's tendency to comply. Jane may have either relatively high or low self-esteem. Low self-esteem will predispose her to comply with Jim's persuasive communications. Jane may vary in the personality characteristic, "trust" (i.e., have a generalized tendency to be more or less trusting of other persons). The greater Jane's trust, the more likely she is to comply.

The reader is encouraged to create various concrete illustrations of the Tedeschi et al. theory. Besides the Jim–Jane example mentioned above, another simple example might be as follows. Imagine that Jim and Art (both shown in Figure 7.1) have high social attraction for one another. They were good friends in high school, have similar backgrounds, and share important attitudes and values. They are discussing plans for a party they will jointly host. The plan is to have the party at Jim's house. But Jim and Art disagree on whether or not to invite Betty and Ralph. Jim likes them very much, but Art has a strong dislike of Ralph. Art might become a "source person" and he might deliver a warning ("You know, Jim, that Ralph will barge in, be arrogant and domineering, and ruin the party for everybody! Let's not invite him and his wife.") Jim thinks the warning over, weighs the overall value and likelihood of compliance versus noncompliance with Art's preference. Because of Art's social attractiveness, Jim finds Art's warning credible, experiences a resultant change in the subjective expected utility associated with the two options before him, and chooses to comply with Art's preference. Betty and Ralph do not get invited.

The major approaches to social power discussed above are similar to and different from one another in a number of ways. They all deal with social power in the context of an interactive relationship between actor a and actor b, where a wants to produce some kind of change in b. Moreover, they all discuss a variety of alternative conditions and actions that might be used by actor a to produce the desired change in b. The approaches differ, however, in the social psychological facets of actors a and b on which they focus. They also differ in the language and general theoretical imagery they employ, indicating the distinct character of the different traditions from which each approach evolved.

The field theorists frame their analyses of power in terms of the cognitive and motivational dynamics of persons' lifespaces. Also, they fix attention on the different motivational bases that actor a might employ to change b's lifespace (reward, coercion, legitimacy, reference, expertise). Kelman's three-process model frames the analysis in terms of attitude and behavior of actor b that actor a wants to change through persuasive communication, and his model addresses the different modes of persuasion that might be used by a to change b (compliance, identification, internalization). Tedeschi's decision game theory emphasizes the various kinds of communications a might deliver to b to modify the subjective expected utility of various courses of action open to b.

## THE BROADER STUDY OF SOCIAL POWER

The approaches emphasized above have been selected from a large theoretical and empirical literature concerned with social power. A few comments are in order to describe that literature in general terms and to indicate how the selected approaches fit into this wider tradition of work.

One useful way to organize the broad power literature has been proposed by Bacharach and Lawler (1981), who distinguish approaches that treat (1) "power as outcome," from those that treat (2) "power as potential," from those that treat (3) "power as tactical action."

Dahl (1957) deals with power as outcome. As Bacharach and Lawler (1981, p. 45) note: "power is equivalent to successful influence, and power that is not successful is not power at all." In other words, this approach does not clearly distinguish a potential cause (power) from a potential effect (result of power use), but rather looks only at an effect (result of power use) and infers power. The reasoning is tautological and circular. For example, one might examine the fact that a tradesman employed by Jim negotiated a favorable subcontract and infer from this outcome something about the tradesman's power *vis-à-vis* Jim. But such an inference would be tautological (i.e., true by definition) and therefore not very informative.

Bierstedt (1950), Wrong (1968), and Molm (1987) analyze power as potential. These authors clearly distinguish the capability actor a might have to influence actor b from a's actual attempt to use that capability to influence b. This way of dealing with power resolves the problem of tautology, and permits a prediction of one or more power effects from one or more power capabilities. This approach also allows the possibility that a power capability, when used, might or might not be effective in producing some result. Thus it opens the way for an analysis of the various conditions under which different kinds of power capabilities may be more or less successful. For instance, Bill might owe his neighbor, Art, a number of important favors. The obligations built up in the relationship between Bill and Art can be thought of as the potential basis of power capability for Art. Art might or might not use these obligations to attempt to induce Bill to undertake some action, say, to paint his shabby house. If Art does attempt to use them to influence Bill, Bill might or might not actually be induced to paint his house. This way of thinking about power is more useful, and it can lead to the formulation of a predictive and testable theory of social power.

Field theory, the three-process model, and the decision game theory approaches selected for background emphasis earlier, along with most other social psychological approaches, treat power as tactical action. This treatment of the topic accepts the distinction between potential power and actual power use, but it goes further to analyze the specific variety of ways power may be used, as well as the specific variety of outcomes that might result. Thus, for instance, French and Raven's reward, coercive, or legitimate bases of social power; or Kelman's means-control, attractiveness, or credibility; or Tedeschi's warnings versus mendations can all be thought of as alternative tactical actions that potentially might be employed to produce various power results.

## THE WEBERIAN TRADITION

The "tactical action" approaches emphasized above do not sharply distinguish power from other modes of social influence. Indeed, power and influence, as concepts, are blended together. The kinds of changes actor a might produce in actor b span the full range of possibilities: changes in behavior, cognition, and affect. Also, the bases of power or modes of social influence used by a to produce changes in b cover an immense variety of conditions: rewards, punishments, threats, promises, persuasion, legitimacy, and so on. In other words, when these background approaches deal with power they incorporate the whole of social influence all at once.

A contrasting position has been stated by Max Weber (1947) and others (Blau and Scott 1962), who have argued that power needs to be sharply delineated as one of several distinct kinds of social influence. The Weberian approach suggests that social influence is a very broad category of interpersonal and social causation (arguably as broad as all of social psychology, perhaps all the social sciences!). From this point of view, it is far too ambitious a task to create a single theory of social power/influence. Rather, it is more useful to clearly demarcate different kinds of social influence, each of which may then become the focus of a more limited (and more manageable) theory or set of theories that identify key determinants and consequences.

The Weberian tradition has distinguished three important types of social influence: (1) power, (2) persuasion, and (3) authority. While many other conditions besides those discussed below are probably necessary to completely define the three forms of social influence, only several of the most important characteristics emphasized by Weber and by Blau and Scott will be included here.

Social power (*Macht*), said Weber, can be defined as "the probability that one actor within a social relationship will be in a position to carry out his own will despite resistance, regardless of the basis on which this probability rests." (Weber 1947, p. 152). Person a exercises power over person b, by overcoming b's resistance to a's will. An armed robber who, brandishing a gun, overcomes resistance in a victim and takes the victim's wallet by force, can be said to have used power. The owner of the sole basis of employment in a one-company town who, through a monopoly on essential jobs, overcomes resistance in townsfolk and requires them to elect a person as mayor whom they do not want to elect, can also be said to have used power. Weber's concept of social power, then, entails as an essential part of its definition some continuing conflict of interest between an agent who uses power, and a subject over whom power is used. The subject complies overtly with the will of the power agent, but, subjectively, continues to resist doing so. If the victim could, he or she would take back his or her wallet, and if they could, the townsfolk would elect someone else mayor. Put differently, compliance with power is provided involuntarily, against the will of one or more persons.

Persuasion, in contrast, can be defined as the process in which person a works through person b's "critical faculties" to reduce b's resistance to her or his own will. In effect, persuasion implies that a convinces b to change subjectively as well as overtly. Presumably in a certain range of cases the critical faculties will be mainly "rational/cognitive," in which case actor a presents a logical argument and/or impressive evidence which together reduce actor b's resistance to a's will.

For example, if Jane provides news clippings on the health hazards of smoking to Jim and gets him to agree with her that it would be smart to stop smoking, she has persuaded him. Her will is that he stop smoking. He comes to act in accord with her will, resisting at first, but eventually he stops resisting and finally does so willingly, voluntarily. On the other hand, such influence might operate through critical faculties that are more "emotional/affective" than "rational/cognitive." Suppose b, a moral, law-abiding woman of high ideals, falls in love with a, an unscrupulous man who frequently breaks the law. Actor a might use his affective/emotional relationship with actor b to convince her to take part in criminal activity. What b initially resists eventually becomes voluntary as a result of the emotional persuasion effected by a.

Authority is distinct from both power and persuasion. According to Weber (1947, p. 152), "Imperative control (*Herrschaft*) is the probability that a command with a specific content will be obeyed by a given group of persons. Discipline is the probability that by virtue of habituation a command will receive prompt and automatic obedience in stereotyped forms, on the part of a given group of persons." Disciplined imperative control captures the essential facets of authority. Person a shares membership with person b in a collectivity (group, organization). Both a and b subscribe to a set of common social norms. On the basis of these norms, a is authorized (is granted the legitimate right) to issue certain circumscribed, collectivity-relevant commands to b in the interest of achieving collective goals. When b receives a legitimate command, he or she is moved to obey it automatically: there is no resistance in b to overcome. A does not need to appeal to b's critical (cognitive or emotional) faculties, in an effort to persuade b to comply. Thus this mode of influence is distinct from persuasion. Also, a does not need to use force or monopoly control of valued resources to overcome b's resistance. Thus, this mode of influence is distinct from social power.

Authority as a distinct mode of social influence operates in many everyday situations—in work organizations, in political and government settings, in churches, in voluntary associations of various kinds. For example, in reference to the work situation shown in Figure 7.1, if Jim, the general contractor, asks the drywall tradesperson to show up at 7:00 A.M. on a given morning and have his or her work completed by 5:00 P.M. that day, then Jim is issuing an authoritative command to the tradesperson, anchored in the formal group (the enterprise) of which both are members. The drywall tradesperson is likely to comply "automatically," without resistance to be overcome, without need of appeal to his or her critical faculties to be convinced, because the tradesperson sees Jim as having a collectively legitimated right to issue the specific work directive. Or suppose Jane, Jim's wife, works as a district court judge. Each time she hands correspondence to John, her secretary, she conveys an implicit command: "Please type this correspondence accurately and soon." John is likely to obey her command without question, and without resistance, because

Jane has a legitimate right to expect him to comply as part of his official occupational duties.

The Weberian approach to authority has been extended and refined in recent work by Zelditch and Walker (1984). These authors distinguish propriety from validity as two kinds of legitimacy, and they distinguish authorization from endorsement as two sources of validity.

To illustrate Zelditch and Walker's (1984) analysis, suppose that part of Jim's construction firm consists of a formally organized office. It has three layers of authority: Jim is on top, an office manager is beneath him, and three secretaries are beneath the manager.

Suppose the manager asks a secretary to type a letter. The secretary might voluntarily comply with the request, because he personally accepts and supports the manager's legitimacy to issue the request. When authority rests on an individual's personal acceptance and support, it rests on the legitimacy of propriety.

Another possibility is that the secretary obeys the manager, but does so involuntarily. The secretary might comply against his will because the manager's authority rests on the legitimacy of validity. The secretary does not personally accept and support the manager's right to request the letter be typed. But the secretary perceives that other significant people in the organization do accept and support the manager's right to issue such a command. Regardless of personal feelings, the secretary might be compelled to obey.

Legitimacy based on validity can stem from two sources. The first source is authorization. It derives from a higher layer of the organization (the boss). The secretary might perceive that the manager is authorized by Jim to request secretaries to type letters. Such authorization rests on formal sanctions (pay, privileges, promotions) that Jim supplies the manager for enforcing legitimate commands given to secretaries.

The second source of valid legitimacy is endorsement. It derives from the same layer of authority. That is, the secretary's peers, the other secretaries in the office, might accept and support the manager's right to request a letter be typed. Endorsement rests on informal sanctions (liking, alliances, displays of friendship) used by peers to compel obedience by the secretary in question to commands made by the manager.

Compared to previous approaches, Zelditch and Walker's analysis is innovative, because it draws the subtle but important distinction between endorsement and propriety as bases of legitimate power (authority).

## FROM WEBER TO EMERSON: POWER-DEPENDENCE THEORY

With the above background in mind, the present chapter now turns to its main focus: a systematic theory of social power and a brief review of the evidence that has thus far accumulated in several distinct research programs to test and extend the theory.

## Expanding the Definition of Social Power

Above, Emerson's concept of social power was defined as the resistance each actor in a relationship can mutually overcome. Several points need to be made about this definition. First, this concept is very similar to Max Weber's concept of social power as a distinct kind of social influence. Both Emerson and Weber emphasize an existing conflict of interest between two actors, a and b. Also, both theorists speak of "overcoming resistance." Thus, this notion, like Weber's notion, suggests that power must not be blended definitionally with persuasion, which implies a reduction of resistance, nor with authority, which implies no resistance. Emerson's concept of power may indeed be related to persuasion and authority. In fact, it can serve (has served) as a basis for carefully forging clear theoretical links to these other forms of influence. But, as a concept, it must be defined in such a way that it is kept clearly distinct from these other forms of influence.

Second, power is defined explicitly as a property of the mutual relationship between a and b. It is a reciprocal part of an established social interaction relationship between the two persons. It does not focus on a one-shot transaction, nor does it focus on the "unilateral" exercise of power. According to Emerson, actor a has power over actor b, who also has power over actor a. Thus, it would be vacuous to say that a given individual "is powerful" without specifying "over whom" he or she is powerful, and without specifying the reciprocal power the other has over him or her.

Third, power is defined explicitly as a potential based in a social structure. It can characterize a given a–b relationship; indeed, it can be a property of profound potential magnitude in a relationship, yet rarely be observed to operate. It can and may occasionally operate. But an important goal is to account for the conditions under which power tends to operate. Also, defining power as Emerson does permits further analysis of the processes of power use and the various possible outcomes of power use, which can be considered separately from the power potentiality itself. We now turn from the concept of power to a theory that clarifies the causes and consequences of power.

## Determinants of Social Power

Emerson notes that persistent human relationships are based on "ties of interdependence," by which he means that each actor, a and b, mediates various valued benefits or resources for the other. A resource is any valued condition or event (including material provisions, and cognitive and/or affective expressions) possessed by one actor and made available to another actor. For example, in the marriage relationship between Jim and Jane the various benefits each actor provides the other—from a comfortable income through sexual fulfillment to fun social contacts—can be thought of as resources. The interaction process through which actors a and b, like Jim and Jane, make resources mutually available is described as "social exchange" by Emerson. For instance, Jim might forego TV football on a weekend to accompany Jane antique shopping, in which case she would benefit. The next weekend, the couple might both watch a TV football game instead of looking for antiques, in which case Jim would benefit.

The descriptive label, "exchange," however, does not imply that Jim and Jane necessarily see themselves as two economically rational actors pursuing their respective self-interests in the same way that a stockbroker pursues his or hers in the marketplace. Their own subjective assessments of their relationship are likely to emphasize such feelings as affection, caring, solidarity, the willingness to stand by one another in times of difficulty, etc. But Emerson argues that an objective theorist can usefully view the a–b relationship over an extended period of time as a structure and process of social exchange. From this objective viewpoint, the interactions that occur between a and b can be understood as a longitudinal series of transactions in which each actor reciprocates various kinds of valued resources. An interesting research issue concerns the degree of congruence between an objective observer's perceptions of the a–b exchange relationship and a's and b's perceptions and interpretations of the relationship.

The central determinant of social power in this theory is mutual resource dependence. The power of a over b is determined by the dependence of b upon a for resources (and vice versa). Dependence can vary from high to low. The greater b's dependence upon a, the more power a has in the relationship. The greater a's dependence upon b, the greater b's power over a. Suppose Jim and Jane rely almost exclusively upon one another as a source for important affective, cognitive, and material benefits, while Art and Doris have a marriage of convenience and each obtains many important benefits from other sources, such as relatives or friends. In comparing the two couples, Jim and Jane would be the relatively more mutually dependent and mutually powerful of the two couples.

Dependence, in turn, is determined by other core variables specified in the theory. One major determinant of dependence is resource value. The greater the value a places on resources obtained from b, the greater a's dependence upon b. For illustration, Jim may value his wife's understanding and affection far more than he values the social life she orchestrates for him (assuming that he is shy, anyway). On the basis of resource value, then, his dependence on his wife (and her power) are determined substantially by the understanding and affection she bestows, but are only trivially determined by the social contacts she facilitates for him.

A second major determinant of dependence is alternative sources of valued resources outside the a–b relationship. The greater the availability of alternative sources to a of resources provided by b, the less dependent a is upon b (and vice versa). Suppose Jim has frequent contact in his travels with various women, and suppose he frequently has affairs with some of these women. However, suppose that Jane is psychologically commited to monogamy, and, in any case, has very few contacts with other men, except when Jim is with her. With reference to sex, resource availability is such that Jim's dependence upon Jane (and her power) are lower: he can obtain sexual fulfillment from various alternative sources, while Jane's dependence upon Jim (and his power) are higher: she is able (psychologically and ecologically) to obtain sexual fulfillment only from him.

## Balance, Imbalance, and Power Use

Power was defined as a reciprocal feature of the a–b relationship. To say that the relationship is reciprocal, however, is not to say that the results of exchange for a and b across a series of transactions are equal in the sense that each actor gives the same quantity or value of resources to the other as the other gives to her or him. Whether the results of exchange are equal or unequal will be determined by the relative power-dependence of a and b.

One logical possibility is that a and b are equally dependent upon one another for valued resources. If so, the a–b exchange relationship is described by the theory as "power-balanced." Jim might rely upon Jane for the resources she provides him to approximately the same extent that Jane relies upon Jim for the resources he provides her. Should a conflict of interest arise between Jim and Jane, power might become activated in the relationship. But, in this case, across a series of transactions, Jim's use of power to overcome resistance in Jane will approximately match Jane's use of power to overcome resistance in Jim, and each of them is likely to achieve roughly equivalent results from exchange in the long run. That is, both Jim and Jane are likely to achieve equally favorable terms of exchange leading to equally favorable net levels of gratification in the long run.

Another logical possibility is that the dependence of one actor is less than the dependence of the other actor. In this case, the exchange relationship is described as power-imbalanced, meaning that one actor, a, has a power-advantage, and the other actor, b, has a power-disadvantage. In the event of a conflict of interest, a is in a position to overcome more resistance in b than b can overcome in a. And in exchange across time the transactions will favor the advantaged actor, who will realize increases in net gratification, while they will work against the disadvantaged actor, who will realize corresponding decreases in net gratification. For example, given that Jane depends more upon Jim than he depends upon her, we might expect the results of exchange to be more favorable to Jim than to Jane. In such a marriage, Jim might provide his income along with a rather remote, preoccupied, self-centered style of behavior, while Jane might provide warm affection, expert childcare, a sympathetic and understanding ear, a fulfilling social life, and generalized attention and deference. Assuming Jane values resources not being provided by Jim, she might be characterized as being exploited by him. Through using his power-advantage, Jim obtains resources of greater quantity or higher quality from his wife in exchange for resources of lower quantity or quality (e.g., he provides less effort, time, attention, and concern to her, than she does to him).

Emerson's theory argues that if an a–b relationship is imbalanced, the person with an advantage will tend to use his or her power potential. This prediction holds, whether or not the actors (such as Jim and Jane in this example) clearly understand or intend the power dynamics occurring in their relationship. In either case, an objective observer can understand those dynamics: Jim is able to achieve resources of increased quantity or value, while Jane is forced to accept resources of decreased quantity or value across a series of transactions, because of differences in the reciprocal level of dependence enjoyed by the two actors.

## Power Balancing

Given that power-advantage in an imbalanced relationship is used, power-dependence theory also predicts that any one of several logically possible balancing actions will occur. These actions are predicted to move the relationship in the direction of power balance.

One possibility, "withdrawal," works through the value determinant of power-dependence. The power disadvantaged actor reduces his or her dependence on the power-advantaged other by gradually lowering the value placed on resources that have been obtained from the other. For example, Jane's dependence on Jim might become less, were she to lower the value she places on the resources he provides to the relationship (e.g., the material level of living he contributes).

A second balancing action, "network extension," stems from the availability of alternative sources of valued resources as a determinant of dependence. In this process, the power-disadvantaged actor lowers his or her dependence on the more powerful other by locating, outside the a–b relationship, alternative relationships within which to obtain the valued resources that have been obtained from that other. For example, Jane might gradually change her stance on monogamy, and eventually form a romantic relationship with another man from whom she can obtain the valued resources (care, concern, attention, etc.) she has not been able to get from Jim.

Third, "status giving" works through the value determinant of dependence in a different fashion. Here, the power-disadvantaged actor increases the value (quantity and/or quality) of resources provided to the more powerful other, thus increasing that other's dependence on the a–b relationship. To vary the example somewhat, suppose that Jim and Jane are "committed" to one another rather than being married. Suppose that Jim is the more dependent, power-disadvantaged person. He might change some feature of his own behavior or attitude so as to enhance the value of what he contributes to the relationship. If Jane is much better educated than Jim, and she values sophisticated conversations, Jim might enroll in night school to expand his formal education and thus enhance the value of his conversations, thereby increasing Jane's dependence on him and increasing his power relative to hers. (See Chapter 6 for a discussion of status processes.)

Fourth, "coalition formation" balances power by reducing the advantaged actor's access to alternative sources of valued resources outside the a–b relationship. This final balancing action might take the form of an implicit alliance between Jane and other women in the community. An unspoken but strongly sanctioned norm prohibiting affairs and supporting monogamy might form among and be sanctioned by the women in the community. "Loose" women who have affairs with other women's husbands will be ridiculed and scorned. The effect of such an alliance or coalition is to restrict availability of sexual resources to each a–b marriage or "committed" relationship, thus increasing the mutual power-dependence of each spouse or partner.

## Power-Dependence in Networks and Groups

The primary focus of the power-dependence principles discussed so far is the dyadic a–b relation, despite the fact that certain ideas (e.g., "network extension," "coalition formation") virtually necessitate consideration of "third parties" in the social environment surrounding the a–b relationship. However, to deal in an explicit way with such broader aspects of the surrounding social environment, Emerson (1972) systematically extended these principles into a theory of complex structural exchange, some major parts of which will be discussed here.

As noted above, one of the fundamental determinants of dependence is "the availability of alternative sources of a valued resource." This determinant of power in an a–b relationship provides an avenue to a more complex social situation, involving an exchange network composed of at least three actors. In Figure 7.1, suppose Jim has begun having an extramarital affair with Bill's wife, Mary. Each relationship, Jim–Jane and Jim–Mary, can be thought of as a power-dependence relation in which the various resources constituting romantic love are exchanged. However, the two relations are "connected," because the exchange that occurs between Jim and Jane is affected by the exchange that occurs between Jim and Mary. What happens in each relationship is contingent in part on what happens in the other relationship.

The romantic resources Jim values are available from two alternative sources, Jane or Mary. If the quantity or quality of such resources are not to his liking in one relationship, he can turn to the other relationship to obtain them. Jim occupies a position of power advantage in this network of connected exchange relations (see Figure 7.1). The theory argues that across time Jim, whether he is fully aware of it or not, will use such advantage, realizing a steady increase in the results of exchange (and his own net satisfaction), while Jane and Mary, being located in disadvantaged positions in the exchange network, will each realize a corresponding decrease in the results of exchange (and net satisfaction).

Importantly, the love triangle illustrates distributive exchange. The romantic resources exchanged among Jim, Jane, and Mary have immediate, consummatory value: given that an actor obtains an expression of romantic affection, it has unqualified value and can be enjoyed by him or her regardless of any other conditions. Such exchange has important implications. First, it implies that the sources of resources are substitutable. What Jim obtains of value from Jane can also be obtained from Mary. Second, distributive exchange implies a structure of competition. For a given actor (e.g., Mary) to obtain relatively more resources means that some other actor (e.g., Jane) will obtain relatively fewer of them. In the love triangle example, the competition between Jane and Mary is the basis of Jim's position of power advantage in the exchange network.

Emerson's theory (1972) also examines a different kind of exchange—productive exchange. It is based on a different kind of resource. The work relationships that link Jim to each tradesperson he hires in the house-building enterprise (see Figure 7.1) are based on productive, rather than distributive, exchange. Each actor in such a situation contributes an instrumental, rather than consummatory, resource. The only way instrumental resources can acquire value is by being interactively combined to create a collective product. The product can then enter distributive exchange as a consummatory resource having value (e.g., being worth money) that can be allocated to the actors who have contributed instrumental resources toward the production of the joint product. The coordination and carpentry that Jim provides as a general contractor, the hole dug by the excavator, the finished interior installed by the drywaller, the pipes and fixtures put in by the plumber, and the wiring and fixtures installed by the electrician only become valuable (attain a dollar value) when they are combined to make a completed house sold in the marketplace. Emerson speaks of the provision of an instrumental resource by each actor in a productive exchange situation as a role performance, and he describes the overall set of such performances as a group or organization composed of a division of labor. In effect, actors are related to one another within a social system, in which each provides a role performance of a given value to help create a collective product. In exchange for a member's contribution, she or he is allocated a portion of the value that results from the collective product (e.g., a given share of the money obtained from the sale of a completed house). Emerson describes the share a given actor gets of the value produced as that actor's group status. For example, Jim's instrumental resources (carpentry and coordination) may constitute a more valuable contribution to the building project than installing the wiring, so Jim's status (his share of the money obtained from the house sale) will be greater than the electrician's status.

With these two important kinds of exchange structure, the distributive exchange network and the productive exchange group/organization, the theory provides a foundation for bridging the micro-social level of the a–b dyadic relationship and the macro-social levels of the exchange network and organized group. One might focus on the social psychology of the individual actor in the context of a dyadic a–b power-dependence relationship. One might move to consider a friendship network based on distributive exchange, such as that depicted in Figure 7.1 among Jim, Jane, and their friends. Or one might focus more globally on a large complex distributive exchange network composed not of individual actors, but of corporate units (small or large), each of which is based on productive exchange among a set of individuals (e.g., a network of industries in a nation's economy or a network of nations in a world economy).

## THEORETICAL EXTENSIONS AND EMPIRICAL RESEARCH INSPIRED BY EMERSON'S THEORY

The principles of power-dependence and exchange discussed above have been extended in several bodies of theoretical/empirical research. Although space limitations do not permit exhaustive coverage of all relevant studies, major lines of work and central findings will be briefly reviewed here.

### Structural Power Use in the Dyad

Molm has investigated "how a structural advantage is transformed into actual behavioral control" within a power-dependence/exchange relation (1987, p. 102; 1989). Her work emphasizes the operant conditioning and learning processes entailed in power interactions. By varying the value of behavior exchange versus the value of an individual task, she has experimentally varied the relative power-dependence of exchange partners, creating structural balance/equality, or imbalance/inequality. In imbalanced exchange relations, she has monitored power use in the form of asymmetrical exchange. In such exchange, a structurally advantaged actor gives little valued behavior in exchange, while a structurally disadvantaged actor gives much valued behavior in exchange.

In one important study (Molm 1987), it was shown "that power use increases with power imbalance" (in a dyad), however, "actual power use often falls considerably below its potential" (Molm 1987, p. 107). Individual dependencies of dyad members affect the power use process. Molm's results show a distinct difference in the behavior of high versus low power users. Low power users simply do not enact behavioral strategies to influence their partners. On the other hand, high power users use effective strategies to create behavior-control contingencies for their partners. When a structurally advantaged actor uses less power than he or she might use, it is often because he or she fails to learn about potential power through behavioral exploration.

In a second major study Molm (1989) examined the use of punishment as a power-balancing process. Assume a reward-power relation that is imbalanced in favor of actor a over actor b. With reference to the less advantaged b, empirical findings showed that "in a relation with high mutual reward dependence, punishment is used more frequently when its magnitude is relatively low; when mutual reward dependence is low, punishment is used more frequently when its magnitude is relatively high" (Molm 1989, p. 1414). Under certain conditions, the use of punishment is effective in increasing a disadvantaged actor's reward from a more powerful other. Used excessively, however, punishment power can lead the more powerful other to merely retaliate (i.e., administer punishments in return) or withdraw from the relation. More research is needed to clarify the intricate links between reward and punishment power processes.

## Two-Party Bargaining

Bacharach and Lawler (1981) extend power-dependence theory in important ways by using it to analyze the tactics often adopted by two parties in a bargaining relationship. After reviewing a large body of theory and research in the economics of bargaining, these authors (1981, p. 40) conclude: ". . . a general theory of bargaining must examine the relationship between the bargaining context, parties' evaluation of each other's bargaining power, and tactical action."

In pursuing this insight, they examined the part played by "tactical concessions," where a party gives something of value to the other party in order to achieve some advantage. Among the important cognitive effects of tactical concessions is a change in parties' images of the bargaining relationship. Instead of perceiving the relationship as one of categorical conflict, where one party's gains equal the other party's losses, the two parties might come to perceive room for mutual compromise and joint gain.

While concession behavior highlights mutually rewarding aspects of tactical bargaining, Bacharach and Lawler also considered the implications of mutually punitive capabilities. One possible implication of such capabilities is "deterrence": because each party recognizes that the other can potentially deliver harm, neither is likely to use the potential. Another possible implication of punitive capabilities is "conflict spiral": because each party recognizes that the other can deliver harm, an escalated cycle of "threat-counterthreat" and "punishment-counterpunishment" emerges (Lawler, Ford, and Blegen 1988).

Another category of tactical action analyzed by Bacharach and Lawler was "tactical dramaturgy," the use of "arguments," "justifications," "explanations," and "rationalizations" by parties to define the bargaining situation advantageously. By defining issues in specified ways, by appealing to common norms, and by "bluffing," actors pursue and achieve their desired outcomes tactically.

Finally, Bacharach and Lawler discuss how the various processes of tactical action interact with the underlying structure of bargaining power to determine the outcome of bargaining. The outcome involves the likelihood and nature of an agreement between parties. Depending upon the relative power of the two parties, and depending on the relative effectiveness of their use of tactical actions, each party stands to benefit more or less from an agreement reached through bargaining.

When the underlying structure of power is unequal, the benefits achieved through bargaining tend to be skewed in favor of one party over another. As a result, the bargaining situation becomes problematic and unstable. (See also Chapter 10 on this topic.)

## Structural Power Use in the Exchange Network

The implications of unequal structural power have been studied in another line of research (Stolte and Emerson 1977; Cook and Emerson 1978; Cook et al. 1983). This research has examined the effects of power position in an exchange network on the results of exchange. The reader will recall that power position is based on the relative availability of alternative sources of valued resources in an exchange network. The dynamics of exchange illustrated hypothetically in the example of a love triangle among Jim, Jane, and Mary have been demonstrated under laboratory experimental conditions in this line of research.

Though the particular procedures used and issues investigated differ among the cited studies, they are similar in some fundamental respects. In a small groups laboratory, four or more college student volunteers are randomly assigned to different locations (cubicles or rooms). Subjects are able to communicate via telephone, computer, or written messages. Across a series of transaction periods, subjects engage one another in repeated pair-wise negotiations. During a given period, a subject may negotiate with up to three other subjects. In each negotiation, subjects attempt to settle on mutually acceptable terms for exchanging units of hypothetical resources. The particular terms settled upon have consequences for the number of ''profit points'' (worth actual money) each subject achieves. The experimental forms are designed (or computers are programmed) to vary among the subjects the relative value and/or structural availability of resources (i.e., positional power-dependence). Some subjects have relatively high and some have relatively low positional power-dependence.

The studies employing variants of these experimental procedures have consistently shown that the subjects with a positional power advantage achieve significantly more profit points than subjects with a positional power disadvantage. Recent studies along this line (Cook et al. 1983; Stolte 1988) have built from the previous work to propose techniques for measuring structural power-dependence in complex exchange networks.

Markovsky, Willer, and Patton (1988) have developed an approach, ''network exchange theory,'' that shares some of the same theoretical goals as the work on exchange networks undertaken by Emerson and his colleagues. However, this approach differs in three basic ways. First, it draws from a more encompassing social exchange perspective that includes Emerson's power-dependence theory, but other exchange studies and theories as well. Consequently, assumptions about the conditions of exchange (i.e., conditions characterizing actors, positions, and relations in networks) are different from the assumptions made by Emerson's theory about those conditions. Second, it uses techniques of theory construction that are more formal (logical, mathematical) than the techniques commonly used by Emerson and his associates. Therefore, the theory is framed in axiomatic terms, and it uses mathematical graph theory tools. Third, network exchange theory employs experimental procedures that are in general ways similar to, yet in specific ways quite distinct from, the procedures used by Emerson and his colleagues. Markovsky, Willer, and Patton's experimental task involves small groups of subjects engaging in a sequence of pair-wise negotiated exchange agreements. In each period, a given pair of subjects must decide on how to divide a pool of 24 counters, with each counter worth one profit point.

Markovsky et al. (1988), in one important study, develop a formal measure of a position's relative power in an exchange network. Called "GPI" (a graph-analytic power index), this measure "simply tallies the number of advantageous paths and subtracts the number of disadvantageous paths to determine each position's potential power" (Markovsky et al. 1988, p. 224). Intuitively, a position is advantaged if, on any occasion for exchange, it is unlikely to be excluded from exchange. Conversely, a position is disadvantaged if it is likely to be excluded from exchange. Excludability is determined by the shape of an exchange network and the conditions of exchange that prevail. A virtue of the GPI measure, according to these authors, is that it shows how the characteristics of an exchange network taken as a whole affect the relative power of each position within the network. Experimental data based on Markovsky et al.'s procedures were collected. These data supported the predictions following from network exchange theory and GPI. However, these data did not support predictions following from an alternative measure of "network-wide dependence" (Dn), that had been developed by Cook, Gillmore, and Yamagishi (1986) in the context of power-dependence theory.

Power-dependence theory, as Emerson originally crafted it, has spawned some exciting debate in the field. New themes are being explored. Variations in concept and method are being tried. Our understanding of power will continue to be refined and extended through such efforts.

---

## Subjective Reactions to Power Dependence

The focus of power-dependence/exchange principles, as Emerson originally formulated them, was on the objective properties of resource exchange relations. Some research, however, has addressed various subjective reactions, e.g., the perceptions and feelings of subjects.

One line of research (Stolte 1978, 1983) examined how power position affects a person's self-evaluation. Subjects negotiated a series of transactions in a laboratory exchange network situation. They then filled out post-experimental questionnaires in which various self- and other-perceptions were measured. This research showed that subjects who enjoy a relatively advantaged power-dependence position have relatively higher "self-efficacy" and "self-worth" perceptions than subjects who are located in a relatively disadvantaged power-dependence position.

Other research (Bacharach and Lawler 1976) determined whether persons use power dependence conditions to assess or estimate power in a manner consistent with Emerson's theory. This study employed vignettes containing depictions of realistic social situations framed in power-dependence/exchange terms. Subjects read a description of a disagreement between a clothing company employer and an employee. Each subject was instructed to take the role of the employee in the depicted situation. The vignette experimentally manipulated the resource value and the resource availability determinants of power dependence characterizing the employee and employer. Afterward, subjects filled out semantic differential scales measuring their perceptions of the employee's and employer's power. In accord with the theory, an employee on whom an employer had high dependence (due to resource value or availability) was seen as having relatively high power, and conversely, an employer on whom an employee had high dependence (due to the same determinants) was seen as having relatively high power. In short, objective structural features of power dependence, as operationalized in the vignette, were perceived accurately and consistently in line with the theory.

Additional research (Hegtvedt 1988) has examined how conditions of power-dependence structure perceptions and estimates of power. Building from the Bacharach and Lawler (1976) study, this research also used vignettes to operationalize power-dependence variables. The vignettes portrayed an interaction between one student needing a paper typed and another student who was willing to do the typing for pay. Subjects took the role of the typist. Consistent with the Bacharach and Lawler study, the results for perceptions of power supported predictions based on power-dependence theory. A typist who was depicted as being relatively less dependent was perceived as being relatively more powerful and, conversely, one who was portrayed as relatively more dependent was seen as relatively less powerful.

These studies show clearly and consistently that objective power-dependence conditions shape a person's perceptions of self and others in ways predicted by Emerson's theory.

---

## Coalition Formation and Organization Processes

Cook and Gillmore (1984) investigated coalition formation as a power-balancing process. They built upon the research on positional power and its use in exchange networks described above. Subjects who experienced power use by an actor with a positional advantage in an exchange network, when given an opportunity to form a coalition, tended to do so as predicted by Emerson's theory. The members of a coalition acted as a unit in negotiating resource transactions with the previously advantaged subject and, thereby, were able to balance the power between themselves and that subject. Consequently, coalition members were able to increase the levels of benefit (i.e., monetary profit) they obtained as a result of exchange.

Bacharach and Lawler (1980) used power-dependence theory, as it applies to bargaining and coalition formation, to study organizational processes. They note that an organization is made up of interest groups reflecting the organizational structure. The various interest groups are in conflict with one another, because each aims to exert some control over activities and policy, but the capacity to exert such control is limited. The more control one interest group has, the less control other interest groups have. The processes of conflict among various interest groups in the organization tend to take the form of either of two kinds of bargaining: (1) "distributive bargaining," where an actor competitively attempts to maximize his or her own (or his or her coalition's) resources at the expense of another person (or coalition), or (2) "integrative bargaining," where an actor attempts to engage in joint problem-solving aimed at cooperatively resolving conflict involving him or herself or his or her coalition. Bargaining, then, is an important tactical mechanism used by members of interest groups to vie for control and organizational influence. This mechanism dynamically links various interest groups together in a resulting organizational structure.

## Judgments: Legitimacy and Justice in Exchange

Complementing the research by Zelditch and Walker (1984) on legitimacy discussed above, several studies inspired by power-dependence theory have investigated the normative judgments subjects make with reference to exchange and power in networks or groups. For example, two studies (Stolte 1983; Cook, Hegtvedt, and Yamagishi 1988) provided a subject in an exchange network a positional power advantage and other subjects a disadvantage. Replicating previous research, these studies showed that positional power was used by advantaged subjects to achieve results of exchange (levels of monetary profit) that were relatively more favorable than the results achieved by the disadvantaged subjects. Included in a post-experimental questionnaire were items measuring the perceived fairness of the results of exchange. Advantaged subjects tended to judge their own results of exchange as relatively more fair, while disadvantaged subjects tended to see their own exchange results as relatively less fair.

The implications of these findings for a theory of the legitimation of structured social inequality (Della Fave 1980) were explored. That theory argued that (1) an actor in a power-advantaged position tends to develop a high self-evaluation (i.e., a sense of competence and efficacy) and consequently comes to attribute the results of exchange to his or her own abilities and to judge his or her own privilege as deserved and fair, and (2) an actor in a power-disadvantaged position develops a low self-evaluation (e.g., a sense of ineptness) and consequently comes to attribute the results of exchange to his or her own inferiority and to judge his or her own deprivation as deserved and fair. The logic of this theory was not supported by the results. Contrary to expectations, subjects' fairness judgments varied with positional power. That is, structurally advantaged subjects saw their own results of exchange as fair, while structurally disadvantaged subjects saw their own results of exchange as unfair. One reasonable interpretation is that the latter actors did not develop a low self-evaluation as a result of their inferior power position, but rather "blamed the system" for their plight.

A concern with legitimacy and justice in exchange led Stolte (1987a, 1987b) to undertake a theoretical analysis to answer two important questions: (1) how does a justice norm form, and (2) why do different justice norms, such as "equality," "inequality," or "equity" form? The analysis bridged Emerson's power-dependence/exchange theory and symbolic interaction theory (Mead 1934; Stryker 1980).

Put briefly, the analysis argued that persons form different kinds of "meaning agreements" reflecting the different kinds of objective circumstances of exchange and power-dependence in which they find themselves. Such meaning agreements mirror what they jointly perceive to be salient causes, and facts of exchange and power, structuring their situation. Under certain conditions, they may agree to form a coalition to work together in pursuit of their respective self-interests. When a coalition or "collective actor" forms, each individual within it, or each individual outside it who is subordinate to it, becomes the object of a collectively communicated norm—a "justice norm."

Depending on the objective circumstances of exchange, a different kind of coalition communicating a different kind of justice norm will tend to form. In an exchange network, where power-dependence is balanced and equal, the norm of "equality" is likely to emerge. Actors are likely to perceive the objective facts of exchange: everyone obtains equal results of exchange. A coalition might form and the facts might be translated into the normative statement, "Everyone ought to obtain equal results of exchange." That which exists objectively and factually becomes thereby that which should exist.

In a different situation, where power dependence becomes imbalanced and unequal, a different kind of collective actor might form. Its members might agree about the objective fact that they are able to obtain relatively more favorable results of exchange than others in the structure are able to obtain. In communication, its members might well convert "what is" into "what ought to be" in the form of the norm, "status/rank inequality." This norm would justify inequality. It would judge advantage for some and disadvantage for others as morally proper.

Finally, in yet a different structure, where actors are engaged in productive exchange, pooling their respective resources to create a joint product, a different collective actor and a different justice norm are likely to form. Under these conditions, "equity" would be likely to emerge, a normative statement that each actor ought to obtain a reward in proportion to the value of the resource he or she has contributed to the collective product.

## SUMMARY

The foregoing analysis underscores the importance of four major themes concerning the nature and impact of social power. First, power as a potential, working through a process, resulting in an outcome, determines the distribution of valued resources among people in a pervasive array of social settings. In primary relations between spouses, parents and children, siblings, and friends, power determines the relative net emotional satisfactions people achieve. In secondary relations between supervisors and subordinates, management and labor, buyer and seller, power determines the relative net benefits (money, information, goods, services, prestige, decision rights, autonomy) people enjoy.

Second, social power, as a distinct mode of influence, entails conflict and the overcoming of resistance. It operates when interests and goals diverge. When a parent and an adolescent child clash over who will use the family car on a given evening, or when management and labor engage in a dispute about working conditions and the wage rate, social power comes to the fore.

Third, social power stimulates a concern in people about issues of equality or inequality and justice or injustice. Whether the resources at issue are material or emotional, if they are of significant value, and if they are distributed unequally, people frequently show concern. A variety of reactions to such concern, from justification or challenge to support or protest, often follow the operation of social power.

Fourth, instead of being a property of the individual person, social power resides in the structure of a social interaction situation. Sometimes it works within a relationship between two people, but often it works within the complex relationships among a set of three, four, or many more people. Different primary and secondary social networks, where variations occur in who interacts with whom, make up the social situations in which power emerges and produces its effects in predictable ways.

## SUGGESTED READINGS

Bacharach, Samuel B. and Edward J. Lawler. 1980. *Power and Politics in Organizations.* San Francisco: Jossey-Bass. Chapters 2 and 3.

Chapter 2 discusses the general characteristics of social power relationships. Chapter 3 clarifies specific kinds of power that vary with circumstances. Drawing from classic and contemporary studies, the two chapters together provide a definitive analysis of the topic.

Emerson, Richard M. 1962. "Power-Dependence Relations." *American Sociological Review* 27:31–40.

This article presents the initial statement of an extremely important theory of power that has had a profound impact on the field. Although tightly reasoned and abstract, it is quite accessible.

_____. 1969. "Operant Psychology and Exchange Theory." Pp. 379–405 in *Behavioral Sociology,* edited by R. Burgess and D. Bushell. New York: Columbia University Press.

This chapter states tersely and clearly the key notions in a structural theory of social exchange that builds from power-dependence processes. Less formal, it is easier to read than other more complete statements of the theory.

Schopler, John. 1965. "Social Power." Pp. 177–218 in *Advances in Experimental Social Psychology,* vol. 2, edited by L. Berkowitz. New York: Academic Press.

This chapter is an important early review of experimental research on power. Most of the work it covers was done by psychologists.

Tedeschi, James and Thomas Bonoma. 1972. "Power and Influence: An Introduction." Pp. 1–49 in *The Social Influence Processes,* edited by J. Tedeschi. Chicago: Aldine.

This article organizes a very large body of theory and research on power as "tactical action." It serves as a useful overview of this approach.

# REFERENCES

Bacharach, Samuel B. and Edward J. Lawler. 1976. "The Perception of Power." *Social Forces* 55:123–34.

_____. 1980. *Power and Politics in Organizations.* San Francisco: Jossey-Bass.

_____. 1981. *Bargaining: Power, Tactics, and Outcomes.* San Francisco: Jossey-Bass.

Bierstedt, Robert. 1950. "An Analysis of Social Power." *American Sociological Review* 15:730–38.

Blau, Peter and Richard W. Scott. 1962. *Formal Organizations.* San Francisco: Chandler.

Cartwright, Dorwin. 1959. "A Field Theoretical Conception of Power." Pp. 183–220 in *Studies in Social Power,* edited by D. Cartwright. Ann Arbor, MI: University of Michigan Press.

Cook, Karen S. and Richard M. Emerson. 1978. "Power, Equity, and Commitment in Exchange Networks." *American Sociological Review* 43:721–39.

Cook, Karen S., Richard M. Emerson, Mary Gillmore, and Toshio Yamagishi. 1983. "The Distribution of Power in Exchange Networks: Theory and Experimental Results." *American Journal of Sociology* 89:275–305.

Cook, Karen S. and Mary Gillmore. 1984. "Power, Dependence, and Coalitions." Pp. 27–58 in *Advances in Group Processes: A Research Annual,* vol. 1, edited by E. J. Lawler. Greenwich, CT: JAI Press.

Cook, Karen S., Mary R. Gillmore, and Toshio Yamagishi. 1986. "Point and Line Vulnerability as Bases for Predicting the Distribution of Power in Exchange Networks: Reply to Willer." *American Journal of Sociology* 92:445–48.

Cook, Karen S., Karen A. Hegtvedt, and Toshio Yamagishi. 1988. "Structural Inequality, Legitimation, and Reactions to Inequity in Exchange Networks." Pp. 291–308 and 507–509 in *Status Generalization: New Theory and Research,* edited by M. Webster, Jr. and M. Foschi. Stanford, CA: Stanford University Press.

Dahl, Robert. 1957. "The Concept of Power." *Behavioral Science* 2:201–18.

Della Fave, Richard. 1980. "The Meek Shall Not Inherit the Earth: Self-Evaluation and the Legitimacy of Stratification." *American Sociological Review* 45:955–71.

Emerson, Richard M. 1962. "Power-Dependence Relations." *American Sociological Review* 27:31–40.

———. 1972. "Exchange Theory: Parts I and II." Pp. 38–87 in *Sociological Theories in Progress,* vol. 2, edited by J. Berger, M. Zelditch, Jr., and B. Anderson. Boston: Houghton Mifflin.

French, John and Bertram Raven. 1959. "The Bases of Social Power." Pp. 150–67 in *Studies in Social Power,* edited by D. Cartwright. Ann Arbor, MI: University of Michigan Press.

Hegtvedt, Karen A. 1988. "Social Determinants of Perception: Power, Equity, and Status Effects in an Exchange Situation." *Social Psychology Quarterly* 51:141–53.

Kelman, Herbert. 1958. "Compliance, Identification, and Internalization: Three Processes of Attitude Change." *Journal of Conflict Resolution* 2:51–60.

Kipnis, David. 1974. "The Powerholder." Pp. 82–122 in *Perspectives on Social Power,* edited by J. T. Tedeschi. Chicago: Aldine.

Lawler, Edward J., Rebecca Ford, and Mary A. Blegen. 1988. "Coercive Capability in Conflict: A Test of Bilateral Deterrence vs. Conflict Spiral Theory." *Social Psychology Quarterly* 51:93–107.

Lewin, Kurt. 1939. "Field Theory and Experiment in Social Psychology: Concepts and Methods." *American Journal of Sociology* 44:868–96.

Markovsky, Barry, David Willer, and Travis Patton. 1988. "Power Relations in Networks." *American Sociological Review* 53:220–36.

Mead, George H. 1934. *Mind, Self, and Society.* Chicago: University of Chicago Press.

Molm, Linda. 1987. "Linking Power Structure and Power Use." Pp. 101–29 in *Social Exchange Theory,* edited by K. S. Cook. Newbury Park, CA: Sage Publications.

———. 1989. "Punishment Power: A Balancing Process in Power-Dependence Relations." *American Journal of Sociology* 94:1392–418.

Stolte, John F. 1978. "Positional Power and Interpersonal Evaluation in Bargaining Networks." *Social Behavior and Personality* 6:73–80.

———. 1983. "The Legitimation of Structural Inequality: Reformulation and Test of the Self-Evaluation Argument." *American Sociological Review* 48:331–42.

———. 1987a. "The Formation of Justice Norms." *American Sociological Review* 52:774–84.

———. 1987b. "Legitimacy, Justice, and Productive Exchange." Pp. 190–208 in *Social Exchange Theory,* edited by K. S. Cook. Newbury Park, CA: Sage.

———. 1988. "From Micro- to Macro-Exchange Structure: Measuring Power Imbalance at the Level of the Exchange Network." *Social Psychology Quarterly* 51:357–64.

Stolte, John F. and Richard M. Emerson. 1977. "Structural Inequality: Position and Power in Network Structures." Pp. 117–38 in *Behavioral Theory in Sociology,* edited by R. Hamblin and J. Kunkel. New Brunswick, NJ: Transaction.

Stryker, Sheldon. 1980. *Symbolic Interactionism.* Menlo Park, CA: Benjamin/Cummings.

Tedeschi, James T., Barry R. Schlenker, and Thomas V. Bonoma. 1973. *Conflict, Power, and Games.* Chicago: Aldine.

Weber, Max. 1947. *The Theory of Social and Economic Organization.* Translated by A. M. Henderson and T. Parsons, and edited by T. Parsons. New York: The Free Press.

Wrong, Dennis. 1968. "Some Problems in Defining Social Power." *American Journal of Sociology* 73:673–81.

Zelditch, Morris, Jr. and Henry A. Walker. 1984. "Legitimacy and the Stability of Authority." Pp. 1–25 in *Advances in Group Processes: A Research Annual,* vol. 1, edited by E. J. Lawler. Greenwich, CT: JAI Press.

# EIGHT

# Justice

KAREN A. HEGTVEDT

## INTRODUCTION

To introduce the topic of fairness in interpersonal relations, I asked my social psychology students to tell me what kinds of situations they view as fair or as unfair. Despite the early hour (8:30 A.M.), the question awakened an outpouring of sentiment and reason. Students had no difficulty enumerating what they thought were unfair situations: increases in tuition to pay for new buildings that few students would use; the exclusion of student representatives on committees allocating funds for social events, gym equipment, and staffing hours for the campus computer labs; sorority and fraternity "back-test files" providing members with an advantage over others in preparing for an exam; lending a friend some item and never seeing it again; and having a roommate who does nothing around the apartment except generate a mess. Irritation, indignation, and even anger colored each person's description of an unfair situation. Along with the emotional coloring, however, there were many reasons why the students saw these situations as unfair. These reasons seemed consistent with what the students knew about the situation and the consequences they encountered. Not all students agreed that each situation constituted unfairness. Little of the discussion focused on what sort of situations students view as fair, except by the implication that the opposites of an unfair situation would be fair.

On the surface, the discussion might appear to be simply a student gripe session. But, in fact, the students' descriptions exemplify what social psychological theories of distributive and procedural justice attempt to explain. "Distributive justice" situations typically involve two or more parties (individuals or groups) who are engaged in social exchange or in the allocation of benefits or burdens. The task these parties face is that of establishing whether a particular distribution (or a distribution pattern) conforms to normative notions of fairness. Situations

described by the students illustrating distributive justice issues include the allocation of tuition money to various projects, the distribution of household tasks among
roommates, and the exchange of items between friends. Similarly, "procedural
justice" perspectives focus on the development of fair procedures underlying the
establishment of a distribution, and on assessments of the violation of these
procedures. The membership composition of an allocation committee or the differential access to information ultimately relevant to the distribution of grades represent procedural justice issues. Generally, the three issues critical to understanding
justice processes in interaction are: (1) How do principles of justice develop? (2)
Why do individuals have different perceptions of injustice? and (3) How do people
respond to unfair situations? A great deal of empirical research addresses these
questions, albeit from different theoretical traditions.

The first question pertains to that which was missing in the earlier discussion:
a definition of what is fair. This chapter opens with a general analysis of the basis
for principles of justice, and the three following sections address each of the
above questions with specific reference to distributive justice. The second section
examines the development of distributive justice principles, with emphasis on the
influence of situational, relational, and personal factors. To address the question
that reflects the disagreement voiced by the students about the unfairness of some
situations, the third section looks at sources of such disagreement in terms of
people's perception of information and social comparisons. Evaluations of a
distribution as unfair lead to the last question regarding responses to injustice.
The fourth section examines individual and collective reactions to distributive
injustice. Because similar questions pertain to the fairness of the procedures
underlying distributions, the fifth section briefly explores these issues as well as
attends to the relationship between procedural and distributive justice. A critique
of the adequacy of existing justice perspectives constitutes the sixth section. The
final section of the chapter highlights basic points necessary to an understanding
of justice processes in social interaction.

## THE BASIS OF JUSTICE PRINCIPLES

At the basis of the development of justice principles are *descriptive* distribution
and procedural rules. The former indicates ways in which benefits or burdens
(outcomes, more generally) may be distributed to two or more recipients, and the
latter represents ways in which parties may proceed toward a distribution decision.

Researchers have examined two broad categories of distribution rules. "Individual deserving rules" dictate that outcomes should be commensurate with the
level of an individual characteristic or combination of characteristics (e.g., contributions, performance, effort, status, needs). By stating, for example, "to each
party according to his or her contributions," these rules highlight an individual-
level characteristic as the basis for deserving a portion of the outcomes being

distributed. In contrast, "outcome distribution rules" ignore individual-level differences and instead pertain to the shape of the resulting distribution of outcomes. These rules, in effect, specify prior to the actual distribution how much each recipient should get. For example, rules requiring an equal division of outcomes or a minimum level of pay set *a priori* constraints on the shape of the outcome distribution.

Initially, most justice research focused on a particular usage of a contributions or performance-based individual deserving rule (Adams 1965; Homans 1974; Walster, Walster, and Berscheid 1978). This usage, termed "equity," specifically includes comparisons between two people in terms of what they bring to the situation (i.e., relevant individual characteristics or "inputs") and what they get from the situation (i.e., their benefits less costs, or "outcomes"). Equity obtains when the ratio of outcomes to inputs for each person is equivalent across actors. In other words, an equity comparison ensures that an individual deserving rule has been applied consistently for a set of people. Thus, for two actors, a and b, the equity formula involves the following:

$$\text{Outcomes}_a/\text{Inputs}_a = \text{Outcomes}_b/\text{Inputs}_b$$

For example, if actor a works twice as hard on a task compared to actor b, then an equitable distribution would ensure that a's outcomes would be twice as high as those of b. Inequitable underreward (overreward) exists when one person receives fewer (greater) rewards than dictated by his or her level of inputs.

Early work emphasizing the equity rule tended to focus primarily on reactions to inequity, as discussed below in the fourth section. Later work, however, emphasized the multiple distribution rules that may underlie notions of distributive justice (e.g., Deutsch 1975; Leventhal, Karuza, and Fry 1980; Reis 1986). The multiple conceptions approach pertains mainly to the development of justice principles; as described further in the next section, research addresses factors affecting choices among three distribution rules—equity (or a contribution-based rule), equality, and a needs-based rule.

In addition to considering multiple distribution rules, researchers more recently have attended to conceptions of procedural justice (Thibaut and Walker 1975; Leventhal, 1980; Lind and Tyler 1988). Procedural rules subject to fairness evaluations pertain to the selection of decision makers, the establishment of "ground rules" for decision making, the means and extent of information gathering, and the mechanisms available for changing decisions.

These distribution and procedural rules provide a means for describing the consequences of exchange and allocation or the steps toward a distribution decision, but they do so *without* reference to justice per se. Justice obtains when behavior in a situation is consistent with a justice principle—either as a guideline for interaction or as a consequence of responses to the violation of the principle. But what distinguishes a justice principle from a distribution or procedural rule? In other words, what does justice mean?

Distribution and procedural rules form the basis of justice principles, but the latter connote far more than a description of a distribution or process. What criteria are used to determine whether a particular rule represents a justice principle in a given situation? First, a justice principle should foster effective social cooperation to promote individual well-being (Deutsch 1975). Second, a justice principle should be impartial to individual interests (Rawls 1971). These two criteria imply that a distribution or procedural rule that benefits the collectivity, not simply self-interests, is likely to be considered just by a number of people. Thus, a third criterion for distinguishing a justice principle is that people share the perception that the rule promotes mutually agreeable exchange or allocation (Reis 1986).

To the extent that a distribution or procedural rule ensures social welfare, appears impartial, and meets with the approval of the people it affects, it represents a "normative" conception of justice. As a normative justice principle, people employ the rule as a basis for ensuring fairness in future distributions or procedures and expect others to similarly use it. As a consequence, individuals experience the fulfillment of their expectations and feel a sense of control in similar situations. For example, assuming the university community perceives as fair a university policy stating that the composition of an allocation committee should include all parties affected by the allocation, then students would expect the administration to appoint some of them to a committee distributing funds for social events, gym equipment, and computer lab staffing. Failure to put students on the committee would stimulate allegations of injustice; but the existing policy gives students a sense of control—they can invoke it to redress the injustice.

The normative conceptualization of justice provides an ideal guide for interaction; it reduces the time and effort necessary to acting justly in a situation and exists as a moral criterion against which to judge the rightness of other distributions or procedures. But, in reality, people often hold differing conceptions of what the justice norm should be. For example, some roommates might feel that everyone should do an equal share of the housework while others might argue that whoever spends the most time in the apartment should do more. Or, fraternity and sorority members might argue that others have chosen not to join the Greek system and thus have no right to complain that access to back-test files is unfair. Resolving these conflicting notions of justice requires an understanding of how justice norms develop as well as an examination of the conditions that foster different notions of justice.

## DEVELOPING PRINCIPLES OF DISTRIBUTIVE JUSTICE

How is it that individuals come to agree that a particular distribution rule is just? A response to that question depends upon the socio-historical and cultural context in which the individuals live as well as their own beliefs, past experiences, and actual interaction. Social psychologists have approached the development of justice principles in two ways.

First, they have theorized about the process by which individuals come to agree implicitly or explicitly on a fair distribution at both the individual and societal levels. An exchange approach provides an explanation for the development of justice rules at both levels of analysis whereas allocation approaches typically focus on the individual level. In addition, socialization processes ensure the transmission of consensual justice beliefs over time. In the giving and taking of resources through exchange, for example, roommates might settle on a fair distribution of household tasks as a result of one agreeing to cook if the other cleans the bathroom. Also, in allocation situations, emphasis rests on decision making or choice processes; for example, in allocating scholarship funds, the group might first set the goals of the distribution and then assess how various distribution rules fulfill the goals. Second, on a more empirical level, researchers have investigated individuals' actual preferences for particular rules under various conditions. For example, do friends prefer to divide up their rewards from a task equally or equitably? Do strangers make the same choices? The empirical studies correspond to theoretical premises but, unfortunately, many of the investigations are not direct tests of those premises.

## Theoretical Approaches to the Development of Justice Principles

The processes underlying the development of consensual perceptions of justice occur at both the societal and the individual levels. At the societal level, the process focuses on what distribution rule generally epitomizes a normative ideal of justice. At the individual level, the process involves socialization, which teaches children normative notions of justice, and actual interaction that allows individuals to come to agreement about the fairness of their exchanges or allocations. It is likely that what people learn through socialization about their society's justice norms conditions the ways in which they develop a sense of fairness in interaction situations.

Most approaches to the development of general justice principles focus on links between individual behavior and societal needs. Walster et al. (1978) first state that individuals will try to maximize their outcomes, but in their second proposition, they suggest that groups maximize their rewards by evolving accepted systems for apportioning resources (rewarding people who treat others equitably and punishing those who do not). Because exchange highlights what individuals contribute to a situation, it heightens concern with proportional rewards and provides the basis for equity as a principle of justice. Such an emphasis also corresponds to the tenets of capitalistic economic systems that promote individualism and the link between investment and profit.

Stolte (1987; Chapter 7, this volume) argues that equity is not the only societal justice norm to emerge from social exchange. Rather, he suggests that variation in the structure of exchange leads negotiating parties to different ''meaning agreements.'' The symbolic meaning conveyed by the negotiated agreement is the basis for transforming actual exchange patterns into normative rules. For example, when people form a coalition to counteract the power of an exchange partner, Stolte predicts that equality will emerge as an agreed-upon justice principle. In contrast, if a situation remains imbalanced despite coalition development, he predicts that some form of equity based on differences in the statuses of exchange partners will develop as a justice principle.

The development of general justice principles ensures legitimacy and stability in a society insofar as they are transmitted to the members of the society. Socialization refers to the process by which individuals become participating members of a society and learn the accepted values, beliefs, and behaviors of their group. Children learn about justice much like they learn about other phenomena: through experience coupled with behavioral reinforcement and punishment, through the development of cognitive capabilities, through observation, and directly through instruction (see Montada 1980).

In Western societies, children's conceptions of justice seem to change with age-related modifications in their cognitive capabilities and their ability to take the perspectives of others. Very young children tend to desire obviously selfish distributions. As they grow older, they opt for the simplicity of equal distributions. When they are able to understand the link between individual contributions and rewards, they begin to favor equitable distributions. Socialization explanations also provide a foundation for understanding why people from different cultural and socioeconomic backgrounds vary in their value emphasis and thus their justice conceptions.

Even with a shared belief in equity as the dominant form of justice, individuals may differentially interpret what is equitable or even believe that another rule provides a more just distribution. Within interaction, beliefs about justice stem from two aspects of a situation.

First, as proposed in their status-value approach to justice, Berger and his colleagues (Berger et al. 1972) explain that people develop stereotyped conceptions of how levels of characteristics represented in groups ''go with'' levels of rewards (called ''goal objects''). The characteristics and the rewards carry status value, which is an evaluation of the prestige ranking attached to them. Although status value is difficult to quantify, its significance to individuals within a social group extends beyond the consummatory value typically attached to inputs and outcomes (i.e., their economic value). For example, a small wage differential between a secretary and a clerk-typist might not purchase that much more food or clothing, but it represents status differences between the two positions showing that the secretary's job is more important. Berger et al. suggest that people expect consistency between the status value of characteristics and rewards. ''Referential standards'' reflect this consistency by defining how the characteristics of ''generalized others'' representing similar individuals correspond to their rewards. When a situation activates individuals' referential standards, they feel entitled to a certain level of benefits. As a consequence, they are likely to promote distribution rules that ensure fulfillment of those expectations. (For a discussion of status processes, see also Balkwell's Chapter 6.)

A second aspect of interaction important to developing shared notions of justice is negotiation (Blau 1964; Stolte 1987). Typically, negotiations involve resources that are divisible and possess consummatory value, although they may also carry status value. To achieve an agreed upon division or exchange of resources requires give and take and eventual compromise. Because negotiating parties may try to get as much of the desired resource as possible (i.e., they are self-interested), their individual conceptions of justice may reflect this initially. But, settlement of competing claims creates a shared conception of justice and a more efficient way to handle future interactions.

To illustrate, consider two people living together for the first time who must work out a division of the household chores. Although the two are from similar cultural and socioeconomic backgrounds, Mary comes from a large family while Amy has no siblings. In Mary's family, everyone helped to keep up the household; her referential standard is that all contribute to chores and each is rewarded by a clean house and other privileges. In contrast, Amy rarely had to "pitch in"; her mother typically took care of all the household tasks. In their new living situation, Mary expects Amy to do half of the housework whereas Amy is comfortable leaving it in Mary's experienced hands. In effect, Mary defines an equality rule as fair in the situation whereas Amy promotes an equity rule, based on experience and skill, as fair. These different beliefs about the fair division of household tasks spur arguments and prevent the completion of any housework. How can these two roommates resolve their competing conceptions of a fair distribution of household labor?

First, Mary and Amy may provide each other with information on their referential standards—what they learned to expect in their own families. Then, each may defend why the other's expectations are inappropriate in the situation. Mary might argue that she is not Amy's mother and thus to expect her to do the housework is wrong. Amy may counter this argument by focusing on her inability to perform chores: she never learned to cook, she has no idea about the uses of various cleaners, pushing a vacuum cleaner strains her muscles, etc. The solution to the impasse between Mary, who refuses to take on all the household chores and Amy, who contends that she lacks the skill to perform such chores depends on what each person is willing to do to come to some agreement. Mary may volunteer to teach Amy how to use various cleaners, how to run the vacuum, and even how to cook. They might work on these tasks jointly for the first month and then evaluate what each person is good at and likes. Through this evaluation, they should achieve some compromise about the division of household tasks. Perhaps Amy will take on all of the cleaning tasks (because they require little skill) while Mary might do the more skilled chore of cooking. The distribution of tasks emerges in accord with preferences and the number of hours each devotes to the household. Assuming that both parties agree that the equitable distribution is fair, the arguments should cease, the apartment be kept clean, and the roommates well-fed.

In contrast to the negotiation illustrated in the example as a means to develop justice principles, in allocation situations a person or group typically faces a decision: how to apportion benefits (or burdens) to a circle of recipients. Although, as described further below, there is a great deal of empirical work on allocation decisions, only one theoretical perspective stands out.

Leventhal et al. (1980) propose a theory of allocation preferences that encompasses concerns with justice. The theory rests on two underlying assumptions. The first assumption is that individuals prefer a distribution that helps them to achieve their goals, which may include fairness, self-interest, obedience to authority, or other pragmatic concerns. The second assumption is that people assess how various types of distribution rules are likely to fulfill their goals. They then choose the rule or combination of rules for which the expectation of fulfilling their goal(s) is the highest.

For example, consider an administrative committee at a private university that must allocate $50,000 in scholarship funds to ten recipients with similar academic performances. The committee values fairness but also pragmatic considerations, such as racial and economic heterogeneity on campus. In making its decision, the committee reviews how each possible distribution rule might help to achieve its goals. An equal distribution of $5,000 each ensures the greatest fairness by indicating impartiality but the amount covers expenses for only one semester. An allocation based on needs would give the three low-income recipients enough for a full year of expenses ($10,000 each) and approximately $2,600 to each remaining recipient. A status-based rule might emphasize racial heterogeneity and thus allocate more money to the two minority recipients. Because the committee pursues multiple goals, it is likely to combine various distribution rules. For example, to ensure fairness, it may provide a minimum level of funds to all recipients. Then, to address pragmatic goals, it may provide minority and low-income students with greater funds; thus $3,500 to each recipient may fulfill concerns with fairness and $3,000 extra to the five recipients who fall into categories defined by the pragmatic goals may fulfill those goals.

In any situation involving goals other than or in addition to fairness, it is likely that the allocation decision will not conform strictly to the normative conception of justice. Such divergence is particularly likely if the goals pursued include self-interest. Although not proposed as specific tests of Leventhal et al.'s allocation preference theory, the empirical studies of allocation highlight factors affecting what appears to be the pursuit of self-interested goals and the conditions under which allocation decisions appear fair.

## Empirical Preferences for Distribution Rules in Allocation Situations

A great deal of research investigates factors affecting individual allocation preferences or "choices among justice rules." Typically, studies involving the allocation of benefits or burdens to a circle of recipients focus on how various factors affect individual choices among equity, equality, and/or needs as distribution rules (see reviews by Cook and Hegtvedt 1983; Major and Deaux 1982; Törnblom 1992). Factors such as situational characteristics, cultural beliefs, relational characteristics, and individual attributes presumably influence the goals that allocators pursue and their expectations about particular distributions. Two general types of studies provide the basis for inferring individuals' allocation preferences: situations involving the individual as a "first party" allocator, apportioning resources to him or herself as well as to other individuals, and situations involving a "third party" allocator who will not receive any portion of the resources.

In terms of situational factors shaping allocation decisions, both first and third party allocators seem to agree about which distribution rules are fair when situational goals of productivity, cooperation, or social welfare are specified (Leventhal et al. 1980). To elicit productivity, allocators typically prefer a performance-based equity rule whereas to increase group harmony and solidarity, allocators generally opt for an equal distribution. Preference for a needs-based individual deserving rule emerges when the situation emphasizes the well-being of group members. The goals enhancing equality and needs-based distribution preferences reinforce the cooperation characterizing family and friendship situations. In contrast, the preference for equity in productivity-oriented situations corresponds to basic underlying tenets of capitalist ideology that promote individualism and competition.

In fact, beliefs about the fairness of income inequalities in capitalistic societies support an equitable distribution of earnings (Kluegel and Smith 1986). The value of individualism in capitalistic societies directs attention to the individual achievements that lie at the basis of equitable distributions. Evidence suggests that people's judgments of the relationship between individual-level characteristics (e.g., education, occupation, sex, race, marital status, family size) and income involve balancing merit considerations with those of need (Alves and Rossi 1978). Individual characteristics, however, influence the assessment of the fairness of income inequalities; people with higher personal incomes or who rate higher on the merit indicators tend to judge income inequalities as more fair.

Generally, cultural beliefs stemming from the ideology or the economic system of a group may influence allocation decisions (Major and Deaux 1982). Theoretically, like situational goals, such beliefs promote certain values that may shape specific allocation goals and thus actual allocation decisions. The similarities in the capitalist ideologies of North American and European countries seem to diminish the influence of other cultural differences on allocation preferences (see Major and Deaux 1982). But, in comparisons between countries with divergent histories and cultural beliefs, differences are evident. For example, Leung and Bond (1984) compare the distribution preferences or presumably collectivity-oriented Chinese students to presumably individually-oriented American students. Their results show that Americans tend to prefer equitable distributions whereas the Chinese tend to favor an equal distribution, especially when the division is between members of the allocator's own group.

In addition to situational and cultural factors, a great deal of research has focused on how the structure and nature of the relationship between the allocator and the recipient group affects the allocation decision. Structural characteristics of allocator/recipient relationships reflect differences in the positions occupied by the individuals; these positions may be defined in terms of the individuals' relative "performances" or contributions to the group task, power over others, or formal roles. The nature of the relationship generally refers to the affective bonds and feelings of obligation between group members.

In the absence of affective bonds, structural characteristics of the relationship tend to exert relatively strong influences on distribution rule choices (Cook and Hegtvedt 1983). When performance is the only basis for differentiating recipients, the typical trend is for allocators who are high performers in a group to select an equity rule, whereas allocators who are low performers tend to choose an equality rule. Similarly, occupants of power-advantaged positions, who fare well in the distribution of material rewards, perceive the distribution as fairer than disadvantaged individuals (Cook and Hegtvedt 1986). Thus, people appear to prefer the rule from which they benefit most. When more than one input distinguishes persons, they appear to differentially weigh inputs in equitable divisions; not surprisingly, allocators weigh more heavily those inputs on which they rate highly. A consequence of these choices is that allocators ensure themselves a relatively large portion of the reward. Their distributions appear to promote their own self-interested claims to material rewards.

The claim an individual makes to material rewards depends in part upon that person's inferences about the causes of the different contributions of the group members. Allocators are more likely to emphasize those contributions that they perceive to be under each individual's control and that directly affect the amount of rewards the group receives (Cohen 1982). For example, allocators who perceive their high performance to be due to their effort on the task rather than due to chance are more likely to make equitable distributions; when they attribute their contributions to luck, they are more likely to prefer equal distributions. It appears that if people can attribute their performances or, more generally, their inputs to something about themselves (e.g., effort, ability) then they are more likely to express self-interested allocation preferences.

The tendency toward self-interest emerges under *impersonal* conditions; that is, when group members are strangers who work independently on related tasks and who anticipate no further interaction with each other. In contrast, under conditions fostering the existence or development of affective bonds, distribution choices appear less self-interested. For example, friends typically employ an equality rule as a basis for distributing rewards despite differences in performance levels whereas strangers opt for an equitable division (Austin 1980). But, even among strangers, if situational conditions draw attention to the needs of other group members, to the role obligations of the allocator, or even to existing normative standards of justice, allocators are likely to refrain from making materially self-interested distributions.

Why does the affective nature of the relationship between allocators and recipient groups alter allocation decisions and, implicitly, the perceptions of just distributions? First, in groups characterized by friendly relations, allocators are likely to be more sensitized to the teamlike behavior of group members and to their obligations as allocators for the team. As a consequence, allocators act more politely, distributing rewards in a manner that benefits others more than themselves. By doing so, allocators present themselves as generous to others and are likely to receive social rewards in terms of thanks and liking as well as favorable evaluations by outsiders. A selfish presentation, in contrast, might engender social costs in the terms of dislike and ostracism. Thus, the second reason for allocators to make less materially self-interested allocations is the potential for social rewards. Ironically, choices for distribution rules that fail to maximize allocators' material rewards may minimize social costs and maximize social rewards and thereby be actually consistent with their self-interests.

To illustrate some of these ideas, imagine a committee of students, faculty members, and administrators who must decide how to distribute recent funds given to the university. Each group occupies a different power position in the university hierarchy and represents different interests; the students want to use the money for scholarships, the faculty advocates expenditures for new faculty positions, and the administration proposes applying the money to the expense of renovating their building. Ultimately, the administrators make the allocation decision. To the extent that there is an arena for sharing interests and forging ties between the diverse groups, it is unlikely that the administrators will devote the funds solely to their own interests, in part for fear of angering the other groups. Rather, the committee is likely to work out a solution that provides each group with a share of the pie and maintains amiable relations. Through the committee's deliberations, they develop a shared conception of a just distribution.

Variation in the emphasis individuals place on the well-being of others is a major explanation for differences in the allocation preferences of men and women. With sex of subject as the most investigated individual-level factor, studies consistently show that female allocators take less for themselves than male allocators do, regardless of whether their inputs are equal to, higher than, or less than their partners' (Major and Deaux 1982). Female allocators' generosity toward their co-recipients may stem from traditional patterns of female gender role socialization that emphasize an orientation toward social relationships (termed an "interpersonal orientation"). In fact, some evidence suggests that, regardless of sex, individuals who are interpersonally oriented tend to pay themselves less than those who are agency oriented, emphasizing traditionally male values of achievement and success (Watts, Vallacher, and Messé 1982). Interpersonal orientation appears to decrease preferences for distributions that materially benefit the allocator. Such an orientation enhances the value of social rewards and the preference for distributions that implicitly or explicitly provide such rewards.

Of course, the use of "third party" allocators who are not co-recipients of the reward eliminates concerns with the role of self-interest on allocation decisions. Such allocators bring to the allocation the impartiality that characterizes just decisions. Their distributions tend to ensure benefits for all group members. In fact, individuals explicitly instructed to produce a fair allocation produce one that clearly differs from those made by co-recipients, who tend to inflate their own rewards (Messick and Sentis 1979).

The correspondence between first and third parties' distribution preferences depends upon the extent to which situational, cultural, relational, and individual factors enhance concerns about social rewards along with material ones. Conditions emphasizing group solidarity goals or values, the affect among recipients, or concerns about others are likely to encourage first party allocators to concentrate on social rewards and costs in the process of choosing a distribution rule. As a consequence, they are more likely to make choices that enhance the welfare of the collectivity and thus coincide with the choices of third party allocators. So even if an individual pursues a self-interested goal, his or her preferences may result in a distribution consensually judged as fair.

The influence of self-interest on allocation preferences and on the process of developing justice principles through negotiation is somewhat paradoxical. But, even when self-interested individuals agree about what sort of distribution rule meets the other criteria of justice (i.e., collective welfare and impartiality), in any particular situation individuals may differentially perceive whether the consensual conception of justice is upheld. Their perceptions depend not only upon their interests, but also upon the information available to them and their knowledge about similar individuals. Ultimately, some may feel unfairly treated while others perceive that the situation is fair. The next section focuses on these sources for potential differential assessments of potential injustice within a situation.

## DIFFERENTIAL ASSESSMENTS OF INJUSTICE

Injustice refers to the violation of an agreed-upon or normative justice principle, typically equity. When individuals attempt to determine whether they are fairly treated, they must assess how their outcomes compare to what they expected based on the distribution principle. Most research on the perception of injustice in interaction focuses on violations of the equity principle. To assess inequity, individuals must first determine the relevance and weighting of various inputs and outcomes in the situation to determine how each individual "measures up" (i.e., their levels of deserving) and then whether the respective ratios of outcomes to inputs is equivalent across all recipients or to some standard. Thus the assessment of justice involves perceptions of rankings and social comparisons.

## Perceptions of Inputs and Outcomes

Typically, theories of equity (Adams 1965; Walster et al. 1978) assume that individuals will similarly perceive the inputs and outcomes of those involved in an exchange or allocation. This simplifying assumption omits consideration of a number of issues raised by other justice researchers, especially in light of developments in the area of social perception processes (see Schneider, Hastorf, and Ellsworth 1979; Chapter 4 of this volume). In the absence of any specific theory addressing the perceptual elements of the assessment of injustice, this section focuses primarily on these issues.

As an illustration, first consider the following scenario. When parents allocate privileges to their teenage children, they must think about what the children have done to deserve the privileges (i.e., the inputs) as well as what privileges are at stake (i.e., the outcomes). Parents might consider grades in school, help provided around the house, care for younger siblings, age, and even gender as inputs while outcomes may pertain to the amount of an allowance, the weekend curfew, use of the car, and increased responsibility. Whether the teenagers perceive the allocation that their parents make as fair depends in part upon what they believe constitutes an input or an outcome, which inputs and outcomes they consider relevant in the situation, and how they weigh those factors.

Beliefs about what constitutes an input or outcome refers most generally to what might be included in each category (see Cook and Parcel 1977). Some factors are obviously either a potential basis for deserving or an outcome because of time ordering, potential for individual change in the factor, or characteristics of the situation. For example, gender and age most likely constitute inputs because of an individual's inability to change them and their presence prior to all other factors. Given the situation described in the example, grades are likely to rate as inputs; in academic situations, however, they may be outcomes. Most ambiguous in the example is "responsibility for oneself." This factor may be an input—something that frees up parents' time and thus is a basis for rewards—or an outcome, as a reward for good behavior. If parents distribute allowance increases according to the responsibility their children take on, but their children consider responsibility as a reward and fail to assume it on their own, then despite their efforts at other tasks, their allowances do not increase nor do they receive more responsibility for themselves; as a consequence the children are likely to feel unjustly treated.

The relevance of an input refers to whether it is included in the equity ratio, whereas weighting focuses on the relative importance or value of a relevant input (Cohen 1982). Individuals are most likely to consider as relevant those inputs they perceive the recipients to have control over, especially if these inputs contribute directly to the production of a particular outcome. For example, to the extent that children's completion of household tasks and care for younger siblings allows both parents to work full-time and generate income, those inputs are highly relevant to decisions about the distribution of children's allowances. The same inputs may be less relevant to the distribution of other outcomes. Of the potential inputs listed in the example, a child's grades may be most relevant for the distribution of car use privileges but irrelevant to the distribution of allowances. The relevance of particular inputs and outcomes ultimately depends upon the nature and context of the distribution. Thus, for example, while parents may consider good grades a relevant basis for some kinds of distributions, teenage friends are less likely to consider them in distributing party invitations.

With the establishment of relevant inputs and outcomes, the next step is to determine the relative weights of these inputs. How important is each input to the outcome to be distributed? Variation in importance stems from the extent of knowledge about the inputs and how well one rates on a given input. For example, a teenager might emphasize how much help he or she has provided a younger sibling but the parents might be unaware of this assistance because both were at work. Or, parents and children might differ on their evaluation of the importance of inputs due to their different interests; the teenager may emphasize his or her outstanding academic performance whereas parents, who need help around the house, might focus on their child's failure to do household chores. By more heavily weighting those inputs on which one does well, individuals ensure themselves a larger share of the distribution.

The assessment of the relevance and weighting of inputs and outcomes generally relies upon the information processing of allocators and recipients. But as implied by the above examples, the process of gathering information underlying justice evaluations is rather subjective. More explicitly, cognitive and motivational biases (see Markovsky, Chapter 4, this volume) color justice assessments.

Cognitive biases, referring to errors in the perception of available information stemming from unequal attention to various elements, include the expectancy bias, the halo/horn effect, and the availability bias. The expectancy bias suggests that judgments are overly influenced by the information that confirms evaluators' expectations based primarily on stereotypes. Such a bias explains why a teenage daughter tolerates her younger brother's greater car privileges; traditionally, men have been expected to drive on dates. The halo/horn bias further emphasizes how stereotypical interpretations of inputs may be misleading. The halo bias refers to consistency in positive evaluations whereas the horn bias indicates consistency in negative evaluations. Parents, for example, might perceive that their daughter who has very high grades also contributes more to the household whereas they may perceive their son who has lower grades to do very little around the house, despite the fact that he may actually do more than his sister. Thus, a consequence of the halo/horn bias is to overlook inconsistency in different input levels, to the detriment of some recipients and the benefit of others. The availability bias represents tendencies to assess events by the ease with which instances are brought to mind; increased familiarity, perceptual salience, or recency heighten attention to events. For example, parents may overemphasize grades in their allocation decisions if these are made on the day report cards come home.

Egocentric biases typically represent the self-interests of the evaluator; these biases may operate directly through interests or indirectly through cognitive biases. Indicators of an egocentric bias include the evaluation of one's own or one's group's inputs or outcomes in a more favorable way than those of another person or group, and giving greater weight to an input on which one rates highly. Such biases reveal the importance of taking the perceiver's position into account in the assessment of justice. Thus, given the different positions occupied by teenagers and their parents, as well as the multiple configurations of inputs and outcomes, it is not surprising that teenagers and parents potentially possess different perceptions of fairness in a situation.

Perceptions of justice are most likely to coincide when: (1) there is a limited number of inputs and outcomes to consider; (2) individuals come to some agreement on the relevance and weighting of various factors; and (3) all parties similarly perceive the available information. Also, explicit statements of what allocators consider in their distribution are likely to result in more similar assessments. For example, job evaluations for promotions and wage increases also involve multiple inputs and outcomes, but less divergent perceptions of justice are likely to emerge in the work situation than in the family situation because of explicit presentation of promotion and wage rules. The assessment of whether justice obtains, however, is incomplete without consideration of the comparisons between individuals and groups.

## Social Comparisons

Social comparisons generally refer to a process by which individuals compare themselves to other people in order to evaluate their own abilities, feelings, and opinions (see Festinger 1954). In the absence of some objective form of measurement, these social comparisons provide a basis for individuals to understand their relative standing within a group. As applied to justice processes, social comparisons help individuals to determine whether a justice principle has been consistently applied to the distribution of outcomes across all recipients. The first comparison that individuals are likely to make is to evaluate whether their own outcomes correspond with outcomes expected on the basis of the appropriate justice principle. Then, individuals may perform several types of social comparisons in order to assess whether justice obtains for others in the situation. These other types of comparisons are described in three different theoretical approaches to injustice: equity theory, status-value theory, and relative deprivation.

The equity approaches (Adams 1965; Walster et al. 1978) focus primarily on the ratios of outcomes to inputs for each party to an exchange. The comparison underlying the assessment of equity is thus between two similarly situated people who are interacting directly or indirectly through their involvement with the same third party. These person-to-person or "local" comparisons provide the basis for determining whether one individual is over- or underrewarded compared to the other person. For example, a worker compares his or her pay for eight hours of work to that of another who works only four hours; equity exists if the first worker receives twice as much as the second. If both earn the same amount, the first worker is likely to feel underpaid *vis-à-vis* the coworker. But the perceived fairness of the second worker's pay remains ambiguous; he or she may also feel underpaid if others doing similar work earn more, or may feel justly paid if those similar others earn the same amount, or may even feel overpaid if similar workers earn what the first worker earned.

Knowing what individuals with characteristics similar to the perceiver earn eliminates the ambiguity resulting from the local comparison. In their status-value approach to justice, Berger et al. (1972) represent this sort of comparison as a referential standard. As previously defined, this standard exists as a frame of reference representing others who possess states of given characteristics that are associated with certain reward levels. To the extent that a situation activates a particular referential standard, individuals compare their outcomes to those expected on the basis of the standard to assess fairness for themselves as well as for their partner. In the work example, the referential standard would be all people doing the same work; if workers in a particular occupation typically earn $80 for eight hours of work, then equitable pay for the first worker would be $80 and for the second worker would be $40. If both workers earned $60, the first would be underpaid and the second overpaid. The referential standard helps to sort out whether one or both of the workers comprising the local comparison are underpaid, equitably paid, or overpaid. Shared sentiments of underpayment are the basis for collective injustice (the same is true for overpayment but such a state is less likely to elicit a negative reaction).

Complementing the individual-to-group comparisons represented by referential standards are group-to-group comparisons, which are represented in the relative deprivation approach to justice (Runciman 1966). Unlike equity and status-value approaches, which include consideration of "inputs," the relative deprivation approach concentrates solely on outcomes. This approach suggests that as individuals' expectations for outcomes increase, they feel relatively deprived if their actual outcomes are not as high as expected. Feelings of deprivation stem from comparing the level of outcomes for members of their group to that of another group whom they define as similar. For example, a group of secretaries at Company a may discover that all secretaries at Company b receive higher wages. Even though wages at Company a have increased over the years, they may still feel relatively deprived compared to their counterparts in the other company. This group-to-group comparison is distinct from the referential comparison insofar as it pertains to people not as individuals but as group members. (A referential comparison might involve a secretary at Company a comparing his or her salary to the average level of compensation for all secretaries in that company or even to all of those in Company b, assuming that he or she perceives similarity to secretaries in Company b).

Of particular importance in assessing justice is the choice of the type of comparison(s) and the actual referent, i.e., which particular person or group (see Masters and Smith 1987). Typically, people choose comparisons that are similar to themselves and proximal—individuals or groups with whom they can identify. In addition, people may choose comparisons that fulfill specific goals; some choices ensure self-enhancing comparisons while others result in neutral or even self-deprecating comparisons. For example, a group of janitors that seeks higher wages may defend their request by comparing themselves to custodial workers employed elsewhere rather than to groundsworkers in the same company.

Most likely, people use a variety of comparisons (see Markovsky 1985). When people select different comparisons, they may disagree about what is just. Extending the above example, the janitors may feel unfairly underpaid when they compare themselves to other janitors, but their employers may think that janitors are fairly paid *vis-à-vis* the groundsworkers (it may be the case that both groups are underpaid in their organization, however).

The structure of and information available in the situation are likely to shape comparison processes by leading individuals to different types and combinations of comparisons. As a result of different comparisons, coupled with variation in underlying perceptions of the relevance and weighting of inputs and outcomes, individuals may differ in their perceptions of justice. These perceptual and comparison processes will have important effects on how people—as individuals or collectivities—react to injustice.

## REACTIONS TO PERCEIVED INJUSTICE

### Individual Responses to Perceived Injustice

Theoretical approaches to individual reactions to perceived injustice focus on behavioral, cognitive, and emotional responses to the violation of the equity rule (Adams 1965; Homans 1974; Walster et al. 1978). The perspectives generally assume that individuals feel some sort of distress or tension when, based on the comparisons of their outcome/input ratio to another person's, they discover that their outcomes are inequitable. The distress varies directly with the magnitude and nature of the inequity and motivates individuals to seek redress for the injustice they suffer.

A large body of empirical research examines individual reactions to inequity (see Cook and Hegtvedt 1983). Several topics are of critical interest. First, what is the relationship between inequity and some form of distress? Second, assuming motivation to redress inequity, what factors influence the restoration of equity?

And, third, how do individuals choose among particular means to redress inequity?

Although the notion of distress is not well-defined, there is consistent empirical support for the expectation that underrewarded people feel the most distressed, followed by overrewarded individuals; equitably rewarded people should feel no distress. Homans (1974) suggests that emotional responses to inequity represent the nature of the distress that individuals feel. When individuals receive less than expected, they should feel angry; in contrast, individuals who receive more than expected should feel guilty.

Empirical results generally support a pattern of emotional reactions that shows the expression of positive emotions among equitably and even overrewarded individuals, and the expression of negative emotions among the underrewarded. There is evidence that overrewarded individuals express more guilt than others, but the threshold is much higher than for anger; overrewarded individuals tend to justify their higher rewards in terms of deserving and thus express generally positive emotions. For example, a babysitter whose going rate is $4 an hour would expect $12 for a three-hour job; if the "employers" pay the sitter only $10, he or she is likely to feel cheated and thus get angry whereas if the sitter receives $15, he or she is likely to assume that the employers were especially impressed with the child care and thus feel happy about the payment.

According to the exchange perspective on inequity (Adams 1965), individuals can attempt to eliminate the distress and restore equity in several ways: (1) altering their actual inputs; (2) altering their actual outcomes; (3) cognitively distorting either their inputs or outcomes; (4) cognitively distorting the other person's inputs or outcomes; (5) changing the object of the comparison from one person to another; or (6) leaving the situation. Walster et al. (1978) classify the first two options as means to restore "actual" equity while the latter options refer to restoration of what they label "psychological" equity. The type of restoration method people choose depends on the nature of the inequity as well as the "costs" of employing the various methods. For example, the underrewarded babysitter is likely to alter his or her outcomes by simply reminding the employer of the going rate for babysitting; the overrewarded babysitter's justification for the additional rewards cognitively distorts his or her inputs. Another strategy for the underrewarded sitter who fears that asking for more money might eliminate this family as a client (i.e., high costs for restoring actual equity) would be to change his or her conception of the going rate to $2.50 an hour or to eat more from the family's fridge while babysitting to compensate for the lower wage.

Most of the research on reactions to inequity stems from traditions involving "productivity" experiments that focus on changes in inputs or "reallocation" studies involving changes in outcomes. Typically, both types of studies involve the following scenario: individuals first work on a task, receiving performance feedback to indicate the level of their inputs, and then they are paid a specific amount which constitutes under-, over- or equitable rewards. In a follow-up session, they again work on a task as a means to assess their reaction to inequity; in the productivity studies, the measure of reactions is their performance level on the task (i.e., increases or decreases in inputs) and in the reallocation studies, the response is in terms of the subjects' own distribution of a second or "bonus" reward. Predictions for the productivity studies are that underrewarded individuals will decrease their inputs whereas overrewarded ones will increase their inputs; predictions for the reallocation studies are that underrewarded people will provide themselves with a greater share of the second reward as compensation for the earlier lower rewards, and overrewarded individuals will compensate those previously underrewarded. Do these predictions hold? In the case of the reallocation studies, evidence is clearly consistent with the predictions. The productivity studies, however, provide mixed results showing relatively consistent support for the prediction for overrewarded subjects but rather inconsistent support for the prediction for underrewarded individuals. This apparent disconfirmation of the prediction for the underrewarded subjects may stem from the nature of the type of reaction observed; underrewarded individuals might not lower their inputs for fear of obtaining even far lower outcomes, yet they might respond to their perceived injustice in other ways.

Unfortunately, despite the many studies on reactions to inequity, no study explicitly examines factors affecting selection of one form of equity restoration over another, or the conditions under which individuals choose not to respond to inequity. The lack of observable reactions in some existing studies may stem from unobserved psychological changes that redress inequity.

In addition, researchers offer other conceptual explanations for the apparent failure of people to redress inequity. Lerner (1980) suggests that individuals may construe events in ways that enable them to believe people get what they deserve. As a consequence of this "belief in the just world," they rationalize their own inequitable outcomes or, with regard to others' outcomes, they may hold the victims responsible for their misfortunes. For example, an executive who discovers that one of her colleagues has just been fired is likely to construct arguments distinguishing herself from that colleague (in order to ward off fears that she may suffer the same fate) and to derogate the colleague's work performance, thereby locating the cause of the dismissal in something about the colleague himself.

The ascription of responsibility for inequity relates to a second explanation for failure to observe inequity reactions: the attributions underlying assessments of inequity (Utne and Kidd 1980). People who perceive another person as responsible for their inequity distress are most likely to seek redress, especially if they feel control in the situation. In contrast, when people locate the cause of the inequity in chance, they are less likely to attempt redress. Extending the example above, if the person who was fired perceives that the dismissal stemmed from his boss's lack of information on his work projects, then he is likely to redress the perceived injustice by appealing to the boss; in contrast, if he is just one of many in a mass layoff, then the individual may do little to redress the perceived inequity.

Thus, to the extent that individuals assess the reasons for a perceived inequity, they gain a better idea of the most appropriate and least costly means to redress the inequity. In addition, in determining reasons for inequitable treatment an individual may discover that others are similarly treated. Continuing with the above example, assuming that everyone included in the mass layoff feels inequitably treated, the shared sentiments of injustice may provide a basis for collective reactions.

## Collective Responses to Perceived Injustice

Collective reactions to injustice involve the coalescing of individuals into a solidarity group that attempts to redress a common plight. Examples of collective responses to injustice include worker strikes, organized boycotts to protest discriminatory practices, and political rebellions. None of the formulations of individual reactions to inequity specifically address collective reactions, yet collective actions begin with individual-level feelings of injustice and perceptions that others share their plight, as determined through referential comparisons. In addition, collective reactions to injustice depend upon group-level power processes and the mobilization of resources, development of organization tactics, and leadership among the less powerful group (deCarufel 1981). Collective reactions to injustice thus highlight a relationship hardly considered by the individual-level perspective: the relationship between power and justice (see Cook and Hegtvedt 1986). It is likely that the power imbalances between groups that result in lower rewards for the power-disadvantaged group stimulates the collective response, while shared feelings of justice cement the solidarity of the deprived group.

Some experimental studies of coalition formation address responses of subordinate group members to inequitable treatment by their leader. Two studies show that when two "weak" members in three-person groups perceive their leader to treat them unfairly, they are likely to form "revolutionary" coalitions against the leader (Lawler 1975; Webster and Smith 1978). Other factors, however, affect the development of revolutionary coalitions. Consistent with Utne and Kidd's (1980) arguments about the effect of attributions on individual reactions to injustice, Lawler and Thompson (1978) find that subordinates who perceive their leader to have high responsibility for their inequity are more likely to revolt than those who perceive their leader to have low responsibility.

Another form of collective reaction focuses on how members of an existing group respond to a distribution rule promoted by a legitimate authority (Martin and Sell 1986). When group members consensually agree that there is another rule that enhances their collective benefit, they are more likely to attempt to overthrow the authority's rule, especially if the rule promoted by the authority is equality. But, an individual's decision to support rejection of the authority's rule grows more difficult when the person must choose between his or her own interests and the interests of other group members. Collective reactions to perceived injustice are thus most likely to emerge when self and group interests coincide. For example, an employer may decide to provide all full-time and part-time workers with the same monetary bonus at the end of the year. An individual who works full-time may agree with other full-timers that the bonuses should be distributed on the basis of how many hours a person has worked in the last year and thus join in a collective response to overthrow the employer's decision. In contrast, a part-time worker might hesitate to join the collective response because he or she benefits from the employer's decision. If there are more part-time workers than full-time workers, an attempt to overthrow the employer's decision would be likely to fail.

People's actual responses to distribute injustice—individual or collective—represent the end result of a series of assessments, both prior to the actual interaction situation as well as within the situation. The prior assessments include the establishment of a normative conception of justice. Within the situation, the assessments involve perceptions of the relevant criteria (i.e., the inputs and outcomes), the comparisons to others, and the evaluation of potential responses. These assessments also pertain to situations involving procedural justice, although as yet theory and research on this topic are less developed than those on distributive justice.

## PROCEDURAL JUSTICE

Research on procedural justice originally stemmed from work on legal attitudes and behavior, with particular emphasis on various legal strategies of conflict resolution (Austin and Tobiasen 1984; Thibaut and Walker 1975). More recently Lind and Tyler (1988) have illustrated the generality of procedural justice issues in a variety of contexts, including interpersonal relationships. Most procedural justice work pertains to only one of the questions posed above for distributive justice: how do procedural justice principles develop? But, in addition, research in procedural justice uniquely links the fairness of procedures to those of outcome distributions.

The theoretical approaches to the development of procedural justice principles note specific descriptive procedural rules which may gain normative status. These rules include: (1) consistency of procedures across persons and across time; (2) suppression of bias; (3) information accuracy; (4) mechanisms to correct bad decisions; (5) representativeness of participants to a decision; and (6) ethical standards (Leventhal et al. 1980).

Leventhal et al. (1980) propose a model similar to their allocation model. They assume that individuals prefer the procedural rules that are most likely to fill the most important goals. For example, if individuals pursue primarily a fairness goal, they are most likely to prefer the rules that promote collective welfare and impartiality, e.g., consistency of procedures across people and bias suppression.

But, as in their allocation model, because of the existence of multiple goals, a preference for any given procedure or combination of procedures does not necessarily ensure justice.

Consideration of different goals also characterize Lind and Tyler's (1988) dual approach to the establishment of procedural justice principles. Their self-interest model suggests that people seek control over decisions because of concerns with their own outcomes; thus people are likely to judge procedures that benefit themselves as fair. In contrast, their group value model suggests that individuals' group identities guide their procedural preferences and thus reflect how beneficial a procedure is to the group.

As reviewed by Lind and Tyler (1988), there appears to be support for both the self-interest and the group-value models of procedural preferences. For example, in studies of conflict resolution, people tend to prefer a method of resolution (termed "arbitration") that provides some control by allowing them to explain their positions to a third party and thus is consistent with the self-interest model. Other studies demonstrate that people evaluate organizational procedures that permit employees to participate in decisions—give them "voice"—as more fair than procedures prohibiting voice. Voice provides a basis for communicating group values. In effect, both of these procedural aspects ensure information accuracy, which presumably affects distributive justice evaluations.

Procedural justice researchers have examined the effects of violations of procedural justice principles on evaluations of distributive justice. If people judge procedures as unfair, they are more likely to assess outcome distributions as unfair also (see Lind and Tyler 1988). Fair procedures, especially those allowing control, make inequitable outcomes more palatable, however.

To illustrate some procedural justice issues, consider what a company president should do to ensure that workers accept revisions in their wage structure. The president should begin by selecting a wage revision committee that consists of representatives from various worker groups. Each committee member should feel that he or she has a voice in the decisions being made. To make the decisions, the committee should gather information from various sources about different jobs and then develop rules associating wage levels with job characteristics. Consistent application of these rules should generate a hierarchy of wages that all committee members perceive as fair. By ensuring procedural justice, the president is likely to obtain a wage distribution that most workers will evaluate as fair.

Theoretical developments in procedural justice are similar to those in distributive justice, with regard to the development of justice principles. Theory and research regarding the processes by which individuals assess procedural injustice and their reactions to perceived injustice, however, hardly exists. A useful strategy may be to integrate distributive and procedural justice perspectives into a single theoretical framework that distinguishes factors influencing one or both types of justice. In doing so, the distributive justice arena may benefit by greater attention to conflict and resolution, while the procedural justice arena may expand to address processes underlying procedural assessments and reactions.

## THE ADEQUACY OF JUSTICE PERSPECTIVES

Most of the social psychological work on distributive and procedural justice focuses on individual evaluations and their effects in small groups. Yet, no single, integrated theory of justice explains the development of justice principles, perceptions of injustice, and reactions to violations of the principles. Perspectives on distributive justice, however, appear to be more complete than those on procedural justice.

The models of allocation preference and procedure preference offered by Leventhal et al. (1980) most directly address the development of justice principles, though they fail to consider the other major justice questions. By emphasizing how given distribution or procedural rules help to achieve an individual's goal in the situation, the models address the development of justice principles as a problem of rational decision making. Thus, to predict which principles are likely to develop requires explicit consideration of individuals' motives. The empirical literature on allocation preferences, however, often fails to specify such motives *a priori*. In addition, these models fail to link individual motives and decisions to the context of the group in which they are embedded. Here, theory seems to lag behind empirical work, which includes consideration of the context, in terms of situational, cultural, and relationship factors affecting allocation preferences.

The equity approaches (Adams 1965; Homans 1974; Walster et al. 1978), rooted primarily in the social exchange perspective, offer some rudimentary theses about the development of equity as a justice principle. Unlike Leventhal et al.'s models, these theses do link the individual to the larger group. The equity approaches also address assessments of injustice by including consideration of local comparisons in the process; such comparisons, however, are a limited means of assessing injustices. And, despite the complexities involved in determining the relevant inputs and outcomes constituting the equity ratio, the perspective inadequately deals with perceptual issues. But, compared to other approaches, the equity perspective provides the most complete treatment of individual reactions to injustice. Research examining the conditions under which individuals select various modes of response to inequity is needed, however.

The status-value approach of Berger and his colleagues (Berger et al. 1972) complements the equity approaches by introducing consideration of referential standards. In terms of the development of particular distributive justice principles, these standards provide a basis for understanding people's reward expectations that may shape negotiations. In addition, a referential standard exists as a point of comparison in the assessment of injustice. This comparison facilitates the potential development of a sense of collective injustice by putting the local comparison into a social context. But, reactions to injustice are outside the scope of the perspective.

If none of the justice perspectives are complete, what would an integrated theory include? As suggested by this chapter, an outline of the components of such a theory involves: *a priori* specification of individual motivations, consideration of social perception and comparison processes, and assessment of response strategies. Of particular importance would be systematic identification of conditions inducing variation in each component.

An understanding of justice processes at the individual level will provide a basis for extending the analysis to the group level. A recurrent theme in the dissection of the three critical theoretical questions was emphasis on the social group: e.g., motivations may focus on collective welfare, structural position affects evaluations of distributions, stereotypes color interpretations of inputs and outcomes, referential standards based on groups help determine perceptions of injustice, reactions to injustice may be collective, and practices within the legal institution highlight aspects of procedural justice. The link between individual- and group-level justice, however, is more complex than simply the influence of group-level phenomena on individual evaluations. Presumably fair individual-level justice principles may produce outcome distributions judged as unfair (Jasso 1983). For example, the development of a justice principle associating job characteristics and wages may provide every worker with a fair wage, but the aggregation of wages may reveal intolerable inequalities among workers in the company. Such conflict between what is fair to the individual and what is fair to the group epitomizes the challenge inherent in creating a just society or maintaining justice in social relationships.

## SUMMARY

When the students in my class listed instances of unfair treatment, they included situations involving themselves as individuals (e.g., coping with a friend's borrowing, with a messy roommate) and as group members (e.g., consequences for students of tuition increases, of monetary allocations for student activities). Their list illustrated concerns in a variety of social relationships, thus highlighting the pervasiveness of justice processes in interaction.

The students agreed on many of the instances of injustice, which suggests the existence of general, consensual principles of justice. But as the review of theories and research in this chapter implies, these principles are not absolute. Although individuals in Western capitalist societies generally accept equity as a normative justice principle, within a specific situation individuals may disagree on what is fair. People invoke different rules of justice, such as when they argue for an equal rather than an equitable distribution. Or, they differentially perceive the types and levels of inputs and outcomes relevant to themselves as well as comparison others. Preferences for different rules or different evaluations of equity depend on a number of factors, including cultural values, individual interests, situational goals, available information, relationships among those affected, and even personal characteristics. As a consequence, justice is relative, not absolute.

The relative nature of justice raises several important issues. First, what is the relationship between justice and self-interest? The empirical literature on the development of justice principles suggests that individuals in impersonal conditions attempt to maximize their material outcomes. Similarly, individuals may use justice principles strategically to obtain outcomes that they value. Variation in individual interests, especially in conjunction with differences in other factors shaping justice preferences and evaluations, are likely to engender competing justice claims. The students disagreed on whether some particular situations were unfair, which indicates the possibility of conflict over what is just. Thus, a second major issue concerns the development and resolution of conflict over different justice claims. Finally, to the extent that affective bonds constrain the pursuit of self-interests (and thus possibly inhibit justice conflict), the relationship between the individual and the group is critical to the understanding of the development of justice rules, the perception of injustice, and the resolution of injustices.

The pervasiveness of justice concerns and the relativity of those concerns raise a number of issues. Even a commonplace, self-serving student gripe session can be a starting point in revealing the complex and multifaceted role of justice in social interaction.

## SUGGESTED READINGS

Cohen, Ronald L. 1982. "Perceiving Justice: An Attributional Perspective." Pp. 119–60 in *Equity and Justice in Social Behavior*, edited by J. Greenberg and R.L. Cohen. New York: Academic Press.

This chapter addresses important aspects of the process of assessing injustice. Cohen provides an extensive analysis of the role of causal and responsibility attributions in making allocation decisions. Emphasis rests particularly on the implications of attribution biases in determining justice.

Cook, Karen S. and Karen A. Hegtvedt. 1983. "Distributive Justice, Equity, and Equality." *Annual Review of Sociology* 9:217–41.

This review article emphasizes the empirical research on individuals' allocation preferences and reactions to inequity. The paper also considers links between social psychological approaches to distributive justice and sociological theories of power, conflict, and social change.

Cook, Karen S. and Toby L. Parcel. 1977. "Equity Theory: Directions for Future Research." *Sociological Inquiry* 47:75–85.

Cook and Parcel provide a comprehensive summary of Adams' (1965) theory of reactions to injustice and Berger et al.'s (1972) approach to activation of justice concerns. The authors critically compare the two perspectives and comment on their limitations as well as their complementarity.

Leventhal, Gerald S., Jurgis Karuza, Jr., and William R. Fry. 1980. "Beyond Fairness: A Theory of Allocation Preferences." Pp. 167–218 in *Justice and Social Interaction*, edited by G. Mikula. New York: Springer-Verlag.

Leventhal et al. attempt to understand fairness issues within the context of allocation decisions. Their chapter reviews empirical evidence and develops expectancy-based theoretical models to explain the selection of distribution and procedural rules within a situation.

Lind, E. Allan and Tom R. Tyler. 1988. *The Social Psychology of Procedural Justice*. New York: Plenum.

In this comprehensive review, Lind and Tyler describe the historical development of concerns with procedural justice and current directions in research. Their particular emphasis is on the applicability of procedural issues in a wide variety of situations.

# REFERENCES

Adams, J. Stacy. 1965. "Inequity in Social Exchange." *Advances in Experimental Social Psychology* 2:267–99.

Alves, Wayne M. and Peter H. Rossi. 1978. "Who Should Get What? Fairness Judgments of the Distribution of Earnings." *American Journal of Sociology* 84:541–64.

Austin, William. 1980. "Friendship and Fairness: Effects of Type of Relationship and Task Performance on Choice of Distribution Rules." *Personality and Social Psychology Bulletin* 6:402–408.

Austin, William and Joyce Tobiasen. 1984. "Legal Justice and the Psychology of Conflict Resolution." Pp. 227–74 in *The Sense of Injustice*, edited by R. Folger. New York: Plenum.

Berger, Joseph, Morris Zelditch, Jr., Bo Anderson, and Bernard P. Cohen. 1972. "Structural Aspects of Distributive Justice: A Status Value Formulation." Pp. 119–46 in *Sociological Theories in Progress*, vol. 2, edited by J. Berger, M. Zelditch, Jr., and B. Anderson. Boston: Houghton Mifflin.

Blau, Peter. 1964. *Exchange and Power in Social Life*. New York: Wiley.

Cohen, Ronald L. 1982. "Perceiving Justice: An Attributional Perspective." Pp. 119–60 in *Equity and Justice in Social Behavior*, edited by J. Greenberg and R. L. Cohen. New York: Academic Press.

Cook, Karen S. and Karen A. Hegtvedt. 1983. "Distributive Justice, Equity, and Equality." *Annual Review of Sociology* 9:217–41.

————. 1986. "Justice and Power: An Exchange Analysis." Pp. 19–41 in *Justice in Social Relations*, edited by H. W. Bierhoff, R. L. Cohen, and J. Greenberg. New York: Plenum.

Cook, Karen S. and Toby L. Parcel. 1977. "Equity Theory: Directions for Future Research." *Sociological Inquiry* 47:75–85.

deCarufel, André. 1981. "The Allocation and Acquisition of Resources in Times of Scarcity." Pp. 317–43 in *The Justice Motive in Social Behavior*, edited by M. J. Lerner and S. C. Lerner. New York: Plenum.

Deutsch, Morton. 1975. "Equity, Equality, and Need: What Determines What Value Will Be Used as the Basis for Distributive Justice?" *Journal of Social Issues* 31:137–50.

Festinger, Leon. 1954. "A Theory of Social Comparison Processes." *Human Relations* 7:117–40.

Homans, George C. 1974. *Social Behavior: Its Elementary Forms*. New York: Harcourt, Brace and World.

Jasso, Guillermina. 1983. "Fairness of Individual Rewards and Fairness of the Reward Distribution: Specifying the Inconsistency Between Micro and Macro Principles of Justice." *Social Psychology Quarterly* 46:185–99.

Kluegel, James R. and Eliot R. Smith. 1986. *Beliefs About Inequality: Americans' Views of What Is and What Ought to Be*. New York: Aldine De Gruyter.

Lawler, Edward J. 1975. "An Experimental Study of Factors Affecting the Mobilization of Revolutionary Coalitions." *Sociometry* 38:163–79.

Lawler, Edward J. and Martha E. Thompson. 1978. "Impact of Leader Responsibility for Inequity on Subordinate Revolts." *Social Psychology* 41:265–68.

Lerner, Melvin J. 1980. *The Belief in a Just World: A Fundamental Delusion*. New York: Plenum.

Leung, Kwok and Michael H. Bond. 1984. "The Impact of Cultural Collectivism on Reward Allocation." *Journal of Personality and Social Psychology* 47:793–804.

Leventhal, Gerald S., Jurgis Karuza, Jr., and William R. Fry. 1980. "Beyond Fairness: A Theory of Allocation Preferences." Pp. 167–218 in *Justice and Social Interaction*, edited by G. Mikula. New York: Springer-Verlag.

Lind, E. Allan and Tom R. Tyler. 1988. *The Social Psychology of Procedural Justice*. New York: Plenum.

Major, Brenda and Kay Deaux. 1982. "Individual Differences in Justice Behavior." Pp. 43–76 in *Equity and Justice in Social Behavior*, edited by J. Greenberg and R. L. Cohen. New York: Plenum.

Markovsky, Barry. 1985. "Toward a Multilevel Distributive Justice Theory." *American Sociological Review* 50:822–39.

Martin, Michael W. and Jane Sell. 1986. "Rejection of Authority: The Importance of Type of Distribution Rule and Extent of Benefit." *Social Science Quarterly* 67:855–68.

Masters, John C. and William P. Smith. 1987. *Social Comparison, Social Justice, and Relative Deprivation*. Hillsdale, NJ: Erlbaum.

Messick, David M. and Kenneth P. Sentis. 1979. "Fairness and Preference." *Journal of Experimental Social Psychology* 15:416–34.

Montada, Leo. 1980. "Developmental Changes in Conceptions of Justice." Pp. 257–84 in *Justice and Social Interaction*, edited by G. Mikula. New York: Springer-Verlag.

Rawls, John. 1971. *A Theory of Justice*. Boston: Harvard University Press.

Reis, Harry T. 1986. "Levels of Interest in the Study of Interpersonal Justice." Pp. 187–210 in *Justice in Social Relations*, edited by H. W. Bierhoff, R. L. Cohen, and J. Greenberg. New York: Plenum.

Runciman, William. 1966. *Relative Deprivation and Social Justice*. London, England: Routledge and Kegan Paul.

Schneider, David J., Albert H. Hastorf, and Phoebe C. Ellsworth. 1979. *Person Perception*, 2nd ed. Reading, MA: Addison-Wesley.

Stolte, John F. 1987. "The Formation of Justice Norms." *American Sociological Review* 52:774–84.

Thibaut, John and Laurens Walker. 1975. *Procedural Justice: A Psychological Analysis*. Hillsdale, NJ: Erlbaum.

Törnblom, Kjell. 1992. "The Social Psychology of Distributive Justice." Pp. 177–236 in *Justice: The State of the Art in Theory and Research*, edited by K. Scherer. Cambridge, England: Cambridge University Press.

Utne, Mary K. and Robert F. Kidd. 1980. "Equity and Attribution." Pp. 63–93 in *Justice and Social Interaction*, edited by G. Mikula. New York: Springer-Verlag.

Walster, Elaine, George W. Walster, and Ellen Berscheid. 1978. *Equity: Theory and Research*. Boston: Allyn and Bacon.

Watts, Barbara L., Robin R. Vallacher, and Lawrence A. Messé. 1982. "Toward Understanding Sex Differences in Pay Allocations: Agency, Communion, and Reward Distribution Behavior." *Sex Roles* 8:1175–88.

Webster, Murray, Jr. and Le Roy F. Smith. 1978. "Justice and Revolutionary Coalitions: A Test of Two Theories." *American Journal of Sociology* 84:267–92.

# NINE

# Affect

## CECILIA L. RIDGEWAY

Emotions and sentiments are much of what makes interacting with others meaningful and important. Yet affect remains the least understood aspect of group processes. Only in recent years have sociologists made a concerted effort to understand how emotions and sentiments are related to the structure of social relationships. This new interest has produced a number of intriguing theoretical efforts to analyze affect processes in the same way that power or status have been analyzed. As yet, however, few of these theories are as rigorously worked out as those for power or status. While all are based on evidence of some sort, most have not been properly tested and refined. As a result, the research considered in this chapter is more speculative than that in other sections. However, it is too important and exciting to ignore. In this chapter, I invite you to be a critical participant at the frontier of developing sociological knowledge.

Affect covers a range of experiences from an intense but transient flush of feeling such as embarrassment or anger to more enduring evaluative attitudes toward others or a group such as "I like that person." Researchers differ in the way they divide up this range. However, this chapter divides it into two general types of experiences. Emotion, as used here, refers to the actual experience of feeling in a situation. Emotions can vary in intensity but they are generally transitory and short-lived. Sentiments, in contrast, refer to relatively stable affective appraisals of a person, relationship, or group. They are ideas or attitudes that summarize past feelings and reflect expectations of future feelings. They are not the direct experience of feeling itself.

To see the difference between emotions and sentiments, consider having a conversation with an old friend. You approach your friend with an established, fairly stable attitude of liking, a sentiment in our terms. In the course of the conversation, some event triggers in you a glow of warmth toward your friend. For a few moments you directly experience your liking for your friend rather than just hold it as an idea. During those moments you are experiencing the emotion of liking, rather than just the sentiment of it.

Unlike sentiments, emotions are always accompanied by bodily sensations. These sensations give emotions their vividness and potential intensity, but they are transitory. For example, regardless of how angry you are, you can only maintain the actual feeling of rage for so long. Although relatively short-lived, emotions are at the root of sentiments. Sentiments toward a person or group summarize the potential for emotion in that relationship; they imply an emotional consequence of the relationship for you. Thus, we must start with emotions to understand affect in groups.

The first step is to gain a general understanding of emotions and the importance of social factors in determining them. Next follows a consideration of theories in the new field of the sociology of emotions and sentiments. These theories describe how aspects of interaction, social norms, and the organization of society shape and control emotions and sentiments. Most of these theories are not specifically concerned with groups and their affective processes. However, they provide essential concepts and ideas about the social determinants and consequences of emotions and sentiments that can be applied to group interaction. The goal of the first half of the chapter is to present these essential concepts and ideas. The second half turns to group processes themselves. It considers theories that employ the earlier concepts to analyze the affective or, as they are sometimes called, "expressive" dimensions of groups.

## THE NATURE OF EMOTIONS

Most people will accept that sentiments, as a form of attitude, will be strongly influenced by social factors. But what is the social content of emotions? People often think of emotions as an elemental force of nature beyond their control and therefore, beyond the influence of society and social structure. They also think of emotions as intensely individual, having more to do with personal psychology than social processes. A classic experiment on how people experience emotions has documented how wrong this view is.

Schachter and Singer (1962) asked how people know what they are feeling. They pointed out that while people experience a very large variety of specific emotions, the physical sensations that underlie these emotions seem relatively vague and undifferentiated. How do people go from fairly general bodily sensations to a sense that they are feeling contempt rather than anger or another emotion? Schachter and Singer reasoned that people rely on cues in their immediate situation to interpret their sensations and cognitively label their emotions. In making this argument, they drew on social comparison theory, which argues that when experience is ambiguous, people compare themselves to others in order to define their reality (Festinger 1954).

To test their argument, Schachter and Singer conducted an imaginative experi-

ment in which male undergraduate volunteers were given an injection of epinephrine, which is essentially adrenalin. This injection was enough to create many of
the bodily sensations that accompany strong emotions: a pounding heart, shaking
hands, and a warm, flushed face. All the participants were told the injection was
a vitamin but what else they were told depended on the experimental condition
to which they were assigned. In one condition they were given an accurate description of the symptoms they were likely to experience, in a second they were
misinformed about what they would feel, in a third they were told nothing about
what to expect. A fourth control condition was exactly like the third condition
except that the participants were given an injection of a neutral placebo rather
than epinephrine.

After receiving the injection, all participants were left to wait for its effects
with another participant, actually a confederate of the experimenter. For half of
the participants, this confederate, who supposedly also had received an injection,
acted in an increasingly euphoric, playful manner including making and throwing
paper airplanes and playing with a hula hoop. The rest of the participants saw a
confederate who acted in an increasingly angry manner, finally ripping up the
study questionnaire in a rage and stomping out.

Schachter and Singer predicted that the participants would interpret their own
bodily sensations in terms of the confederate's reactions and decide they were
feeling an emotion similar to his. That is indeed what happened. Participants
reported feeling anger or happiness depending on the situational cues the confederate's behavior provided them. As Schachter and Singer expected, this effect was
stronger for the second and third conditions. That is, it was weaker for participants
who had been accurately informed about the symptoms they would experience
since they did not need to rely on the situation to interpret their sensations. The
effects were also weaker for participants who received a placebo. Without physical
sensations, participants did not think they were experiencing a strong emotion
regardless of how the confederate behaved.

This study demonstrates quite clearly that the emotions we feel are a joint result
of bodily changes and a social process by which we cognitively interpret what
those changes mean and how they should be labelled. It is this social process of
interpretation that makes emotions a proper topic for sociological inquiry. It
means that the social structure within which the person is embedded affects what
emotions are experienced and how he or she acts on those emotions.

Since Schachter and Singer's initial study, most researchers have accepted the
importance of social factors in determining emotion. A debate has raged, however, over the extent of the role played by these factors. The "social constructionists" suggest that the causal processes behind emotions are almost entirely social
(e.g., Hochschild 1979; Gordon 1981). They accept Schachter and Singer's argument that the physiological base of emotions is so undifferentiated that it is the
social processes of norms and interpretation that determine what we feel and when
we feel it.

Others, the "positivists," have argued that Schachter and Singer's results have been overinterpreted (e.g., Kemper 1978, 1987). These researchers claim that the physiological states underlying emotions as distinct as anger or happiness are in fact different and that people do not generally confuse these emotions on the basis of social cues. But even the positivists acknowledge that physically different emotions are few compared to the variety of felt emotions. Kemper (1987), for instance, argues that there are only four neurochemically distinct states that underlie all emotions. These correspond to what he calls the "primary" emotions of fear, anger, depression, and satisfaction or happiness.

There simply is not enough evidence yet to say for certain whether the physiological base of emotions is entirely undifferentiated or, if it is not, exactly how many physically different states are involved. One thing we can say for certain, however, is that the physiological base of emotions is *relatively* undifferentiated compared to the great variety of meaningfully different emotions we feel. Thus biological changes alone are almost never enough to tell us what we are feeling. They must be considered in combination with social information about our situation. Recognizing this point, Kemper (1987) has called for a compromise between the positivist and social constructionist positions. He suggests that a small number of bodily states are transformed into a potentially infinite variety of emotions by means of the situational cues available and the cultural rules through which the person has learned to interpret those cues.

The recognition that emotion involves both bodily factors and a variety of social factors is represented in current definitions of emotions. While the exact wording varies, researchers now agree (Thoits 1985, 1989) that emotions have at least the following elements: (1) appraisals of the situation that evokes the emotion, (2) changes in bodily or physiological sensations, (3) some kind of display of expressive gestures, whether free or inhibited, and (4) a cultural label applied to specific constellations of one or more of the first three components.

This definition makes it clear why a sociology of emotions is not only possible, but essential to the understanding of emotional experience and its effects on social behavior. Three of the four defining elements of emotion are social.

The bodily changes of emotions are initially triggered by a socially shaped appraisal of the situation. When you step into a dark room and realize that there is someone waiting in there, it is your appraisal of the social situation as threatening that causes the rush of adrenalin that you feel. When you next realize that it is a surprise party organized by friends, it is that subsequent appraisal that changes your feelings to relief and happiness. Thus, even the initiation of emotion involves a process of social interpretation, a learned reading of situational cues.

The third element in the definition suggests that your own and others' facial, hand, and body gestures will be among the important cues you use to understand the bodily changes evoked by your appraisal of the situation. Only a very few of these gestures are automatic results of the bodily changes connected with emotions. Most, instead, are shaped by learned norms of expression (Ekman 1984). For instance, in some cultures, grief is expressed by loud crying and lamenting but in others, it is expressed by a rigid, quiet manner. Finally, the fourth point indicates that the way you interpret all the situational cues and decide what you are feeling depends on cultural rules that tell you what kind of emotions there are and what their signs are.

You will note that this description of the social factors involved in the process of interpreting and, indeed, fully experiencing emotion goes well beyond the rather simple view suggested by Schachter and Singer's social comparison argument. It is not only cues in the immediate situation that are important, but also cultural rules from the larger society. Furthermore, people do not simply compare themselves to others in the situation but rather engage in an elaborate process of perceiving and interpreting information according to social rules and relationships. Recent work in the sociology of emotions and sentiments has uncovered a number of key aspects to this process of socially constructing emotions. Many of these aspects are vital to understanding affective processes in groups. It is to these recent analyses that we turn now.

## THE SOCIOLOGY OF EMOTIONS AND SENTIMENTS

### Social Interaction and Emotion

Kemper (1978, 1987, 1990), one of the pioneers in the sociology of emotions, has pointed out that most emotional reactions arise from people's involvement in social interaction. Most events that have emotional significance to us occur in our dealings with others. Kemper bases his social interactional theory of emotion on this observation.

During interaction, people continually appraise the situation in order to know how to act. Kemper asserts that the aspect of that appraisal most likely to elicit emotion will be the assessment of the *social position* in which the person has been placed relative to others in the situation. From a review of previous research, Kemper concludes that there are two dimensions of positional relationships between people that are most important in eliciting emotion. These are power and what will be called "regard."[1] Power refers to the ability to coerce. Regard refers to the degree of liking, appreciation, or respect in which you or another are held in the situation. The implications, real or imagined, of a given situation for maintaining or changing your power or regard in relation to others is a potent trigger for emotion.

Kemper goes on to argue that particular relationships of power and regard between individuals give rise to very specific emotions. For instance, an insufficiency of power in relationship to another person causes anxiety. He further

---

1. In Kemper's (1978, 1987) theory, the dimension I call "regard" is termed "status." Since the term "status" is used to mean something else in this chapter (as well as in other chapters in this book), I have taken the liberty of relabeling Kemper's dimension as "regard" to avoid confusion.

proposes that certain outcomes of power and regard produce biologically built-in bodily reactions that are the basis for his four primary emotions (Kemper 1987). Here we see Kemper's positivist bent.

Kemper makes an additional point that is useful in understanding the affective processes of groups. How you react to a given power or regard outcome depends not only on the interactional outcome itself but also on who or what you perceive to be responsible for that outcome. Did you bring it on yourself, did the other person do it, or was it caused by a third party such as someone else or the environment? Others besides Kemper have pointed out that this attribution of causal responsibility is important in shaping not only the specific emotion felt but also the direction of behavior, if any, that is motivated by the emotion (Kelley 1984). For instance, if something causes you to lose regard in relation to another, not only how you feel but also what you do about it will depend on whether you think it is your own fault or the fault of others.

Kemper's theory has not been tested directly. Furthermore, his argument that particular types of power and regard relationships evoke very specific emotional reactions is somewhat controversial. Even more contested is his assertion that some of these reactions are biologically built-in. However, many researchers accept Kemper's basic point that most emotions result from the real or imagined outcomes of interaction with others. Kemper has also marshalled substantial evidence for his claim that the fundamental aspects of these relationships that evoke emotional responses have to do with power and regard. Finally, there is also evidence that the attribution of causal responsibility for an emotion-triggering event is an important determinant of the emotion felt and the behavioral response to the event (Kelley 1984).

## Norms and Emotion

Kemper's (1978) theory acknowledges the impact of the larger cultural context within which interaction takes place, but puts primary emphasis on interactional dynamics themselves in shaping emotions. The work of Hochschild (1979, 1983, 1989) and Gordon (1981, 1989, 1990), two social constructionists, reverses this emphasis. Their research reveals important insights into the way emotions are regulated and even created by social norms. As a result of this regulation, what we feel is connected to the way our society is organized and what it values, and is not necessarily identical in all respects with what people feel in very different societies (Gordon 1990).

There are at least two important types of emotion norms that affect interaction in groups. Both are part of what Gordon (1989, 1990) calls a society's "emotion culture." The first are widely shared cultural beliefs about what emotions there are, termed the society's "emotional vocabulary," and the particular cues by which these emotions are to be recognized. These norms form the fourth element of our definition of emotions. Societal norms that define specific emotions and the signs that indicate them are an essential element in determining what we feel. A good example is a cultural belief in the emotional experience of romantic love. Most western societies, unlike some others, have clear normative beliefs that the feeling of romantic love exists and is an important emotion that can be recognized by a distinct series of cues.

The second type of emotion norms is situationally specific. Hochschild (1979) has pointed out that social settings in our society carry conventional rules for feeling as well as behavior. You are supposed to feel sad, not happy, at a funeral. "Feeling rules," as Hochschild calls them, specify the *extent* of feeling appropriate in the situation (you can feel too much or too little), the *direction*, either positive or negative, of the proper emotion, and the appropriate *duration* of the feeling. Associated with feeling rules are "display rules" (Ekman 1982) that indicate the nature and intensity of expressive behavior appropriate to a situation. As anyone who has gone to a dull, boring party knows, in order to achieve the goals of a given social setting, it is every bit as important that participants live up to feeling rules as it is that they conform to behavorial rules.

Feeling and display rules are embedded within the larger emotion culture of a society and reflect the social structure, values, and concerns of that society (Hochschild 1979, 1983). In particular, the feeling and display rules attached to different roles in organizations and groups reflect the *power* of the position as well as the goals of the group and the values of the society within which it exists. In our society, for instance, the roles of boss and employee allow the more powerful boss to express annoyance at the employee but do not condone an equally annoyed response from the employee. In a fascinating study of flight attendants, Hochschild (1983) documents how some work roles in our society demand that their occupants express certain required feelings as part of their job. This in effect treats such employees' feelings as a commodity that the employer buys with a paycheck.

As with other social norms, most people endeavor to conform to feeling and display rules. When they fail to do so, they are often subject to criticism from others and upset with themselves as well. For whatever reason, events in a situation do not always straightforwardly evoke emotions that are normatively appropriate. Sometimes you are not happy at a party or sad at a funeral. In such situations, Hochschild (1979) argues, people engage in "emotion work." That is, people actively try to change their feelings to match what they should feel according to the feeling rules they have learned. They do this by deliberately manipulating the components or elements of emotion in the hope that if they get one or two of the elements in line with the rules, the rest will fall into place. They may manipulate the cognitive element of emotion (corresponding to the appraisal of the situation in our definition) by trying to think thoughts that will evoke the proper emotion. Or they may try to change their bodily sensations by, for instance, breathing deeply to quiet themselves down. Finally, they may alter their expressive gestures in the hope that this will actually make them feel the required emotion. This is what people do when they try to smile or not cry in order to feel happier.

It is a sign of how seriously people take feeling and display rules and how important they are for smooth interaction that when a person persistently fails to express the proper feelings, he or she comes to be seen as an emotional deviant (Thoits 1985). Associates may even come to see the person as "emotionally disturbed" or "not normal." Thoits (1985) has described how, when people struggle and repeatedly fail to manage their emotions "properly," they often label themselves as mentally ill and seek help of some sort.

## Sentiments and Emotions

Thus far we have discussed emotions, but said little about sentiments. Kemper (1978) would consider sentiments to be the more enduring emotions produced by a relationship in which the structure of power and regard is relatively stable. But what about the idea that the sentiments between people in a relationship may be basically stable over time and yet the people still experience a lot of emotional ups and downs in the short run? "Affect control theory" is a sociological approach that addresses the relationship between more stable sentiments and transient feelings in interaction (Heise 1979; Smith-Lovin and Heise 1988; Smith-Lovin 1990). This theory is distinctive in that it is not only precisely formulated conceptually, but also it is empirically based as well. It is a broad scoped theory that applies to interaction in any kind of situation.

Affect control theory claims that the meanings and expectations we associate with the social roles we play, personal attributes, other people, social actions, and social settings are essentially affective in nature. They are sentiments. A sentiment about something can be represented in terms of three dimensions: how good or bad you feel the object is (evaluation), how powerful or weak it is (potency), and how active or passive it is (activity). These dimensions are drawn from Osgood's cross-cultural assessments of the meanings people associate with things using a series of bipolar adjectives known as the "semantic differential" (Osgood, May, and Miron 1975).

David Heise (1979), the founder of affect control theory, argues that people learn "fundamental sentiments" or affective meanings for different social roles, kinds of people, settings, etc., considered "out of context." Fundamental sentiments summarize a society's emotion culture by embodying the affective meanings attached in that society to culturally defined social roles, settings, and the like. On the other hand, when people interact with others, they form "in context" impressions of themselves, the others, the setting, and the events that are occurring. These "transient sentiments," as Heise labels them, reflect people's attitudes toward an event or role, given the other events and people present in the situation. In the range from emotions to stable sentiments, transient sentiments occupy a midpoint. They too can be summarized in terms of evaluation, potency, and activity.

The central assumption of affect control theory is that people are motivated to make their transient sentiments match or confirm their fundamental sentiments. Heise proposes that when interaction events throw transient sentiments out of line with fundamental sentiments, this triggers emotions, flashes of negative feelings that motivate the actors to engage in some counter behavior to bring the sentiments back in line. Imagine, for instance, that you are enacting the Expert to a Novice (fundamental sentiments) and the Novice surprises you by asking something that you cannot answer. This creates transient sentiments in the situation (the Incompetent Expert, the Knowledgeable Novice) that are inconsistent with the fundamental sentiments, triggering in you a negative emotion. Feeling disturbed, you try to compensate by, perhaps, giving an officious speech about all you know that the Novice does not.

Affect control theory argues, then, that fundamental sentiments drive people's behavior in interaction and are an important source of the emotions they feel in the situation (Smith-Lovin 1990). People try to structure interaction in the first place to create transient sentiments that confirm fundamental sentiments. They also engage in reconfirming behaviors to try to manage the inevitable emotional upsets brought on by events that the person cannot completely control. Usually this works and fundamental sentiments are maintained.

Sometimes, however, disconfirming events are so extreme or repeated that the person cannot adequately compensate for them. When this happens, the problematic situational sentiments actually change the fundamental sentiments themselves. If, for example, you come out of high school with an understanding of yourself as a Good Math Student but have persistent difficulties in advanced college math courses, you will gradually alter that self-concept, maybe to something like Average Math Student. So fundamental sentiments remain stable by driving interaction, transient sentiments, and emotional reactions to confirm them, but interactional events do eventually alter them. (Note the similarity this suggests between the operation of affect and status processes in groups.)

This overview of research in the sociology of emotions and sentiments suggests a number of concepts and insights that are useful for analyzing affect processes in groups. For Kemper (1978, 1990), the position of power and regard you hold in a group, how interactional events affect those positions, and who you perceive as responsible for those events are all important determinants of your emotions in the group. Gordon (1981, 1990) and Hochschild (1979, 1983) offer insights into the importance of norms or "emotion culture" for what is felt and expressed. These norms include a society's emotional vocabulary as well as situationally specific feeling and display rules. Affect control theory documents how more stable sentiments drive transient sentiments and emotions in interaction but, in turn, can be modified by them. Now let us turn to theories and accounts that focus specifically on group interaction. As we shall see, these theories apply the concepts we have reviewed, along with others, to analyze affective processes in groups.

## GROUP PROCESSES AND AFFECT

As with sociological studies of emotion and sentiments generally, systematic analyses of affective processes in groups are still in the formative stage. But while no comprehensive theory of affective processes exists, theoretical analyses of a few aspects of them have been developed. These theories developed from observations of groups, but only a few have been subjected to adequate independent tests. Many of the theories also require more conceptual development. This is speculative ground, then, and the reader should keep this in mind. However, available theories allow us to trace the outlines of affective group processes.

The group processes perspective on affect differs from that of most research on the sociology of emotions and sentiments. Rather than focusing on emotions or sentiments per se, group processes work concentrates on the structure of interaction among actors. Emotions are seen as intervening variables that are triggered by events in interaction. Emotions, in turn, shape people's behavioral reactions to those events, which may include displays of expressive or affective behaviors.

Because emotions can determine behavior, they have the potential to maintain or change the structure of relationships that govern interaction in the group. Two aspects of this structure are central to group processes analyses: the status structure and the affective structure. The status structure describes the pattern of deference and influence among group members. The affective structure represents the pattern of liking (or disliking) among the members. Members hold a structure of sentiments toward one another. These two structures are generally similar to Kemper's (1978, 1987) dimensions of power and regard. If Kemper's theory is correct, they both should have emotional significance for the members.

Chapters 5 and 6 of this volume deal with the emergence of a status structure. This chapter will simply take the status structure as a given and examine how it both affects and is modified by affective processes. The focus here will be on the affective structure of a group and how it emerges and shapes behavior in interaction.

Contemporary analyses of group processes and affect really began with Bales' (1950, 1953) pioneering work. Thus our starting point is Bales' research and subsequent theoretical analyses of the questions he raised about status and affective behavior in groups. These analyses illustrate how the development of affective relations is virtually inevitable in any group. Furthermore, such relations will be affected by status processes. The next section turns to an account of the way expressive behavior accumulates to create the more stable sentiments of an affective structure and the relationship between this structure and future expressive behavior. This leads to a discussion of cultural norms for groups and their effects on the emergence of affective structure. The last section considers how the relationship between the affective and status structures can modify status differences in a group.

## Status and Affect

Bales argued that in goal-oriented groups, the status structure is based on task-related behaviors. However, this structure will not be stable and the group will not achieve its goal unless the group members also maintain harmonious interpersonal relations by means of positive ''socioemotional'' behaviors. These are what we have termed ''affective'' or ''expressive'' behaviors and include being helpful or friendly or in some other way expressing evaluative feeling toward another member.

In the course of discussing group goals and how to achieve them, argued Bales, disagreements inevitably develop. Disagreements create tensions that must be resolved through positive socioemotional behavior if group solidarity is to be maintained. Thus the task and socioemotional dimensions of interaction are interdependent but somewhat competitive with one another. This point is a basic insight of Bales' that provides a framework for our understanding of affect processes in groups. It suggests that there will be no groups without affective processes. It also suggests that status processes will have an effect on affective relations and vice versa.

In a well-known series of studies, Bales and Slater (1955; also see Slater 1955) proposed that group members manage the interdependent but competing demands of goal accomplishment and affective relations by developing separate task and socioemotional leaders. The task leader is the person the members rank as having the best ideas and the socioemotional leader is the one ranked as best liked. Although an interesting suggestion, subsequent research showed that this separation of task and socioemotional leadership only occurs under specialized conditions such as when the task leader lacks legitimacy in the group (Burke 1967, 1971). How then does the process of task discussion, out of which the status hierarchy emerges, affect emotions and socioemotional behavior? The question is important because most groups begin with some kind of discussion of collective goals and concerns.

Recently, Ridgeway and Johnson (1990) proposed a new theoretical analysis of this question, at least for some types of groups. This analysis provides a more detailed specification of Bales' insight that even the most neutral discussion of task concerns in a group is likely to produce events that trigger emotional reactions and expressive behavior. This, in turn, sets the stage for the emergence of an affective structure.

Ridgeway and Johnson limited the scope of their analysis to groups where the members are motivated to accomplish a collective task and are initially emotionally neutral to one another. They began with the assumption that an informal status structure had evolved in the group. Employing expectation states theory, they represented this structure as an order of performance expectations (Berger, Conner, and Fisek 1974; Berger et al. 1977; Berger and Zelditch 1985; Webster and Foschi 1988). Recall from Chapters 5 and 6 that such expectations are the anticipations members form for the likely usefulness of one member's contributions to the group's task compared to another's. Thus high status members are expected to make more useful or valuable contributions to the task than low status members.

Ridgeway and Johnson started with Bales' point that working on a collective task inevitably means some choice among different task ideas, with the result that some members' suggestions will be accepted and others' will not. Even if purely task-oriented in intent, such agreements and disagreements evoke an emotional reaction in the group member who receives them. According to evidence marshalled by Kemper (1978, 1987) and others (e.g., Berkowitz 1982), people experience pleasurable emotions as a result of exercising mastery or competence in their interactions with their environment and negative feelings when their efforts to exercise such competence are blocked. An agreement with your task suggestion confirms your effort to exercise competence over the task, but a disagreement pulls your efforts up short.

As our earlier discussion indicated, the precise emotions you make of this "gut reaction" depends on your appraisal of the situation. This appraisal will differ depending on whether you are higher or lower in the status hierarchy than the person who agreed or disagreed with you. First, consider disagreements. Ridgeway and Johnson (1990) propose that the emotion you feel when someone disagrees with you depends on whether you attribute responsibility for the disagreement to yourself (my idea was bad) or the other (the person doesn't know what he or she is talking about). This is an application of our earlier discussion about the way attribution of responsibility for an event affects the emotion it produces. If you think the disagreement was the other's fault, you are likely to feel annoyed, but if you think it was your fault, you will probably feel depressed.

The catch, according to Ridgeway and Johnson, is that your position in the status structure will determine whether you hold yourself or the other responsible for the disagreement because status positions are associated with performance expectations. They propose that if you hold an equal or higher status position and therefore, performance expectation, for yourself compared to the other, you will assume that the disagreement was the other's fault. After all, you are as good or better than the other at the task. Consequently, you will feel annoyance toward the other. On the other hand, if you hold a lower status position and corresponding performance expectation for yourself compared to the other, you will assume that you are wrong and feel depressed.

This has important implications for the group because the emotions of annoyance and depression motivate you to behave toward the other in very different ways. If you feel annoyance, say Ridgeway and Johnson, you are likely to express negative socioemotional behavior toward the other in an effort to discourage further annoying disagreements. You may say something to the other in a critical, sarcastic, or unfriendly tone. This is the way high status members are likely to react to lower status disagreers.

On the other hand, if you feel depression because you conclude that the disagreement was your own fault, it makes no sense to express negative behavior toward the other. Thus, low status members are unlikely to snap back at higher status disagreers. This creates an inequality in the expression of negative socioemotional behavior. Higher status members will express more of this negative behavior than low status members. Empirical evidence from groups shows that this is in fact what happens (Slater 1955; Wood and Karten 1986).

The situation of agreement is rather different, according to Ridgeway and Johnson. Again, your status position may affect who you hold responsible for the agreement and, consequently, the nature of the positive emotion you feel. If the agreer is of lower status you may feel pride or satisfaction. If he or she is of equal or higher status an emotion like gratitude may be more likely. But the difference here is that all these positive emotions incline you to reward the agreer by expressing positive socioemotional behavior toward him or her as a way of encouraging future pleasurable agreements. As a result, the status order does not block or inhibit the expression of positive, friendly behavior as a response to agreement.

Ridgeway and Johnson argue that once friendly behavior is expressed toward a group member, that member is likely to reciprocate in kind. Consequently, agreement can set off chains of positive socioemotional exchange that encourage the development of group solidarity. Solidarity is the strength with which the group is bound together by members' connections with one another and the group as a whole. Since positive, friendly behaviors serve as rewards, the more they are exchanged in the group, the stronger the association for the members between rewards and the group. This association develops not only for those who receive the rewards but also the other members who witness their exchange. Once the group is viewed as rewarding, the members have in effect formed a positive attitude or sentiment toward it. Such sentiments are an important element of group solidarity.

Although the status order does not inhibit the expression of positive socioemotional behavior, as we have seen, it does reduce the occurrence of negative socioemotional behavior by making low status members feel depressed rather than angered by a disagreement. This reduction is especially large because it is low rather than high status members who are most likely to receive disagreements in the first place. Putting the effects of agreements and disagreements together, we should see more positive socioemotional behaviors in a group than negative ones. Again, this is what the empirical evidence does show (Bales and Slater 1955; Bales and Hare 1965; Anderson and Blanchard 1982).

Ridgeway and Johnson's analysis provides an explanation for what we know about the distribution of positive and negative affective behaviors in task groups. However, it still has to be tested before we can be sure of its accuracy. In the meantime, it does suggest two important points. First, emotional reactions and consequent affective behavior will take place eventually even in the most neutral group simply out of the process of trying to work together. This means that virtually every group is likely to develop some kind of affective structure of who likes whom. Second, this structure will be deeply intertwined with the status structure rather than independent of it. In a task group, the development of the affective structure is likely to be driven by the status structure.

A second line of research, also derived from Bales' original insights, further illustrates how the status structure shapes affective reactions (Meeker and Weitzel-O'Neill 1977; Ridgeway 1982). But this research also shows how affective reactions influence the success of efforts to change the status structure. Once again, the starting point is Bales' suggestion that the task-related behaviors that are the basis of status can create affective tensions in a group. Ridgeway and Johnson discuss disagreements as one way this can occur. This other line of research suggests a second way. When a person for whom the group holds low performance expectations (i.e., a low status member) tries to assertively present his or her ideas in order to gain greater influence and status, negative reactions can be triggered. Meeker and Weitzel-O'Neill (1977) and Ridgeway (1982) argue that the other group members see such influence attempts as a selfish and illegitimate grab for power since they presume the low status member is not very competent. Consequently, they often react with annoyance and disapproval and the low status member's influence attempt fails. They begin to form a negative sentiment toward this "pushy" and "uppity" person. The result is that negative emotions, socioemotional behaviors, and sentiments triggered by an effort to change the status structure are used to punish the changer and maintain the status quo. It is worth noting that this legitimacy analysis is similar to the analysis Burke (1967, 1971) used to explain the circumstances under which task leaders would be so resented that separate socioemotional leaders emerged in groups.

An unfortunate implication of this legitimacy analysis concerns groups whose members differ in external status characteristics such as race or sex. As Chapter 6 notes, members of such groups tend to form lower performance expectations for those whose characteristics carry less status value in society than others (e.g., women versus men in a mixed-sex group). This analysis implies that if a woman in a mixed-sex group acts assertively to gain substantial influence, she may evoke negative emotional reactions that frustrate her efforts. In fact, there is evidence that this "backlash" effect occurs. Carli (1990) found that when women used assertive language to present their ideas to men in task-oriented dyads, they were actually less influential than when they spoke tentatively and their male partners saw them as less trustworthy. In contrast, when women tried to influence other women, or men tried to influence men or women, they were more successful if they used assertive rather than tentative language.

Since this discouraging backlash effect is an emotional reaction, Meeker and Weitzel-O'Neill (1977) suggested that women in mixed-sex groups might be able to counter it by accompanying their assertive influence attempts with positive, friendly socioemotional behavior. Ridgeway (1982) tested this suggestion and found that it worked. When a competent woman in an otherwise male, four-person group accompanied her assertions of task ideas with evidence that she was trying to be friendly, helpful, and "group-oriented," she became quite influential. When her task suggestions were accompanied by evidence that she was motivated by self-interest, her influence was very low. Men in otherwise female groups, on the other hand, were highly influential regardless of whether they expressed friendliness and group orientation, or self-interest. This was as expected since men in such groups do not face legitimacy problems when they speak up to gain influence.

The good news in these results is that women and others whose external status characteristics disadvantage them in a group can overcome their legitimacy problems and achieve high influence if they combine their assertive task behavior with expressive indications of a friendly, cooperative intent. They can use affective behavior to help change their position in the status structure. In fact, Meeker and Weitzel-O'Neill (1977) suggest that efforts to speak up and be influential without provoking resistance may partly account for women's slightly higher rate of positive socioemotional behavior in groups, compared to men. However, there is bad news in these results as well. They suggest that women often must be "nice" as well as competent to achieve high influence and status in mixed-sex groups, an added burden of emotional work that men do not face.

This research implies that negative emotional reactions to "illegitimate" challenges to the status structure can lead to negative sentiments toward the challenger. Ridgeway and Johnson (1990) also suggest how flashes of emotion sparked by interaction produce behaviors that accumulate to affect group solidarity. But precisely how do incidents of emotion and the affective behaviors they produce accumulate to create an affective structure in a group? This is the next question I will consider. Recent theories have begun to indicate some answers (Berger 1988; Johnston 1988; Smith-Lovin and Heise 1988).

## Affect: Interaction and Structure

Affective events apparently accumulate through a multistage process to create the more stable sentiments that make up a group's affective structure. The process begins when something in your interaction with another triggers a positive or negative emotion. This emotion can vary from quite mild to very intense but, of course, the stronger the emotion the greater its impact on the formation of a sentiment towards the other. If the experience of positive or negative emotion recurs as interaction with the other continues, you come to expect such experiences whenever you are with that other person. Assuming subsequent events confirm this expectation, you go on to attribute a more stable sentiment to yourself ("I like x") and, usually, you also attribute characteristics to the other that justify your liking ("x is a nice or attractive person").

Berger (1988) has begun to develop an expectation states theory of affect processes that describes the creation of affective structures in a multistage process similar to this. He calls the expression of positive or negative feelings toward another "affective behavior." We will also term it "expressive behavior." Berger limits his theory to groups or situations in which such affective behavior is considered appropriate according to the norms of the larger society. Thus, the theory applies to relatively intimate or personal groups. This is a point that we will return to later.

If some event in such a group triggers a reasonably intense positive or negative emotion in an actor, and the actor reacts by also treating the other in an evaluative, emotional way, Berger suggests that this "activates" or begins a process of affectively-oriented interaction. As positive or negative affective behavior is exchanged between the actors (e.g., compliments, endearments, sarcastic comments, threats) the actors form "affect states" that characterize their emotional orientation toward one another at the moment. Such states are something like the transient sentiments described by affect control theory. Affect states are expectations about affective relations between the actors in a specific situation rather than stable sentiments toward the people involved. (Note the correspondence between "affect states" in this theory and the concept of "performance expectation states" discussed in other chapters of this volume.)

Affect states can be mutually positive, mutually negative, or have one actor positive toward the other while that other is negative toward the first actor. Affect states have both cognitive (i.e., informational) and emotional components. Furthermore, affect states imply certain behaviors that a society's emotion culture defines as appropriate to them. Thus, the affect state of mutual hate implies certain classes of behavior between the actors. Berger argues that while affect states are operating, they organize and drive the actors' behavior toward one another. He proposes that they do this in a "univalent" way. That is, while you are in a positive affect state toward another, you treat the other in purely positive terms. Similarly, a negative state motivates purely negative behaviors.

Berger's suggestion of univalence during affect states is unusual and potentially controversial. However, it does capture the "single-mindedness" of emotionally driven behavior. In a bitter argument with someone, you do not usually mix in some friendly behaviors or think of the other's good qualities, even if later you wish you had.

The very one-sidedness of interaction in affect states makes them unstable and transient. Something in the heated argument, for instance, may cause one of the actors to start laughing. If the other laughs too, the affect state may switch from mutually negative to mutually positive. The emotionally-oriented interaction that creates and is shaped by affect states is itself usually relatively short-lived. Other considerations eventually arise in the interaction, or other actors intervene and the affect process is "deactivated." The affective episode passes.

Although relatively brief, such affective episodes can have long-term effects. Berger (1988) suggests that the behavior that occurs during them can cause the actors to form a more enduring sentiment towards the relationship. After a friendly exchange you may decide that "I like that person" and the other may form a similar attitude toward you. This represents the formation of a more stable affective structure for the group, in this case one of mutual liking.

Behavior during an affective episode often has a second effect as well, which can help solidify the affective structure. Johnston (1988) argues that actors frequently assign affective personality characteristics to "the other" on the basis of an affective exchange. For instance, the friendly exchange that caused you to decide that you liked the other may also make you attribute to the other characteristics such as warmth or kindness. As Johnston notes, the emotional "one-sidedness" of the affect states formed during such an episode mean that the characteristics assigned to the other are likely to be correspondingly positive or negative.

The emergence of a more stable affective structure as well as the assignment of supporting personality characteristics shape the likelihood that future affective episodes will occur between the actors. The more intense the sentiments of the affective structure (in either a positive or negative fashion), the more likely future expressive episodes are to be activated.

Once expressive exchange is triggered again, the affective structure and supporting personality characteristics will shape the nature of the new episode. The situational affect states formed during an exchange are now likely to confirm the affective structure. For instance, if the structure is one of mutual liking, the expressive exchanges that are triggered are more likely to be friendly. Consequently, mutually positive situational affect states are also likely.

"Likely," however, does not mean "always" or "necessarily so." Affect states are formed on the basis of incidents in the moment and these can be quite unpredictable. It is quite possible for two people whose affective structure is mutually very positive to find themselves in a shouting match driven by a mutually negative situational affect state. However, their more stable positive sentiments may help them moderate their negative behavior during the episode and may also encourage them to deactivate the argument sooner. Thus an affective structure shapes and stabilizes expressive exchanges in a group, but does not completely control them. If repeated expressive exchanges occur that disconfirm the affective structure, they will change both the personality characteristics assigned and the affective structure itself.

Berger and Johnston formulated this expectation states analysis of affect processes on the basis of clinical observations of distressed marriages. Since the theory has not been tested it must be viewed as suggestive at this point. Also, as both Johnston (1988) and Berger (1988) note, the theoretical formulation itself is not fully developed. Many questions remain, including, for instance, how affective processes are deactivated. However, the basic outline of the processes described, although formulated in different terms and different in focus, is not too dissimilar from that suggested by affect control theory (Smith-Lovin and Heise 1988). The substantial empirical basis of affect control theory suggests that the basic processes described by Berger and Johnston do occur in some form.

## Normative Blueprints and Affective Interaction

Berger's idea that interaction in groups is characterized by episodes in which two or more members engage in emotionally oriented exchanges is an intriguing way to conceptualize affective processes. However, Berger limits the scope of his analysis to groups that are defined by the society as ones where intimate interaction is appropriate. What about other groups? What about the work groups that Ridgeway and Johnson or Meeker and Weitzel-O'Neill discuss? Berger's analysis can be extended to these groups too. However, to do so, the societal norms that define these differing kinds of groups must first be considered.

Elsewhere I have suggested that our societal culture contains norms or rules that define the principal types of interaction appropriate to the forms of small groups common in the society (Ridgeway 1983). These social rules provide normative "blueprints" that tell us how to enact a "committee" or a "friendship" or a "roommate group." They frame our orientation toward the situation and our initial expectations for what kinds of behavior and events should occur. It is these social rules that Berger refers to as defining the appropriateness of intimate interaction in a given situation. Affect control theory also asserts the existence of such norms with the evidence it provides that people in U.S. society share normative views of the evaluation, potency, and activity associated with different social "settings" (Smith-Lovin 1988). Among other things, the blueprint norms for a type of group contain feeling rules and display rules that describe the kind of emotional reactions and affective behavior considered appropriate to the group setting.

The blueprint norms for intimate groups such as a family or romantic attachment require periods of affective interaction. If no emotional exchanges occur in your romantic relationship, you will feel something is wrong. It is not a "real romance" according to cultural rules. On the other hand, the blueprint norms of task groups like a committee prescribe a cool, work-oriented atmosphere in which emotional episodes are kept to a minimum.

Yet, as we have seen, there are no groups without affect processes. Even in work groups, agreements and disagreements are likely to trigger some exchanges of emotionally driven behavior, even though the emotion is generally fairly mild. Challenges to the expected order also spark emotional reactions. I argue that these quieter exchanges in task groups operate according to the same basic affective processes as the more intense and frequent expressive episodes of more intimate groups. That is, they too are triggered by an emotion-arousing event (e.g., a disagreement or a status challenge) that causes affective behavior. This behavior leads to the formation of situational affect states (e.g., annoyance or gratitude) between the interactors that shape the episode, can lead to the formation of more enduring sentiments toward the relationship, and cause the assignment of supporting affective personality characteristics (e.g., "she is cooperative" or "he is self-interested").

The difference, however, is that in task groups, the blueprint norms encourage the rapid deactivation of affective exchanges rather than their prolongation. This deactivation occurs through emotion work members do to bring their feelings and behavior back in line with task group norms (Hochschild 1979). If the interactors themselves do not turn away from their affective exchange (whether it be arguing or friendly joking), others will intervene to return the group to work concerns. As Ridgeway and Johnson (1990) point out, the status structure assists in this control of affective behavior by inhibiting lower status members from responding with expressive interchanges when higher status members disagree with them.

Blueprint norms also set the stage for the events that trigger emotionally oriented interaction in the first place and so, can play a role in the activation of affective episodes. Sometimes this is inadvertent. In task groups, for instance, blueprint norms emphasizing a work orientation occasionally result in status struggles because some members do not agree on a resolution after an initial statement of arguments. A lower status member refuses to defer, or more equally ranked members each refuse to cede to the other. Ridgeway and Johnson (1990) argue that events like this usually provoke anger first in one and then the other disagreer, leading to a cycle of negative exchanges. In Berger's terms, an episode of affective interaction has been activated. Members may develop polarized affective sentiments during status struggles because of their emotional quality. Since this polarized structure involves liking some members and disliking others, it erodes the mutual-liking element of group solidarity. Because of these potentially negative consequences and because of the blueprint norms for emotional neutrality in task groups, other members are often uncomfortable with status struggles and sometimes intervene to stop or deactivate them (Ridgeway and Diekema 1989).

Blueprint norms, then, shape the way members react to an event that arouses emotion in one or more members. In task groups, members work to contain and deactivate the emotionally driven behavior that may occur. As a result, the total amount of affective interaction is less in such groups and they generally develop less intense affective structures. In more intimate relationships members encourage expressive exchanges, especially if they are positive, with the result that such groups develop much more intense affective structures. We see that a group's blueprint norms shape the emotion work its members perform, resulting in the group's management (but not complete control) of the activation and deactivation of affective episodes and the resulting emergence of an affective structure. Yet the basic nature of affective processes is similar in all groups.

Berger (1988) notes that affective processes, like status processes, are contributors to the larger process by which people in a group develop situational role identities that govern their interaction over time. In relatively short-lived task groups like some committees, status processes may almost entirely determine the generation of situational role identities. But in more enduring groups and in more intimate groups like friends and family the role of affective processes is much greater (although status processes also remain important). How do the status and affective structures of groups combine to shape behavior? Hochschild (1983) and Ridgeway and Johnson (1990) give some suggestions about the impact of the status structure on affective behavior and the emergence of the affective structure. Meeker and Weitzel-O'Neill (1977) and Ridgeway (1982) also show how affective behavior triggered by the status structure can influence the success of efforts to change that structure. But how does the more enduring structure of sentiments that emerges from these transitory affective exchanges in turn modify status behavior in the long run? This is the next question to consider.

## Affective Structures and Status Structures

Several expectation states theorists (Shelly, Webster, and Berger 1989; Shelly 1988; Webster 1980; Berger 1988; Johnston 1988) argue that the affective structure can either exaggerate or reduce differences in status-related behaviors such as participation rates and influence over group decisions. They propose that when the affective structure is "congruent" with the status structure, differences in participation and influence are amplified. The two structures are congruent when high status members are also the best liked and low status members are the least well liked. Some evidence indicates that this is the most common situation (Shelly 1988). When the two structures are "incongruent," differences in participation and influence are moderated. Incongruence occurs when the distribution of liking does not coincide with the distribution of status.

The question of congruence and incongruence is complicated because while status structures imply inequalities in power and prestige, affective structures are often equality structures of mutual liking or disliking. However, the common structures of mutual liking or disliking are only true equalities when the *degree* of liking or disliking is close to equal for all parties. When one person likes another much less than he or she is liked in return (or dislikes more than he or she is disliked), that person is in an advantaged position in an unequal affect structure. This is sometimes called the "principle of least interest" because the person with the least emotional interest in the relationship has the most power.

When high status members are better liked (or disliked less) than low status members (i.e., there is congruence), the power and influence of the high status members is increased. Low status members not only think the high status members are competent, they also like them and want to please them. As a result, low status members are even more likely to listen to and accept the ideas of high status members than they would otherwise. Shelly (1989) reports preliminary data from a pilot experiment that supports this prediction; reviews of other research seem to support it as well (Shelly 1988).

Johnston (1988) has also applied this congruence principle to her very interesting analysis of relations between divorced spouses. When status and affect inequalities converge, she argues, spouses are particularly likely to develop rigid, polarized behavior and correspondingly polarized role identities in the relationship. Under some circumstances, these can inhibit the open communication necessary to resolve potentially destructive problems.

Consider a wife who loves her husband more than he loves her. The husband is also of much higher status than she, being perhaps older, richer, and more powerful in the world. In this structurally congruent and unequal situation, the wife is likely to feel committed to the relationship but also powerless within it. She will be eager to adapt her behavior to her husband, letting him define the situation. This leads to a complementary polarization of roles where if he likes to talk, she will listen quietly; if he likes to be quiet, she will keep up the conversation. Seeing each other in these opposite behavior patterns, the spouses attribute personality characteristics to justify or explain them. He is domineering and cold, she is warm but passive and dependent. They now begin to interpret any ambiguous communication in terms of these polarized traits. They can no longer say anything to one another that does not seem to confirm their opposite ways of acting and feeling. They become trapped in destructively rigid roles that make open communication almost impossible when problems develop. This is not an inevitable scenario when affective and status inequalities are large and congruent, but it is a possible one, a risk created by the structure of the relationship.

Incongruence between status and affective structures can occur either because the affective structure is an equal one and the status structure is unequal or because those who are high in one structure are low in the other. The inequality of participation and influence created by the status structure should be reduced in incongruent cases, as Shelly's (1989) pilot evidence also confirms. This suggests that if there are status differences between two group members, but they are mutual friends (an equality affective structure), the low status member should participate more and have more influence than if the two were not friends (or the friendship was not mutual).

We saw earlier that the status structure can constrain or amplify affective exchanges. Shelly, Webster, and Berger's (1989) work suggests that the affective structure can similarly constrain or amplify status differences. This brings us back to Bales' insight that both status and affective structures are fundamental to groups. Virtually no group is without them. Although there is sometimes tension between the two structures, they are interdependent so that what changes one, affects the other.

## SUMMARY

The theories we have reviewed provide a general outline for affect processes in groups. The very process of talking together about a shared interest or goal causes events that trigger emotional reactions. Thus episodes of affectively-driven behavior are activated in all kinds of groups. A society's blueprint norms for the group, however, and the feeling and display rules they contain, determine whether members work to quickly deactivate or encourage such affective episodes. When expressive interaction occurs, it leads to the formation of situational affect states that govern the affective behavior of the moment. From these, in turn, more enduring sentiments may develop, resulting in the emergence of an affective structure of liking in the group. This structure stabilizes but does not entirely control future expressive interaction. Furthermore, the affective structure is interdependent with the status structure. Your status position affects your exposure to events with emotional consequences such as agreements and disagreements, as well as your emotional reaction to them. In this way status has an impact on the affective relations you form in the group. These affective relationships, in turn, modify status differences among the group members.

This account of affective processes is based on clinical observations of groups and suggestive evidence in the research literature. It also makes use of basic concepts and findings in the sociology of emotions. These include evidence that the very emotions we experience are socially constructed because they are based on interpretations of events as well as bodily sensations. Furthermore, power and regard in interaction are especially potent triggers for emotions. This account of affect processes in groups draws as well on the sociological concepts of "emotion culture," "feeling and display rules," and "emotion work," and on evidence of the effect of stable sentiments on interaction. Together, these are encouraging indicators about the basic validity of the account. However, they do not constitute a proper test of the theories involved. To emphasize again, most of the ideas presented in this chapter are still untested and must be kept in critical perspective. Rigorous empirical tests are the most pressing goal of future research. Only then can an analysis of affect assume the central place it should have in our knowledge of group processes.

## SUGGESTED READINGS

Berger, Joseph. 1988. "Directions in Expectation States Research." Pp. 450–74 and 522–28 in *Status Generalization: New Theory and Research*, edited by M. Webster, Jr. and

M. Foschi. Stanford, CA: Stanford University Press; Johnston, Janet R. 1988. "The Structure of Ex-Spousal Relations: An Exercise in Theoretical Integration and Application." Pp. 309–26 and 509–10 in Webster and Foschi, eds., *op. cit.;* Shelly, Robert K. 1988. "Social Differentiation and Social Integration." Pp. 366–76 and 512–13 in Webster and Foschi, eds., *op. cit.*

These three articles present new expectation states theories of affect processes in groups. The "Theories in Progress" section of the chapter by Berger (pp. 463–72) gives a general overview of these theories. The Shelly chapter discusses congruence and incongruence of affective structures and status structures. Johnston's intriguing chapter integrates expectation states theories of affect, status, and control processes and uses the results to explain why some divorced couples become locked in destructive, ongoing battles.

Gordon, Steven. 1981. "The Sociology of Sentiments and Emotion." Pp. 562–92 in *Social Psychology: Sociological Perspectives*, edited by M. Rosenberg and R. Turner. New York: Basic Books.

This influential review article provides a good discussion of the classic issues involved in understanding emotions. Taking a social constructivist stance toward the problem, it offers an excellent discussion of the ways in which emotions are social phenomena.

Hochschild, Arlie R. 1979. "Emotion Work, Feeling Rules, and Social Structure." *American Journal of Sociology* 85: 551 75.

This fascinating and very readable article introduces the concepts of "feeling rules" and "emotion work" and discusses how the emotion management they describe is related to the requirements of middle class jobs and attitudes.

Kemper, Theodore D. 1990. "Social Relations and Emotions." Pp. 207–37 in *Research Agendas in the Sociology of Emotions*, edited by T. D. Kemper. Albany, NY: SUNY Press.

This chapter provides a brief introduction to Kemper's "positivist" theory of the way interactions with others in relation to power and regard generate most emotions.

Smith-Lovin, Lynn. 1990. "Emotion as the Confirmation and Disconfirmation of Identity: An Affect Control Model." Pp. 238–70 in Kemper, ed., *op. cit.*

In this chapter, Smith-Lovin gives a clear and accessible introduction to affect control theory and the way it conceptualizes emotion as part of the process of confirming or disconfirming fundamental sentiments about identities through the transient sentiments aroused in interaction.

Thoits, Peggy A. 1989. "The Sociology of Emotions." *Annual Review of Sociology* 15: 317–42.

This review article takes up where Gordon leaves off. It provides a thorough, readable, and thoughtfully critical review of research and theory in the new field of the sociology of emotions.

## REFERENCES

Anderson, Lynn R. and P. Nick Blanchard. 1982. "Sex Differences in Task and Social-Emotional Behavior." *Basic and Applied Social Psychology* 3:109–39.

Bales, Robert F. 1950. *Interaction Process Analysis: A Method for the Study of Small Groups*. Cambridge, MA: Addison-Wesley.

———. 1953. "The Equilibrium Problem in Small Groups." Pp. 111–61 in *Working Papers in the Theory of Action*, edited by T. Parsons, R. F. Bales, and E. A. Shils. Glencoe, IL: Free Press.

Bales, Robert F. and A. Paul Hare. 1965. "Diagnostic Use of the Interaction Profile." *Journal of Social Psychology* 67:239–58.

Bales, Robert F. and Phillip E. Slater. 1955. "Role Differentiation in Small Decision-Making Groups." Pp. 259–306 in *The Family, Socialization and Interaction Processes*, edited by T. Parsons and P. E. Slater. Glencoe, IL: Free Press.

Berger, Joseph. 1988. "Directions in Expectation States Research." Pp. 450–74 and 522–28 in *Status Generalization: New Theory and Research*, edited by M. Webster, Jr. and M. Foschi. Stanford, CA: Stanford University Press.

Berger, Joseph, Thomas L. Conner, and M. Hamit Fisek. 1974. *Expectation States Theory: A Theoretical Research Program*. Cambridge, MA: Winthrop.

Berger, Joseph, M. Hamit Fisek, Robert Z. Norman, and Morris Zelditch, Jr. 1977. *Status Characteristics and Social Interaction: An Expectation-States Approach*. New York: Elsevier.

Berger, Joseph and Morris Zelditch, Jr., eds. 1985. *Status, Rewards, and Influence*. San Francisco: Jossey-Bass.

Berkowitz, Leonard. 1982. "Aversive Conditions as Stimuli to Aggression." Pp. 249–88 in *Advances in Experimental Social Psychology*, vol. 15, edited by L. Berkowitz. New York: Academic Press.

Burke, Peter J. 1967. "The Development of Task and Social-Emotional Role Differentiation." *Sociometry* 30:379–92.

———. 1971. "Task and Socio-Emotional Leadership Role Performance." *Sociometry* 34:22–40.

Carli, Linda L. 1990. "Gender, Language, and Influence." *Journal of Personality and Social Psychology* 59:941–51.

Ekman, Paul. 1982. *Emotion in the Human Face*. Cambridge, England: Cambridge University Press.

———. 1984. "Expression and the Nature of Emotion." Pp. 319–43 in *Approaches to Emotion*, edited by K. R. Scherer and P. Ekman. Greenwich, CT: JAI Press.

Festinger, Leon. 1954. "A Theory of Social Comparison Processes." *Human Relations* 7:114–40.

Gordon, Steven L. 1981. "The Sociology of Sentiments and Emotion." Pp. 562–92 in *Social Psychology: Sociological Perspectives*, edited by M. Rosenberg and R. H. Turner. New York: Basic Books.

———. 1989. "Institutional and Impulsive Orientations in Selectively Appropriating Emotions to the Self." Pp. 115–36 in *The Sociology of Emotions: Original Essays and Research Papers*, edited by D. D. Franks and E. D. McCarthy. Greenwich, CT: JAI Press.

———. 1990. "Social Structural Effects on Emotions." Pp. 145–79 in *Research Agendas in the Sociology of Emotions*, edited by T. D. Kemper. Albany, NY: SUNY Press.

Heise, David R. 1979. *Understanding Events: Affect and the Construction of Social Action*. New York: Cambridge University Press.

Hochschild, Arlie R. 1979. "Emotion Work, Feeling Rules, and Social Structure." *American Journal of Sociology* 85:551–75.

_____. 1983. *The Managed Heart: The Commercialization of Human Feeling.* Berkeley, CA: University of California Press.

_____. 1989. *The Second Shift: Working Parents and the Revolution at Home.* New York: Viking-Penguin.

Johnston, Janet R. 1988. "The Structure of Ex-Spousal Relations: An Exercise in Theoretical Integration and Application." Pp. 309–26 and 509–10 in *Status Generalization: New Theory and Research,* edited by M. Webster, Jr. and M. Foschi. Stanford, CA: Stanford University Press.

Kelley, Harold. 1984. "Affect in Interpersonal Relations." *Review of Personality and Social Psychology,* vol. 5, edited by P. Shaver. Beverly Hills, CA: Sage.

Kemper, Theodore D. 1978. *A Social Interactional Theory of Emotions.* New York: Wiley.

_____. 1987. "How Many Emotions Are There?" *American Journal of Sociology* 93: 263–89.

_____. 1990. "Social Relations and Emotions: A Structural Approach." Pp. 207–37 in *Research Agendas in the Sociology of Emotions,* edited by T. D. Kemper. Albany, NY: SUNY Press.

Meeker, B. F. and P. A. Weitzel-O'Neill. 1977. "Sex Roles and Interpersonal Behavior in Task-Oriented Groups." *American Sociological Review* 42:92–105.

Osgood, Charles E., W. H. May, and M. S. Miron. 1975. *Cross-Cultural Universals of Affective Meaning.* Urbana, IL: University of Illinois Press.

Ridgeway, Cecilia L. 1982. "Status in Groups: The Importance of Emotion." *American Sociological Review* 47:76–88.

_____. 1983. *The Dynamics of Small Groups.* New York: St. Martin's Press.

Ridgeway, Cecilia L. and David Diekema. 1989. "Dominance and Collective Hierarchy Formation in Male and Female Task Groups." *American Sociological Review* 54:79–93.

Ridgeway, Cecilia L. and Cathryn Johnson. 1990. "What Is the Relationship Between Socioemotional Behavior and Status in Task Groups?" *American Journal of Sociology* 95:1189–212.

Schachter, Stanley and Jerome Singer. 1962. "Cognitive, Social and Physiological Determinants of Emotional State." *Psychological Review* 69:379–99.

Shelly, Robert K. 1988. "Social Differentiation and Social Integration." Pp. 366–76 and 512–13 in *Status Generalization: New Theory and Research,* edited by M. Webster, Jr. and M. Foschi. Stanford, CA: Stanford University Press.

_____. 1989. "Power and Prestige in Complex Social Structure: Affect, Authority and Status." Research proposal to the National Science Foundation, Washington, DC.

Shelly, Robert K., Murray Webster, Jr., and Joseph Berger. 1989. "Congruent Structures of Affect and Status." Paper presented at the American Sociological Association Annual Meeting, San Francisco.

Slater, Phillip E. 1955. "Role Differentiation in Small Groups." *American Sociological Review* 20:300–10.

Smith-Lovin, Lynn. 1988. "The Affective Control of Events Within Settings." Pp. 71–101 in *Analyzing Social Interaction: Advances in Affect Control Theory,* edited by L. Smith-Lovin and D. R. Heise. New York: Gordon and Breach.

_____. 1990. "Emotion as the Confirmation and Disconfirmation of Identity: An Affect Control Model." Pp. 238–70 in *Research Agendas in the Sociology of Emotions,* edited by T. D. Kemper. Albany, NY: SUNY Press.

Smith-Lovin, Lynn and David R. Heise. 1988. *Analyzing Social Interaction: Advances in Affect Control Theory.* New York: Gordon and Breach.

Thoits, Peggy A. 1985. "Self-Labelling Processes in Mental Illness: The Role of Emotional Deviance." *American Journal of Sociology* 92:221–49.

———. 1989. "The Sociology of Emotions." *Annual Review of Sociology* 15:317–42.

Webster, Murray, Jr. 1980. "Integrating Social Processes." Research proposal funded by the National Science Foundation, Washington, DC.

Webster, Murray, Jr. and Martha Foschi, eds. 1988. *Status Generalization: New Theory and Research*. Stanford, CA: Stanford University Press.

Wood, Wendy and Steven J. Karten. 1986. "Sex Differences in Interaction Style as a Product of Perceived Sex Differences in Competence." *Journal of Personality and Social Psychology* 50:341–47.

# TEN

# Conflict and Bargaining

REBECCA FORD

This chapter concerns social conflict—a phenomenon that can take the form of an argument between spouses over the division of household chores, a wage dispute between labor and management, a land dispute between environmentalists and private industry, or a military war between two countries. As these examples demonstrate, conflict takes many forms, and affects all levels of social organization—it can emerge between two or more individuals, groups, or even nations.

Regardless of the particular form it takes, or the level of social organization at which it occurs, all social conflict involves two or more interdependent parties with divergent interests. Interdependence refers to the degree to which the choices and behaviors of each party affect the other. Parties have divergent interests if it is difficult for them to simultaneously realize their goals. Two women who both desire the same promotion, divorced parents who both seek sole custody of their only child, a firm which tries to cut costs while workers seek higher pay and more benefits, all illustrate interdependent parties with divergent interests.

Parties in conflict may opt to handle their differences in one of several ways. They may withdraw from the situation to avoid further confrontation, they may try to dominate the other through force or violence, or they may engage in bargaining—a form of give and take—in an effort to deal with their differences. Of these three, bargaining is unique, in that it alone has the potential to provide *both* parties with something they want.

Like conflict, bargaining varies substantially across social contexts. It may be formal and explicit, or informal and tacit. Formal, explicit bargaining is officially recognized, and involves direct communication between two parties who exchange a series of offers and counteroffers over some issue. Explicit bargaining takes place when labor and management sit down at the bargaining table to negotiate the size of a wage increase for employees. In contrast, informal, tacit bargaining is not officially recognized and parties do not directly communicate. Instead, they usually try to outmaneuver or coordinate with each other, usually at a distance, without direct communication (Lawler 1992). Tacit bargaining occurs when two motorists jockey to be the first through an intersection, and when shoppers who have lost each other in a busy mall reunite by anticipating where the other will go (Schelling 1960).

Bargaining also varies in another important respect—the extent to which it is integrative or distributive. Integrative bargaining situations offer some potential for both bargainers to maximize their outcomes; the integrative potential in a situation is most likely to be discovered by bargainers who adopt a joint problem-solving approach to conflict. In contrast, in a distributive bargaining situation, bargainers' outcomes are often negatively related, so that gains for one imply losses for the other. Distributive bargaining discourages joint problem-solving. The difference between these two kinds of situations is illustrated by the case of two sisters who quarrel over an orange. One wants the peel for a cake; the other wants to drink the juice. They resolve their differences distributively, by cutting the orange in half, rather than integratively, by giving one sister all the peel and the other all the juice (Follett 1940).

The qualitative difference between these two kinds of bargaining contexts pushes bargainers to use different kinds of "tactics" to handle negotiations. A tactic is a move, or set of moves, used by a bargainer to influence the other, and can be classified as hostile or conciliatory. Hostile tactics, like threats and punishments, occur more frequently in distributive bargaining, while conciliatory tactics, like concessions and trade-offs, are used more often in integrative bargaining (Bacharach and Lawler 1981; Pruitt and Rubin 1986).

In this chapter, the discussion of conflict is organized around the conceptual distinction between explicit and tacit bargaining and between hostile and conciliatory tactics. By way of overview, the chapter begins by presenting several definitions of conflict, and then goes on to discuss individual needs and preferences versus social structures as two sources of conflicting interests. Following that, explicit versus tacit bargaining is discussed in more detail. Next, the chapter focuses on bargaining tactics, hostile and conciliatory, and how these are used in tacit and explicit bargaining contexts.

## DEFINING CONFLICT

There are many ways to define conflict (see, for example, Coser 1956; Schelling 1960; Pruitt 1981). This is not surprising, given the range of forms it takes, and given that it may emerge at any level of social organization. Some theorists define conflict in terms of incompatible activities or behaviors (Deutsch 1973). For example, the efforts of wildlife conservationists to save endangered species, such as the black rhinoceros, are incompatible with the activities of big-game poachers. Others have defined conflict in terms of incompatible goals (Pruitt and Rubin 1986). A car buyer's goal to spend as little as possible is incompatible with the dealer's goal to get the buyer to spend as much as possible. Finally, some theorists (Tedeschi, Schlenker, and Bonoma 1973) combine these two perspectives, and define conflict as an "interactive state in which the behaviors and goals of one actor are to some degree incompatible with the behaviors and goals of some other actor or actors."

As this last definition makes clear, conflict is a *social* phenomenon; if the pursuit of one party's preferences and interests does not affect the other, there is no conflict. Tedeschi's definition also involves the idea that conflicts vary in severity. The more opposed parties' interests are, the more severe the conflict. This implies that conflicts can be placed on a continuum, ranging from situations in which parties' interests are not at all opposed, to those in which their interests are completely opposed.

When parties have compatible interests, their primary concern is with coordinating their activities so as to produce the best possible outcome for both. In contrast, parties whose interests are diametrically opposed are primarily concerned with dominating or overcoming their opponents. This kind of situation is referred to as "pure" conflict. Fortunately, pure conflict does not occur very often—rather, parties are more likely to discover that their interests partially coincide, and partially conflict (Schelling 1960).

When interests overlap in this way, the situation is referred to as "mixed motive." Mixed motives refer to the presence of incentives to cooperate, as well as to compete, with the other (Schelling 1960). In a bargaining context, the benefits associated with reaching agreement provide the incentive to cooperate; the benefits associated with reaching an agreement in one's favor provide the incentive to compete.

Bargainers may cooperate with one another by giving up something of value; this may mean yielding on a given issue, or trading off on other issues. Bargainers this compete with one another by refusing to yield but insisting that the other do so, by deceiving each other about their true interests, and so on. Mixed motive situations typically entail a great deal of uncertainty and ambiguity for the parties involved, since neither can be sure the other will not respond to the incentive to act in its own interest.

Concretely, there is probably no limit to the number of things which may cause conflict; people may conflict over the purchase price of a car, the "right" school to attend, religious issues, the death penalty, who has the right to vote, how to run the country, and so on. However, more abstractly, conflicts can be traced to one of two sources: divergent interpersonal preferences, or divergent interests that are embedded in social structures (i.e., enduring, patterned behaviors).

Interpersonal conflicts occur because *individuals* often have incompatible personal beliefs, attitudes, values, goals, etc. For example, a husband and wife may come into conflict because they cannot agree on the type of car to buy; she may prefer a sports car, while he may prefer a luxury sedan. In contrast, structural conflicts occur because the *positions* within social structures have divergent interests attached to them. In a formal organization, the position of "manager" is associated with a set of interests which are not dependent upon the particular person the organization hires. The structure of one organization may be such that — managers benefit from sharing information, while the structure of another may make sharing information costly. Such differences may exist regardless of individual preferences for sharing information. Overall, structural conflicts tend to be more difficult to resolve than interpersonal conflicts, primarily because social structures are more permanent, and are seldom under complete control of those who occupy positions in the structure (Lawler 1992; Lawler and Ford 1993).

## BARGAINING AND NEGOTIATION

Whether conflicts are interpersonal or structural in origin, bargaining and negotiation may be used in an effort to either resolve or at least manage differences between conflicting parties. Minimally, bargaining refers to the give-and-take of two or more interdependent parties in conflict. Each party perceives some benefit associated with settling the conflict, or else they would not engage in bargaining. At the same time, each would like a settlement at least as good as, if not better than the other (Hamner and Yukl 1977).

As noted previously, bargaining varies along two continua: the extent to which it is formally recognized by the parties involved, and the extent to which bargainers attend to the cooperative or competitive features of a mixed motive situation (Bacharach and Lawler 1980). Bargaining that is formally recognized by the parties involved is termed "explicit bargaining." According to Chertkoff and Esser (1976), explicit bargaining presupposes that two parties have divergent interests, that they can communicate with one another over the issue at stake, and that mutual compromise is possible. If neither party is able or willing to yield, then there is nothing to bargain over. Intermediate solutions are necessary for explicit bargaining to take place. For example, there are no obvious intermediate solutions to the current conflict between conservationists who are trying to preserve the Brazilian rain forest and gold miners who want to cut it down to get at Brazil's gold reserves, but a range of solutions are usually possible in salary disputes. Workers can agree to accept less money, or fewer benefits, while management can agree to give a larger salary increase or provide other benefits to workers. Finally, explicit bargaining requires that the parties be able to exchange provisional offers that do not fix the final outcome of the negotiation until all involved agree.

In contrast, informal bargaining, or "tacit bargaining," does not involve an open exchange of provisional offers and counteroffers; consequently, there is less potential for compromise. In tacit bargaining, the "negotiation" is implicit and takes place through parties' efforts to outmaneuver one another, or to coordinate with one another (Schelling 1960; Bacharach and Lawler 1980; Murnighan 1991;

Chertkoff and Esser 1976). Typically, communication channels do not exist in tacit bargaining, or if they do, the parties involved tend not to use them (Deutsch and Krauss 1962; Bacharach and Lawler 1981).

By way of illustration, Schelling (1960) describes a scenario in which two people have parachuted out of a plane, and have become separated from each other during the drop. Each has a map, and knows that the other also has a map, but neither knows where the other is, and neither has any way to communicate with the other. Time is of the essence if they wish to be rescued. According to Schelling, the parachutists are likely to examine their maps and try to anticipate a logical place to rendezvous, such as a landmark, or crossroads. In short, tacit bargainers often converge upon solutions which are conspicuous or prominent in some way.

Both tacit and explicit bargaining contexts can be distributive or integrative. Distributive bargaining tends to be competitive; bargainers are primarily concerned with their own interests, because if one bargainer does well, it is generally at the other's expense. Competitive bargainers are more reluctant to yield, trust one another less, and have more difficulty reaching agreement than bargainers who are cooperatively oriented. In contrast, in the integrative situation, bargainers are more cooperative and more concerned with finding solutions that produce high joint outcome. Integrative bargaining is more likely to succeed when bargainers attach differing priorities to a set of issues, when resources are not scarce, and when they trust one another (Pruitt 1981).

## BARGAINING TACTICS

The contrast between distributive and integrative bargaining parallels a contrast between two kinds of tactics bargainers can use to influence bargaining outcomes: hostile and conciliatory tactics. Recall that tactics refer to a move or set of moves used by a bargainer to influence an opponent (Bacharach and Lawler 1981). Hostile tactics (threats, punishments, insults, etc.) communicate a desire to compete with, intimidate, or resist the other, and are more likely to be the focus of a distributive bargaining context, where bargainers are concerned with reaching an agreement in their own favor. Conciliatory tactics (promises, compliments, rewards, concessions, etc.) communicate a desire to cooperate with and get along with the other (Bacharach and Lawler 1981; Lawler, Ford, and Blegen 1988), and are more likely to be the focus of an integrative bargaining context, where bargainers are more concerned about reaching a mutually beneficial agreement.

Both kinds of tactics depend upon social influence processes for their effectiveness; one party can do well at the other's expense only if the other allows it. Likewise, mutually satisfactory solutions are possible only if both parties will consent to it (Pruitt and Rubin 1986). This implies that use of a given tactic is a separate issue from whether that tactic actually produces the desired outcome.

For example, workers may try to intimidate management into giving them higher wages by walking off their jobs. However, this tactic may backfire, and the striking workers may simply be replaced or fired.

## HOSTILE TACTICS

The form that hostile tactics take depends partly upon whether the bargaining context is tacit or explicit. In tacit bargaining, hostile tactics can take the form of implied threats, or competitive moves and countermoves by one or both parties. In this sense, competition reflects the extent to which a party chooses what is best for it individually, without regard for the other. In contrast, in explicit bargaining, hostile tactics take the form of explicitly stated threats and punishments. In both kinds of contexts, research is concerned with three themes: (1) What factors foster the use of hostile tactics; (2) How do hostile tactics affect bargaining outcomes, including prospects for agreement; and (3) When are hostile tactics effective means of gaining compliance?

## TACIT BARGAINING

Tacit bargaining has been primarily, though not exclusively, the province of game theorists. There are many game theories, but all seek to identify the *best* strategy for a rational actor, who must make decisions in an interdependence situation. The term ''strategy'' means the choices an actor makes while taking into account all possible choices of other actor(s). Rational actors are those who are motivated to maximize rewards and minimize costs. As noted above, interdependence means that each actor's outcomes are jointly determined by his or her decisions and those of another. Game theorists have been concerned with how the structure of payoffs or incentives in a situation affects the choices of rational actors, and how those choices affect both individual and collective outcomes (Schelling 1960; Rapoport 1966).

### Social Dilemmas

Game theories have been especially concerned with choices made in ''social dilemmas.'' These situations have two important characteristics: first, they offer identical incentive structures, i.e, the same set of both positive and negative consequences to all actors. Second, when each actor pursues his or her individual interests, all receive poorer outcomes than if they had not tried to further their own interests (Messick and Brewer 1983).

A classic example of a social dilemma is the ''tragedy of the commons'' (Hardin 1968). According to Hardin, English herdsmen who wished to expand their herds without buying more land began grazing their herds on the commons, a pasturage of land for members of a community to use as they pleased. In the short run, individual herdsmen were able to expand their herds at a relatively low cost. However, in the long run, the commons were overgrazed and ruined, because no herdsman wished to be the first to reduce the size of his herd to allow the grass in the pasture to be replenished.

Many social problems, e.g., income tax evasion, depletion of natural resources, and overpopulation, are social dilemmas that arise as the result of individual pursuit of personal interests (Messick and Brewer 1983; Schelling 1960). If most people in a society conserve natural resources, then it is safe for a few to engage in wasteful practices. However, if one person is tempted to behave this way, it is safe to assume that all will be subject to the same temptation, and eventually, most will engage in wasteful behavior. In this way, an entire society can lose important natural resources, e.g., water, clean air, and oil.

Perhaps the most famous social dilemma is that of the "prisoner's dilemma" (Luce and Raiffa 1957). This situation is usually described in terms of two persons who are arrested on suspicion of commiting a serious crime. Each is taken to a separate cell, in order to prevent communication about an alibi. The district attorney knows that they have committed a serious crime, but only has enough evidence to convict them on a lesser charge. The district attorney tells the prisoners individually that each has two choices: confess or keep quiet. If both choose to keep quiet, both will be convicted of the lesser charge, and both will be sentenced to two years in prison. If both choose to confess, then both will be prosecuted for the more serious crime, but will only serve seven years, since both cooperated with the state. However, if one prisoner confesses, while the other keeps quiet, the one who confesses will go free for helping to convict the other of the more serious crime. The one who keeps quiet will be prosecuted to the fullest extent of the law and will receive a life sentence. The situation the two suspects face is shown in Figure 10.1. Prisoner A's outcomes are shown above the diagonal line; prisoner B's outcomes are shown below the diagonal line.

The dilemma each prisoner faces is whether to confess or keep quiet, keeping in mind that the number of years each will serve in prison depends on the choices made by *both* prisoners. Assuming that each prisoner wishes to minimize time spent in prison, the best thing for each *individual* prisoner is to confess, *regardless of what the other does*. By confessing, the individual will *either* get his or her best outcome (freedom), or will defend against his or her worst possible outcome (life in jail). Of course, if *both* prisoners reason the same way, both will confess, and both will serve seven years, whereas if both refuse to confess, each will spend only two years behind bars. This dilemma reveals how individual pursuit of interests often leads to destructive collective outcomes.

Because of its simplicity and elegance, the prisoner's dilemma has been extensively studied in the laboratory, where the outcomes at stake may be represented by points or money, rather than prison sentences. In these studies, certain conven-

Figure 10.1.   Prisoner's Dilemma

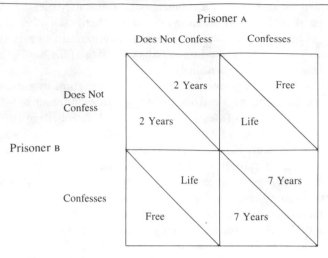

tions are observed in representing the matrix, e.g., A's outcomes are always shown above the diagonal in each cell, while B's are always shown below. In addition, each combination of choices is represented as follows: r stands for the "reward payoff" associated with mutual cooperation, or keeping quiet; p represents the "punishment payoff" associated with mutual competition, or confession; t stands for the "temptation payoff," received by the party who competes (confesses), when the other cooperates (keeps quiet); and s represents the "sucker's payoff" and goes to the party who keeps quiet (cooperates) while the other competes (confesses) (Luce and Raiffa 1957; Rapoport and Chammah 1965, 1966). The magnitude of the payoffs must be in the following order for the structure to be called a "prisoner's dilemma": t > r > p > s. In addition, t + s/2 < r. This latter condition shows there is no benefit to taking turns in receiving s, since the average of t and s is still less than r. Taken together, these two conditions create the "push" to compete at the individual level (Rapoport and Chammah 1965).

In some situations, actors find themselves in a prisoner's dilemma over time, and must decide between competition and cooperation several times in succession. Rapoport (1966) compares this kind of situation to the one where the actors choose only once. As described above, when played only once, competition is the rational choice for both parties, because the party who chooses cooperation will receive s if the other chooses to compete. In turn, if both choose to compete, the worst that will happen is that both will receive p. While p is not as good as r or t, it is preferred to s. Thus, if A cannot be certain that B will cooperate, competition is the safest course of action. In that way, A will either receive t or avoid s.

Over time, however, Rapoport suggests that a different outcome initially seems plausible for the following reason: both parties presumably realize that it is in their interest to begin with cooperation, because the opponent would likely retaliate for a competitive choice on the next exchange. Thus, mutual cooperation seems likely in the face of immediate retaliation for a competitive choice. However, Rapoport notes that when the relationship comes to an end, both parties will inevitably be tempted to compete with the other, because there is no further possibility of retaliation. Without the threat of retaliation, the rational party will choose competitively on the last exchange in order to obtain t, or to avoid the risk of s. In effect then, the tacit agreement to cooperate unravels.

To demonstrate this point, Rapoport considers a situation in which two parties agree to engage in a series of ten exchanges—neither wishes to be punished by retaliation on a subsequent exchange, so both decide to begin by cooperating. However, as each comes to realize on the last exchange, it is in each party's interest to compete with the other because they can either get t or defend against s. Of course, once both actors realize that the outcome of the tenth exchange will be mutual competition, they have no incentive to cooperate on the ninth exchange. This means that the outcome of the ninth exchange will also be mutual competition. If both apply the same logic to each of the preceding exchanges, they will both choose to compete on each and every exchange. In this way, both incur losses when they could have enjoyed mutual profits.

As this example implies, actors who know when the relationship will end are especially likely to be caught up in mutual competition. By the same token, it also implies that there is some possibility for cooperation to evolve if actors do not know when the relationship will end. The literature on cooperation in the prisoner's dilemma is taken up in a subsequent section on the use of conciliatory tactics in tacit bargaining.

## Threats in the Prisoner's Dilemma

In a standard prisoner's dilemma, the "prisoners" are not allowed direct communication with one another. However, some studies have modified this and allowed limited direct communication about the choices the players make. In one research tradition, developed largely by James Tedeschi and his associates (1973), a subject with no threat and punishment capability faced a "programmed other" that could threaten and punish the subject if the subject did not choose cooperatively.

These researchers were interested in compliance to threats, and theorized that credible threats would generate more compliance than those which were not credible. In turn, they argued that threat credibility is affected by several things, including the magnitude of the threatened punishment, the source's past conduct, the source's status, and the wording of the threats.

One study in this set (Horai and Tedeschi 1969) examined the impact of past conduct and the magnitude of punishment on compliance by varying the frequency with which the programmed other followed through on threats, and by varying the magnitude of the punishment the programmed other could levy. They found that compliance was greater when the programmed other consistently punished noncompliance, and when the threatened punishment was larger.

A second study (Faley and Tedeschi 1971) tested the hypothesis that threats from high status individuals are more credible than threats from low status individuals. In this study, ROTC (Reserve Officer Training Corps) cadets of varying levels of status and authority interacted with a programmed other they believed to be either high or low in status. As anticipated, high status cadets were less intimidated by threats from a low status other, while low status cadets were more intimidated by threats from a high status other.

A third study, which examined threat wording (Schlenker et al. 1970), contrasted compellent threats with deterrent threats. Compellent threats specify action the target must perform in order to avoid being punished, e.g., "clean your room, or you will not receive your allowance." Deterrent threats specify action the target must not engage in, e.g., "Do not fail the exam; if you do, you will not get your allowance." By varying the wording of threats sent by the programmed other in this manner, Schlenker and his colleagues found that compellent threats were more credible and perceived to be more coercive than deterrent threats. The primary reason for this seems to be that compellent threats require that the target actually take some action to avoid being punished. Taken together, these three studies suggest that credible threats are an effective means of influence in a conflict of interest situation.

## Trucking Game Research

Hostile tactics were also the focus in another kind of tacit bargaining context, called the "Acme-Bolt trucking game." Developed by Deutsch and Krauss (1960, 1962), this game assumes that two trucking companies, Acme and Bolt, are each paid to deliver goods from a starting point to a destination point. Each company is paid for delivered cargo, minus costs incurred during the trip. Company costs are a function of the time in seconds it takes each company to make the trip.

Each company has two routes to its destination point: a short, one-lane road common to both companies, and an indirect route that takes longer to travel. If both try to use the short route at the same time, they will meet head-on, and neither will be able to reach its destination unless one backs up. If the longer route is taken, it costs the company taking it more money. Thus, Acme and Bolt have to decide who will take the short route first, and who will back up (Deutsch 1987).

Deutsch and Krauss found that eventually, Acme and Bolt learned to coordinate their efforts by taking turns at using the short route, so that their companies were actually able to make a profit. However, they also found that if they gave one of the companies a gate, which that company could use to block the other from using the short route, both companies lost money. Further, if both companies had gates to obstruct one another, they lost even more money than if only one of them had a gate. When both parties had gates, both were more likely to use the gate to block the other and to refuse to move from the short route. Overall, this line of research suggests that when one or both parties have the capability to impose costs on each other, they will use that capability, and both will suffer costs (Deutsch 1987; Lawler 1986).

## EXPLICIT BARGAINING

Most studies of hostile tactics in explicit bargaining contexts have used some form of Siegel and Fouraker's (1960) "bilateral monopoly" game. Briefly, this game involves two parties, a lone buyer and a lone seller of some commodity, who each wish to maximize his or her profits by negotiating over the price at which the commodity will be bought or sold. Generally, the outcomes of buyer and seller are negatively related; the higher the price, the greater the seller's profit; the lower the price, the greater the buyer's profit.

Both parties have information on their own profit at each possible agreement level; occasionally they are given information on their opponent's profits as well. Buyer and seller then exchange a series of offers and counteroffers until an agreement is reached, or until some time limit is met. Both are individually oriented, which means that they wish to maximize their own outcomes, and are unconcerned about the other party's outcomes. This differs from a competitive orientation, which implies that each party wishes to outdo the other, and from a cooperative orientation, which implies that each is concerned about the other's outcomes. In this context, hostile tactics, based on each party's coercive capability, take the form of explicit threats of damage, and actual damage to the opponent's outcomes.

### *Two Theories of Coercive Power*

The Deutsch and Krauss trucking game research (1960, 1962) and the Tedeschi et al. (1973) studies of threat effectiveness have served as the point of departure for a theory that links coercive capability to the use of hostile tactics in explicit bargaining. On the one hand, the trucking game studies show threat and damage tactics to be rather ineffectual means of influence because they cost the source as well as the target, and embroil both parties in a costly use–counteruse spiral of resistance. The central ideas of this body of research are now captured by "conflict spiral theory." On the other hand, the idea that threats can be effective under some conditions is now part of "bilateral deterrence theory" (Lawler 1986).

Lawler (1986) formulated these two theories to address two primary issues.

The first of these is the effect of "total power." Total power refers to the sum of both bargainers' power capabilities. The second issue concerns the impact of "relative power." Relative power is the amount of power difference between two bargainers. Both theories are concerned with how increases or decreases in both total and relative power affect the use of hostile tactics (see Chapter 7 for a general discussion of the concept of "power").

Consider bilateral deterrence theory first. When bargainers have equal power, bilateral deterrence theory predicts that increases in total power leads both bargainers to use fewer hostile tactics, while decreases in total power leads both to use more hostile tactics. This is called the "total power prediction," and it occurs when total power changes for two reasons. First, both bargainers fear "retaliation," or a response in kind, from the opponent for any acts of aggression they might initiate. A given actor's fear of retaliation is based on the coercive strength of his or her opponent—the more powerful an opponent, the more retaliation costs the opponent can impose in response to hostile tactics, and the less likely an actor is to use hostile tactics.

Second, both actors' use of hostile tactics is affected by their expectation of attack by the opponent. A given actor's expectation of attack is a function of his or her own coercive capability—the more powerful an actor is, the lower that actor's expectation of attack. Conversely, the less powerful an actor is, the greater that actor's expectation of attack. This means that when the total power in the relationship is high, both bargainers have higher fear of retaliation and lower expectation of attack, and consequently use fewer hostile tactics overall. However, when the total power in the relationship declines, bargainers have less to lose through retaliation, have higher expectations of its use by the other, and are both more likely to use hostile tactics (Lawler 1986).

When bargainers have unequal power, bilateral deterrence theory predicts that both bargainers will use more hostile tactics than when they have equal power. This is called the "relative power prediction." The primary reason for the difference between equal and unequal power bargaining relationships is that high and low power actors interpret the meaning of a power difference differently. In the face of a power difference, high power actors stress the retaliation aspects of the situation, and use more hostile tactics because they have less to fear. In contrast, low power actors use more hostile tactics because they have a greater expectation of attack. The important point is that *both* high and low power actors use more hostile tactics than parties having equal power (Lawler 1986).

Now consider conflict spiral theory. The most basic predictions of this theory are *opposite* those of bilateral deterrence theory. As total power increases, bargainers are *more* likely to use hostile tactics. According to conflict spiral theory, this effect is due to the "temptation" to use power, as well as the expectation of attack. Temptation refers to each party's perception of the benefits associated with power use, and is based on that party's coercive capability. The more powerful a party is, the more tempted it will be to use its power to affect bargaining outcomes.

Both parties are also affected by their expectation of attack, which, in this theory, is a function of the opponent's coercive capability. The more coercive capability the opponent has, the higher a party's expectation of attack, and the more likely the party is to use hostile tactics. In sum, conflict spiral theory suggests that greater levels of total power in an equal power relationship leads to more temptation and higher expectation of attack for both parties, which combine to produce more use of hostile tactics by both parties (Lawler 1986).

Conflict spiral theory's relative power prediction also differs from that of bilateral deterrence theory. The former predicts that when bargainers have unequal power, they are both less likely to use hostile tactics than equal power bargainers. As before, equal and unequal power relationships differ because high and low power actors do not interpret the power difference in the same way. In this theory, high power actors focus more on the expectation of attack, while low power actors are more concerned about the temptation to use power. In the face of a power difference, the high power actor's expectation of attack and the low power actor's temptation to use power both go down, leading both actors to use fewer hostile tactics than parties with equal coercive power (Lawler 1986).

These theories have been tested in two experiments, which pitted bilateral deterrence against conflict spiral theory (Lawler, Ford, and Blegen 1988). These studies used a two-party bargaining setting similar to the Siegel and Fouraker setting described above. The experiment manipulated the magnitude of coercive power available to the parties, and allowed them to exchange offers and counteroffers and administer hostile tactics (threats or actual damage) to one another. The results of both experiments found support for the total and relative power predictions of bilateral deterrence theory over conflict spiral theory; equal power bargainers used fewer hostile tactics than unequal power bargainers, and increases in the magnitude of power capability for each reduced equal power bargainers' inclination to use hostile tactics. However, Lawler and his colleagues suggest that it is premature to reject conflict spiral theory, as there are likely to be special conditions under which its predictions hold. For example, it may be that when the use of hostile tactics provides some direct benefit to the user, as would a tax or a tariff, the predictions for conflict spiral theory will be realized. (See also the discussion of these theories appearing in Chapter 2 of this volume.)

## Other Hostile Tactics

Pruitt and Rubin (1986) describe another set of hostile tactics which they term "contentious tactics." Parties use contentious tactics when they try to compete with or impose their preferred solution on another. Examples of contentious tactics include ingratiation, gamesmanship, persuasive argumentation, and imposing time pressure. Ingratiation tactics involve giving compliments, gifts, and the like to the opponent in the hope of inducing that actor to concede more. In contrast, gamesmanship is designed to keep the opponent off-balance, e.g., stalling when the opponent wishes to move quickly, and moving quickly when the opponent wishes to take more time. Ingratiation and gamesmanship are only effective if the other is unaware of the actor's actual intentions (Pruitt and Rubin 1986).

While ingratiation and gamesmanship operate indirectly on the opponent's aspirations to do well, persuasion tactics operate directly on the opponent's aspirations by presenting logical arguments that are designed to induce the opponent to yield. They can be effective if the actor can argue that he or she legitimately needs or deserves a favorable outcome to the conflict. A person who claims that he or she will lose his or her job if the conflict is not resolved, or a company that tells employees it will go bankrupt if it gives them a raise, are both using persuasive argumentation (Pruitt and Rubin 1986).

Time pressure, in the form of a deadline, is also a direct tactic which can be used to further yielding in an opponent. As Pruitt (1981) points out, a deadline may get the other to yield if that party believes that negotiations will break down with no agreement in sight. Obviously, for this tactic to be successful, the other party must really believe that the actor will withdraw from the negotiations when the deadline passes, even if no agreement has been reached. Several studies have shown that deadlines can be effective in getting the other to yield (Rubin and Brown 1975; Pruitt 1981), but this effect seems to be strongest when the bargainers have a cooperative orientation (Carnevale and Lawler 1986). When bargainers have an individualistic orientation, and are concerned only about their own outcomes, deadlines can exacerbate conflict (Carnevale and Lawler 1986).

## CONCILIATORY TACTICS

Like hostile tactics, the form that conciliatory tactics take depends in part on the context in which they are used. In tacit bargaining, conciliatory tactics are represented by cooperative moves or countermoves, e.g., choosing to not confess in the prisoner's dilemma. In explicit bargaining, conciliatory tactics refer to promises, rewards, and concessions, i.e., offers and counteroffers during bargaining.

### Tacit Bargaining

In tacit bargaining contexts, research has focused on two closely related questions: first, what are the consequences of cooperating in a mixed-motive situation; and second, what is the most effective way to induce the other to cooperate? To answer these questions, researchers have contrasted two general strategies, noncontingent versus contingent, in a prisoner's dilemma played over a series of trials, to determine which is most effective. The term "contingent strategy" means a strategy in which an actor's choices depend upon those made by the opponent. For instance, an actor might choose to retaliate by competing every time the opponent chooses to compete, and cooperating every time the opponent cooperates. On the other hand, a noncontingent strategy is one in which the actor engages in a series of predetermined moves, e.g., consistent cooperation, consistent competition, or some mixture of these, regardless of what the other does.

In an extensive review of research on contingent and noncontingent strategies, Oskamp (1971) concludes that consistent cooperation in the prisoner's dilemma produces more cooperation than does consistent competition. However, contingent strategies produce more cooperation than noncontingent strategies having the same overall level of cooperation. In fact, one consequence of noncontingent cooperation is that the actor using it is very likely to be seen as weak and easily intimidated.

Of all the contingent strategies in a prisoner's dilemma, "tit for tat" is probably the best known. Tit for tat is defined as a strategy that cooperates on the first move in a prisoner's dilemma, and thereafter echoes whatever the opponent did on the previous exchange. Several studies (Axelrod 1984) show that tit for tat is better than most strategies that can be devised, and at least does no worse than other strategies it has been paired with. Thus, Axelrod considers tit for tat to be a very effective strategy.

According to Axelrod (Axelrod and Hamilton 1981; Axelrod 1984), tit for tat is effective in inducing cooperation for several reasons. First, it is a "nice" strategy that never punishes the other first. Second, others cannot take advantage of it—the opponent who competes against tit for tat will experience swift retaliation. Third, it is a "forgiving" strategy; tit for tat always resumes cooperation as soon as the opponent does so, and does not hold a grudge by punishing the opponent again at a later date. Fourth, tit for tat is a simple strategy, and can generally be easily recognized (Axelrod 1984; Rubin and Brown 1975).

Overall, these four characteristics enable tit for tat to survive in a variety of strategic environments. If it interacts with another "nice" strategy, i.e., one that cooperates, both will do well, because both will enjoy the fruits of mutual cooperation. If the other is tempted to be "nasty," i.e., switch to competition in order to obtain the temptation payoff, it will immediately experience punishment for that choice, and so learn that there are costs to being "nasty." Likewise, if tit for tat interacts with a "nasty" strategy that tries being nice, tit for tat immediately rewards that choice by cooperating. In sum, Axelrod sees tit for tat as a strategy that teaches others how cost effective cooperation can be.

However, tit for tat does have several limitations. For example, Axelrod's thesis assumes that payoffs correspond to a prisoner's dilemma situation, which may or may not be the case. Second, it is entirely possible that one actor hates the other and wishes to do away with that person on a permanent basis. Third, tit for tat's success rests on the assumption that the first party to compete can be clearly identified. This may not be the case, given that parties may well differ in their interpretation of the starting point of the situation—a common occurrence in conflict situations. Finally, it is very difficult for tit for tat to survive in a completely hostile environment; without other cooperators, tit for tat will always be on the defensive, and will never recoup the loss incurred by its first cooperative move (Blalock 1989; Axelrod and Hamilton 1981).

Other research has considered the effects of shifts in strategy during a prisoner's dilemma game, e.g., what happens when a party initially cooperates, but shifts to a tit for tat strategy at some later point in the game? This kind of strategy has been dubbed the "lapsed saint" strategy, and is sometimes contrasted with the "reformed sinner," in which the party begins by competing, and then shifts to a tit for tat strategy (Oskamp 1971). Several studies show that the reformed sinner produces more cooperation after the shift than does the lapsed saint strategy. However, once the opponent experiences tit for tat for a sufficient period of time after the shift, the cooperation levels produced by these two strategies become indistinguishable (Oskamp 1971).

## Explicit Bargaining

In explicit bargaining, conciliatory tactics are substantially more complex than in tacit bargaining; bargainers must make a number of decisions about the size of opening offers, e.g., small versus large, as well as the size and frequency of subsequent concessions (Hamner and Yukl 1977). This complexity makes it more difficult to provide bargainers with advice about the most effective concession strategy.

Several studies report that small opening offers are more effective than large opening offers in getting the opponent to yield. Apparently, a large initial offer by one bargainer can convey an impression of weakness, thereby increasing the opponent's aspirations, making that party less willing to yield (Komorita and Brenner 1968; Yukl 1974; Hamner and Yukl 1977).

While making a tough opening offer is more effective than making a soft one, an extremely tough concession stance throughout the remainder of the bargaining can make it more difficult to reach agreement. Some research shows that bargainers who make small opening offers can avoid an impasse if they either match the size of the other's concessions, or offer just slightly less than the opponent on each concession (Chertkoff and Esser 1976; Yukl 1974; Lawler and MacMurray 1980). However, if a bargainer does open with a large initial offer, it is best to switch to a much tougher subsequent concession stance, because it can communicate that one is reasonable, yet not weak (Lawler and MacMurray 1980).

## Conciliatory Tactics and Bargaining Power

In explicit bargaining, conciliatory tactics have been linked to a form of power called "dependence power" (Bacharach and Lawler 1980, 1981). Richard Emerson (1962, 1972a, 1972b) offers the most complete conceptualization of dependence power. According to Emerson, the power of actor a is a function of actor b's dependence on a. B's dependence on a is a function of two things: the extent to which b values outcomes obtained in the relationship with a, and the number of alternative sources of this outcome b can obtain in other relationships. The more b values outcomes obtained in the relationship with a, and the fewer alternative sources of this outcome b has, the more power a has over b (Bacharach and Lawler 1981; see also Stolte's Chapter 7 in this volume).

Although not explicitly formulated to deal with bargaining per se, Emerson's power-dependence theory has been extended to deal with such phenomena (Bacharach and Lawler 1981; Lawler and Bacharach 1986, 1987). In the context of bargaining, power-dependence theory implies that three facets of the power relationship affect bargaining outcomes. One facet is a bargainer's absolute power, or his or her power regardless of the opponent's power. Second is relative power, which is the degree to which bargainers differ in their dependence on one another. The third facet is the total amount of dependence in the relationship, which refers to the sum of both bargainers' dependence.

From a dependence perspective, a's concession behavior is a function of a's dependence on b, or b's absolute power. This means that the greater a's dependence on b, the more likely a is to make concessions to b. Within a bargaining relationship, there is likely to be more conciliation as bargainers' mutual dependence increases, i.e., as the total power in the relationship increases, but less conciliation within the relationship as one party becomes more dependent than the other, i.e., as relative power increases.

To illustrate the workings of these facets of power dependence, consider a labor-management dispute in which union members are seeking a hefty pay raise, but management is resisting. If management has few alternative sources of labor, and highly values the workers' contributions, then the union has a bargaining advantage, and is less likely to make concessions to management. Conversely, if union members have poor job prospects, and highly value their current employment, management has a bargaining advantage, and is less likely to make concessions to the union. However, if both union and management have poor alternatives and highly value current outcomes, both are likely to be more conciliatory.

To determine if the alternatives and value of each party play an important role in influencing that party's tactical concessions, Bacharach and Lawler (1981) conducted an experiment that manipulated each of the four dimensions of dependence: a's alternatives and value, and b's alternatives and value. Subjects played the role of negotiator, ascribed either high or low value to the outcomes at stake, and had either a high or low probability of getting a good agreement with an alternative bargaining group.

This study found that when negotiators thought they had a good chance of reaching agreement with an alternative party, they made fewer concessions in the initial bargaining session. When both parties had a poor chance of reaching a good agreement with an alternative other, they were much more likely to reach agreement during the initial bargaining session. This is consistent with the basic dependence notion that a party's concessions are a function of its dependence on another, and not of the latter's dependence on the former.

In addition, the study found that greater value did not necessarily lead to more yielding. In fact, Bacharach and Lawler observed that when actors who ascribed higher value to bargaining outcomes bargained with opponents who ascribed lower value to bargaining outcomes, the former was actually more resistant to yielding. These authors suggest that actors who place high value on bargaining outcomes exert more tactical effort in the form of a tougher concession stance than do those who place lesser value on bargaining outcomes.

## Conciliatory Tactics and Conflict Resolution

A substantial body of research has also focused on the relationship between conciliatory tactics and conflict resolution, especially the kind of agreement to which bargainers consent. Three of these tactics are: logrolling, expanding the pie (Pruitt 1981; Pruitt and Rubin 1986) and unilateral initiatives (Osgood 1962; Boyle and Lawler 1991). Although all of these tactics can be used to facilitate conflict resolution so that parties may reach agreement, logrolling and expanding the pie are tactics used to reach integrative agreements, while unilateral initiatives are used when negotiations have broken down and one party tries to induce the other to concede again.

Logrolling can be used to integrate both bargainers' needs if the bargaining involves multiple issues, and the bargainers assign differing priorities to these issues. Logrolling simply means that the bargainers trade off on the issues, so that each is able to get what he or she desires most (Pruitt 1981). For example, consider a situation in which employees seek a 10 percent pay raise, and a 10 percent increase in health care benefits, and management is unwilling to yield on both issues. If the increase in health care benefits is more important to employees, while holding the line on wages is more important to management, management may suggest that it will improve health care benefits by 10 percent, if employees will forego a raise. In this way, both parties do better than if management had consented to give a 5 percent raise and increase health care benefits by 5 percent.

Expanding the pie can integrate bargainers' interests if a new option can be invented that reconciles both parties' interests, or if the pool of available resources can be expanded (Pruitt 1981; Pruitt and Rubin 1986). Consider two siblings who live at home with their parents, are both enrolled in college classes, but conflict over the use of the family's only personal computer for writing papers, doing homework, and the like. While the parents might insist that the students compromise by taking turns with the computer, the students' needs can be integrated with the purchase of an additional computer, which expands available resources.

While integrative bargaining offers the possibility of maximizing joint gain across both bargainers, it is not a foregone conclusion that bargainers will realize the integrative potential in many conflict situations (Pruitt and Rubin 1986; Pruitt 1981). Instead, many bargainers settle for compromise, which typically requires parties to split the difference between their preferred outcomes. Compromise is illustrated by the case of the two sisters discussed earlier, who split the orange in half, by a buyer and seller who meet halfway between the buyer's initial offer and the seller's initial demand, and by two countries seeking control of additional territory, who divide the area equally between them. According to Pruitt, fear of prolonged conflict, lack of trust, time pressures that constrict the search for other solutions, and a cultural norm of "fairness," which dictates equal division of resources, are all reasons why bargaining may end in compromise (for a discussion of theories of justice, see Chapter 8, this volume).

Recent research also suggests that perceptual and judgmental errors may affect bargainers' ability to discover integrative solutions to their conflicts (Thompson and Hastie 1990). In two studies designed to examine the link between social perception and integrative agreements in bargaining, Thompson and Hastie arranged to have subjects serve as either the buyer or seller of a new car. In the first study, the buyer and seller had to negotiate four issues: financing, warranty, delivery date, and tax. Of these, financing was most important to the seller, while an extended warranty was most important to the buyer. The objective of this multiple issue task was to assess bargainers' skill in estimating the relative importance of each issue to their opponent. To the extent that bargainers can accurately determine that they and the opponent assign differing priorities to the issues at stake, the prospects for integrating the interests of the two parties are substantially greater.

Results from this study indicate that bargainers tended to enter into negotiations with a distributive orientation, and did not anticipate opportunities for integrative agreements. This means that they did not initially realize that they and the opponent assigned different values to the four issues. However, this judgment error did decline during negotiations, apparently because the bargainers exchanged information about their interests. Bargainers who realized the integrative potential early on were able to engage in more advantageous trade-offs, and thus made more profit from the negotiations than those who did not.

In the second study, the buyer and seller had to negotiate eight issues: warranty, financing, radio, number of options, price, delivery date, color, and tax. The buyer and seller ranked the first four differently, were completely compatible on color and tax, and completely incompatible on price and delivery date. The study then assessed the extent to which bargainers could in fact detect the compatible issues. Accuracy in detecting compatible interests is also essential to mutually beneficial trade-offs. As expected, many bargainers had difficulty in ferreting out the compatible issues, and consequently settled for suboptimal outcomes.

Sometimes conflict escalates to the point that negotiations break down, and bargainers find themselves at an impasse, but do not wish to invite an outside mediator. When this happens, each bargainer is reluctant to be the first to yield, as doing so may create the impression of weakness in the other's eyes (Pruitt 1981). However, if both remain resolute, and adopt overly tough concession stances throughout the bargaining, there is little likelihood that the conflict will be resolved (Hamner and Yukl 1977). To deal with this dilemma, bargainers may adopt a strategy known as Graduated and Reciprocated Initiatives in Tension-Reduction, or GRIT (Osgood 1962).

Osgood originally developed GRIT as a strategy for de-escalating the arms race between the United States and the former Soviet Union. However, GRIT can potentially be used in any situation where an impasse results from a buildup of hostility (Pruitt 1981; Boyle and Lawler 1991). To break the impasse, Osgood suggests that one bargainer must gain the other's trust without inviting exploitation. The way to do this is by initiating a series of conciliatory gestures, which should be small, so as to avoid the impression of weakness, yet large enough to be taken as sincere. Osgood also suggests that the party initiating the conciliatory gestures retain its ability to retaliate against acts of exploitation.

In one of the few studies of GRIT's implications in an explicit bargaining context, Boyle and Lawler (1991) examined how unilateral initiatives and immediate retaliation for acts of aggression affect an actor's concession behavior. This study established an impasse between a real bargainer and a programmed other by having the latter issue several threat and damage tactics, and make no concessions early in the bargaining. Next, the programmed other engaged in a series of unilateral concessions, or did not, and either retaliated against damage tactics by the real bargainer or did not.

The results of this study show that unilateral initiatives do indeed increase the opponent's trust, which in turn leads that party to concede more and use fewer hostile tactics. The results for the programmed other's retaliation tactic were somewhat more complicated; briefly, in the short run, retaliation by the programmed other increased the real bargainer's use of hostile tactics. In the long run, however, retaliation by the programmed other decreased the real bargainer's use of such tactics. In contrast, when the programmed other did not retaliate for acts of aggression, the real bargainer used more of them over time. Boyle and Lawler conclude that the real bargainer probably viewed the programmed other as weak and vulnerable when it did not retaliate against acts of aggression. Overall then, this study provides substantial support for the basic implications of the GRIT strategy when explicit negotiations have reached an impasse.

## Third Party Tactics

Sometimes bargainers cannot resolve differences on their own. When this happens, they may seek assistance from a third party. In formal bargaining, third party intervention usually involves mediation or arbitration. Mediators, e.g., divorce counselors, attorneys, etc., act only in an advisory capacity, while arbitrators, e.g., judges, have the power to render binding judgments. Like ordinary bargainers, both mediators and arbitrators rely upon hostile as well as conciliatory tactics to affect bargaining outcomes (Pruitt 1981; Kressel and Pruitt 1989).

A particularly interesting set of studies on mediator tactics has been undertaken by Peter Carnevale and his associates (Carnevale 1986; Carnevale, Conlon, Hanisch, and Harris 1989; Carnevale and Conlon 1988; Harris and Carnevale 1990). Although these studies examine a variety of mediator tactics, the present discussion limits itself to hostile and conciliatory tactics, which Carnevale terms "pressing," and "compensation," respectively. Pressing involves the use of threats to reduce one or both bargainers' aspirations to get them to be more conciliatory with one another. Compensation involves the promise of rewards to induce conciliation.

According to Carnevale, mediators are most likely to press when they place a low value on the disputing parties' aspirations, and when they believe that the disputants are unlikely to reach agreement on their own. When this happens, mediators are likely to see coercion as the only way to reach a settlement. Second, pressing is likely to be used when time constraints are imposed on the bargaining. As a bargaining deadline approaches, e.g., a contract renewal, mediators are likely to regard pressing as the only viable means of resolving the conflict.

To test these ideas, Carnevale and his colleagues conducted several studies involving a simulated organizational dispute. In one study, subjects played the role of a "product manager" trying to mediate a dispute between two managers employed by a securities firm. The mediators were led to have either high or low concern for the manager's outcomes, and either high or low perception of common ground between the managers. As predicted, mediators were most likely to press when they had low concern for the parties' aspirations, and when they thought the parties were unlikely to find a satisfactory solution on their own. Mediators were most likely to use conciliatory tactics when they were highly concerned about the parties' aspirations, but also thought the parties were unlikely to find a satisfactory solution on their own.

A second study (Carnevale and Conlon 1988) tested the notion that mediators are more apt to rely upon pressing in the face of time constraints if they have been unable to resolve their own differences. As before, this study involved a simulated organizational dispute between two managers. In addition, time pressure was manipulated by varying the number of rounds bargainers had to resolve their differences. As expected, time pressure increased the mediators' use of pressing, and decreased their use of conciliatory behaviors.

Harris and Carnevale (1990) also looked at how the mediator's ability to press or compensate affects conciliation between bargainers themselves. Interestingly, they found that mediators who had more concern about the bargainers' aspirations, and who could provide them with benefits, were actually less successful in getting bargainers to concede to one another than were mediators who were less concerned about bargainers' aspirations and could punish them for not conceding. Thus, the ability of mediators to provide an alternative source of rewards may actually reduce bargainers' inclination to resolve their own differences.

## SUMMARY

This chapter briefly overviews social psychological theory and research on conflict and bargaining. Conflict emerges when interdependent parties have incompatible interests, and can be dealt with by means of withdrawal, domination, or bargaining. However, only bargaining has the potential to provide both parties with something they want.

Bargaining is an important influence process; the form it takes depends upon whether it is openly recognized and how bargainers' interests are related. Tacit bargaining is not openly acknowledged, and bargainers do not make use of verbal communication. Explicit bargaining is openly recognized, and bargainers directly communicate offers, counteroffers, and agreements. Both tacit and explicit bargaining may be either distributive or integrative. In distributive bargaining the parties' interests are negatively related so that a gain for one on the issue being negotiated implies a loss for the other. However, in integrative bargaining the parties' interests are positively related so that yielding produces gains for both.

Integrative and distributive bargaining tend to be characterized by different kinds of influence processes. Conciliatory tactics are more likely to prevail in integrative bargaining, while hostile tactics are more likely to dominate in distributive bargaining. Both kinds of tactics are important, because both affect prospects for conflict resolution.

Research shows that cooperation can be difficult to maintain in bargaining. Even conciliatory bargainers may have difficulty in locating integrative solutions, and may settle instead for a compromise. In contrast, competition appears easier to maintain. For example, a competitive equilibrium prevails in the prisoner's dilemma, trucking game bargainers readily block their opponent's progress, and parties in explicit bargaining frequently use threat and damage tactics against the opponent.

Cooperation is difficult to sustain for two principal reasons. First, conflict situations generate substantial mistrust—neither can be sure that the other will not respond to incentives to compete. In addition, hostile action against another can provide rewards in the form of concessions or favorable agreements. Second, cooperation may be taken as a sign of weakness, and may be exploited.

Despite these tendencies, some conditions produce more conciliation than others. In the prisoner's dilemma, cooperation can evolve in a long-term relationship where competition is swiftly punished. In the trucking game, bargainers can learn to coordinate their interests if they do not have "weapons" to use against the other.

Other research findings indicate that, in explicit bargaining, higher levels of coercive power in an equal power relationship lead to less use of hostile tactics, thereby improving prospects for agreement. High mutual dependence also increases conciliation because both bargainers ascribe high value to the outcomes at stake, and neither has other alternatives to choose from. Retaliation, when combined with small concessions, can break an impasse in negotiations; when bargainers experience retaliation for acts of aggression, they are less likely to take advantage of conciliatory overtures. Finally, bargainers who exchange information with each other, and who adopt a problem-solving orientation, make more concessions and reach more agreements.

## SUGGESTED READINGS

Bacharach, Samuel and Edward J. Lawler. 1981. *Bargaining: Power, Tactics, and Outcomes.* San Francisco: Jossey-Bass. Chapter 2.

This chapter discusses the essential role of dependence in bargaining and its implications for the tactical decisions bargainers must make at the bargaining table.

Deutsch, Morton. 1980. "Fifty Years of Conflict." Pp. 46–77 in *Retrospectives on Social Psychology,* edited by L. Festinger. New York: Oxford University Press.

In this chapter, Deutsch overviews the progress that has been made in conflict theory and research over five decades. The discussion is organized around his conceptual distinction between conflict as a constructive or destructive social process.

McGrath, Joseph E. 1984. *Groups: Interaction and Performance.* Englewood Cliffs, NJ: Prentice-Hall. Chapter 9.

This chapter examines the handling of mixed-motive conflicts in four kinds of task situations: negotiations, bargaining, social dilemmas, and coalitions.

Murnighan, J. Keith. 1991. *The Dynamics of Bargaining Games.* Englewood Cliffs, NJ: Prentice-Hall.

This readable book overviews a wide range of bargaining games and their defining characteristics. Typical strategies and outcomes are discussed in games which apply to dyads, small groups, and large collectivities.

Pruitt, Dean G. and Jeffrey Z. Rubin. 1986. *Social Conflict: Escalation, Stalemate, and Settlement.* New York: Random House. Chapter 4.

In this chapter, Pruitt and Rubin discuss the tactics of contending, i.e., the tactics bargainers use when they try to impose their preferred solution on the opponent. A range of tactics, including ingratiation, persuasive argumentation, promises, and threats are discussed.

## REFERENCES

Axelrod, Robert. 1984. *The Evolution of Cooperation.* New York: Basic Books.
Axelrod, Robert and William D. Hamilton. 1981. "The Evolution of Cooperation." *Science* 211:1390–96.

Bacharach, Samuel B. and Edward J. Lawler. 1980. *Power and Politics in Organizations.* San Francisco: Jossey-Bass.

———. 1981. *Bargaining: Power, Tactics, and Outcomes.* San Francisco: Jossey-Bass.

Blalock, Hubert M., Jr. 1989. *Power and Conflict: Toward a General Theory.* Newbury Park, CA: Sage.

Boyle, Elizabeth and Edward J. Lawler. 1991. "Resolving Conflict Through Explicit Bargaining." *Social Forces* 69:1183–204.

Carnevale, Peter J. 1986. "Strategic Choice in Mediation." *Negotiation Journal* 2:41–56.

Carnevale, Peter J. and Donald E. Conlon. 1988. "Time Pressure and Strategic Choice in Mediation." *Organizational Behavior and Human Decision Processes* 42:111–33.

Carnevale, Peter J., Donald E. Conlon, Kathy A. Hanisch, and Karen L. Harris. 1989. "Experimental Research on the Strategic-Choice Model of Mediation." Pp. 344–67 in *Mediation Research,* edited by D. G. Pruitt, K. Kressel, and associates. San Francisco: Jossey-Bass.

Carnevale, Peter J. and Edward J. Lawler. 1986. "Time Pressure and the Development of Integrative Agreements in Bilateral Negotiations." *Journal of Conflict Resolution* 30:636–59.

Chertkoff, Jerome M. and James K. Esser. 1976. "A Review of Experiments in Explicit Bargaining." *Journal of Experimental Social Psychology* 12:464–86.

Coser, Lewis. 1956. *The Functions of Conflict.* New York: Free Press.

Deutsch, Morton. 1973. *The Resolution of Conflict.* New Haven, CT: Yale University Press.

———. 1987. "A Theoretical Perspective on Conflict and Conflict Resolution." Pp. 38–50 in *Conflict Management and Problem Solving: Interpersonal to International Applications,* edited by D.J.D. Sandole and I. Sandole-Staroste. New York: New York University Press.

Deutsch, Morton and Robert M. Krauss. 1960. "The Effect of Threat Upon Interpersonal Bargaining." *Journal of Abnormal and Social Psychology* 61:181–89.

———. 1962. "Studies of Interpersonal Bargaining." *Journal of Conflict Resolution* 6: 52–76.

Emerson, Richard M. 1962. "Power-Dependence Relations." *American Sociological Review* 27:31–40.

———. 1972a. "Exchange Theory, Part I: A Psychological Basis for Social Exchange." Pp. 38–57 in *Sociological Theories in Progress,* vol. 2, edited by J. Berger, M. Zelditch, Jr., and B. Anderson. Boston: Houghton Mifflin.

———. 1972b. "Exchange Theory, Part II: Exchange Relations, Exchange Networks, and Groups as Exchange Systems." Pp. 58–87 in *Sociological Theories in Progress,* vol. 2, edited by J. Berger, M. Zelditch, Jr., and B. Anderson. Boston: Houghton Mifflin.

Faley, Thomas and James T. Tedeschi. 1971. "Status and Reaction to Threats." *Journal of Personality and Social Psychology* 17:192–99.

Follett, Mary P. 1940. "Constructive Conflict." Pp. 30–49 in *Dynamic Administration: The Collected Papers of Mary Parker Follett,* edited by H. C. Metcalf and L. Urwick. New York: Harper and Brothers.

Hamner, Clay W. and Gary A. Yukl. 1977. "The Effectiveness of Different Offer Strategies in Bargaining." Pp. 137–60 in *Negotiations: Social Psychological Perspectives,* edited by D. Druckman. Beverly Hills, CA: Sage.

Hardin, Garret. 1968. "The Tragedy of the Commons." *Science* 162:1243–48.

Harris, Karen L. and Peter Carnevale. 1990. "Chilling and Hastening: The Influence of Third Party Power and Interests on Negotiation." *Organizational Behavior and Human Decision Processes* 47:138–60.

Horai, Joann and James T. Tedeschi. 1969. "Effects of Credibility and Magnitude of Punishment on Compliance to Threats." *Journal of Personality and Social Psychology* 12:164–69.

Komorita, Samuel and Arline R. Brenner. 1968. "Bargaining and Concession Making Under Bilateral Monopoly." *Journal of Personality and Social Psychology* 9:15–20.

Kressel, Kenneth and Dean G. Pruitt. 1989. "Conclusion: A Research Perspective on the Mediation of Social Conflict." Pp. 394–436 in *Mediation Research*, edited by D. G. Pruitt, K. Kressel, and associates. San Francisco: Jossey-Bass.

Lawler, Edward J. 1986. "Bilateral Deterrence and Conflict Spiral: A Theoretical Analysis." Pp. 107–30 in *Advances in Group Processes: A Research Annual*, vol. 3, edited by E. J. Lawler. Greenwich, CT: JAI Press.

———. 1992. "Power Processes in Bargaining." *Sociological Quarterly* 33:17–34.

Lawler, Edward J. and Samuel B. Bacharach. 1986. "Power-Dependence in Collective Bargaining." Pp. 191–212 in *Advances in Industrial and Labor Relations*, vol. 3, edited by D. R. Lipsky and D. Lewin. Greenwich, CT: JAI Press.

———. 1987. "Comparison of Dependence and Punitive Forms of Power." *Social Forces* 66:446–62.

Lawler, Edward J. and Rebecca Ford. 1993. "Metatheory and Friendly Competition in Theory Growth: The Case of Power Processes in Bargaining." Pp. 172–210 and 471–74 in *Theoretical Research Programs: Studies in the Growth of Theory*, edited by J. Berger and M. Zelditch, Jr. Stanford, CA: Stanford University Press.

Lawler, Edward J., Rebecca Ford, and Mary A. Blegen. 1988. "Coercive Capability in Conflict: A Test of Bilateral Deterrence vs. Conflict Spiral Theory." *Social Psychological Quarterly* 51:93–107.

Lawler, Edward J. and Bruce MacMurray. 1980. "Bargaining Toughness: A Qualification of Level of Aspiration and Reciprocity Hypotheses." *Journal of Applied Social Psychology* 10:416–30.

Luce, R. Duncan and Howard Raiffa. 1957. *Games and Decisions*. New York: Wiley.

Messick, David M. and Marilynn B. Brewer. 1983. "Solving Social Dilemmas: A Review." *Review of Personality and Social Psychology* 4:11–44.

Murnighan, J. Keith. 1991. *The Dynamics of Bargaining Games*. Englewood Cliffs, NJ: Prentice-Hall.

Osgood, Charles. 1962. *An Alternative to War or Surrender*. Urbana, IL: University of Illinois Press.

Oskamp, Stuart. 1971. "Effects of Programmed Strategies on Cooperation in the Prisoner's Dilemma and Other Mixed-Motive Games." *Journal of Conflict Resolution* 15:225–59.

Pruitt, Dean G. 1981. *Negotiation Behavior*. New York: Academic Press.

Pruitt, Dean G. and Jeffrey Z. Rubin. 1986. *Social Conflict: Escalation, Stalemate, and Settlement*. New York: Random House.

Rapoport, Anatol. 1966. *Two-Person Game Theory: The Essential Ideas*. Ann Arbor, MI: The University of Michigan Press.

Rapoport, Anatol and Albert M. Chammah. 1965. *Prisoner's Dilemma: A Study in Conflict and Cooperation*. Ann Arbor, MI: The University of Michigan Press.

——. 1966. "The Game of Chicken." *American Behavioral Scientist* 10:10–28.

Rubin, Jeffrey Z. and Bert R. Brown. 1975. *The Social Psychology of Bargaining and Negotiation.* New York: Academic Press.

Schelling, Thomas. 1960. *The Strategy of Conflict.* New York: Oxford University Press.

Schlenker, Barry R., Thomas V. Bonoma, James T. Tedeschi, and W.P. Pivnik. 1970. "Compliance to Threats as a Function of the Threat and the Exploitiveness of the Threatener." *Sociometry* 33:394–408.

Siegel, Sidney and Lawrence E. Fouraker. 1960. *Bargaining and Group Decision-Making.* New York: McGraw-Hill.

Tedeschi, James, Barry Schlenker, and Thomas V. Bonoma. 1973. *Conflict, Power, and Games.* Chicago: Aldine.

Thompson, Leigh and Reid Hastie. 1990. "Social Perception in Negotiation." *Organizational Behavior and Human Decision Processes* 47:98–123.

Yukl, Gary A. 1974. "Effects of the Opponent's Initial Offer, Concession Magnitude, and Concession Frequency on Bargaining Behavior." *Journal of Personality and Social Psychology* 29:322–35.

# INDEX

Abstractness, 7
Acme-Bolt trucking game, 240–41
Action opportunities, 102, 123
*Ad hoc* explanations, 6–7
Affect, 87–88, 205–26
Affect control theory, 212
Affect states, 220–21
Affective exchange, 223
  and personality traits assigned, 221
Affective structure, 214, 215
  and status structure, 224–26
American Psychological Association, 64
American Sociological Association,
  viii, 64
Anecdotes, reliance on, 82–83
Arbitration, 250 52
Assumptions, 18
Attribution theory, 78–79, 109
Authority
  definition of, 158
  and knowledge claims, 43–44
  and legitimacy, 159, 196
  and power, 158
Availability bias, 190
Axioms, 18

Bargaining, 36, 88, 167–68, 171, 231–
  53
  competitive, 235, 239
  and conciliatory tactics, 232, 235,
    244–50
  distributive, 171, 232, 235
  explicit, 231, 234, 241–44, 246
  and hostile tactics, 232, 235, 236,
    242, 243–44
  integrative, 171, 232
  tacit, 231–32, 234–35, 236, 244–46
  two-party, 167–68
Behavior
  fundamental sequence of interaction,
    104–107, 123

socioemotional, 97–99, 215, 217
task, 97–99, 215, 216, 223
Belief-maintaining effect, 81–82
Beneffectance, 78
Bilateral deterrence theory, 36, 167,
  241–42
Bilateral monopoly game, 241

Causation, 28, 48, 83, 210
Circular explanation, 5–6, 123, 156
Coalitions, 164, 170–71, 182, 196
Coercive power, 151, 241–43
Cognitive bias, 190
Cognitive conservatism, 78
Cognitive dissonance theory, 77
Collective orientation, 109–10, 122, 130
Collective outcome, 237
Common sense
  definition of, 4
  explanations using, 5–13
  limitations of, 5–13
  versus scientific theorizing, 4–13
Compliance, 152
Conditional versus unconditional
    statements, 10–11
Conflict, 88, 231–53
  definition of, 231, 232–34
Conflict resolution
  and conciliatory tactics, 248–50
Conflict spiral theory, 36, 167, 241–42
Congruence in status and affective
    structures, 224–25
Consensual perceptions of justice, 181
Consensus, 100
Construct theory, 77
Contentious tactics, 243
Contiguous events, 8–9
Contingent strategy, 244–45
Contradiction, 10
Contrast effect, 75
Control groups, 53